A SHORT HISTORY OF WESTERN PHILOSOPHY
IN THE MIDDLE AGES

A SHORT HISTORY
OF WESTERN PHILOSOPHY
IN THE MIDDLE AGES

by

S. J. CURTIS, M.A., Ph.D.

*Senior Lecturer in Education, and Honorary
Lecturer in Mediaeval Philosophy, the University
of Leeds*

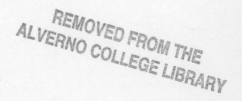
MACDONALD & CO., (Publishers) LTD.

LONDON

First published 1950

Made and printed in Great Britain by Purnell and
Sons, Ltd., Paulton (Somerset) and London

CONTENTS

		PAGE
Foreword, by Dorothy L. Sayers.		vi
Author's Preface		ix
Introduction		11

CHAPTER

I. The Precursors of Mediæval Philosophy: St. Augustine, the Pseudo-Dionysius and Boethius . 13

II. John the Scot, an Original Thinker of the 9th Century . 35

III. The Universals Controversy: Abelard . 48

IV. St. Anselm of Canterbury . 70

V. John of Salisbury, the Historian of the Universals Controversy . 81

VI. Mediæval Universities and Schools . 87

VII. Arabian Philosophy: the Controversy concerning the Intellect . 105

VIII. Early 13th-century Thinkers: Alexander of Hales, Robert Grosseteste and Albert the Great . 124

IX. St. Thomas Aquinas . 134

X. St. Thomas Aquinas, continued . 156

XI. The Moral and Political Philosophy of St. Thomas Aquinas . 181

XII. Representative Franciscans of the later 13th Century: St. Bonaventure and Roger Bacon . 202

XIII. Duns Scotus . 217

XIV. William of Ockham and his Followers . 229

XV. Nicholas of Cusa . 245

XVI. Mediæval Mysticism . 254

Appendix I. Chronological Chart . after 278

Appendix II. Chief Philosophical Works of St. Thomas Aquinas . 279

FOREWORD

By Dorothy L. Sayers

THERE is something curiously moving and impressive about the mediæval Schoolmen. From the cloistered retreats to which learning had been driven by the tumults of the Dark Ages, they emerge into the sunlit bustle of town and university, exuberant with vitality, filled with an enormous and zestful intellectual appetite. For us, accustomed to hearing the intellect stigmatized as "cold" and "remote from life," there is something almost disconcerting about the passionate excitement of these men who riot in the streets of Paris for the right to read Aristotle, split dialectical hairs with the fervour of *balletomanes* comparing the entre-chats of rival ballerinas, and hug Logic to their arms like a bride. Their massive tomes of disputation stagger us by their sheer bulk and tireless accumulation of minute particulars. They are in love with learning; no labour can bore or weary them; to dwell on detail is an inexhaustible delight. Theirs is the spring-like energy of the First Renaissance—fresher than the Second, with a sweeter, sharper tang in the air; less sumptuous and sensuous in colour, sparer and more athletic in its severe intellectual lines.

We note, as we watch them at work, their intense absorption in the processes of thought and the psychology of the conscious. We may be inclined to blame them for not giving more attention to the experimental science which we value so highly; but the mediæval man was consistent in choosing to understand and perfect the instruments of thought before looking for subjects on which to use them. The dying Socrates had bequeathed this choice to the Greeks, and when the Arabians brought Aristotle to the West, they put into the eager hands of the clerks the Ariadne-clue with which to explore the fascinating labyrinth of the human mind. Is it

vi

possible to abstract valid general concepts from the welter of individual objects presented to the senses? What is the mysterious relation between will and judgment? How, exactly, does a desire pass over the "threshold of assent" to issue in an act? These problems held them enthralled; and if we, despairing of any final solution, have turned to look for an explanation "below the threshold," yet in all our conscious, day-to-day thought and actions we still interpret ourselves to ourselves in the terminology developed by the Schoolmen from the Greek philosophers.

Impressive too, and exhilarating, is the encounter and exchange between Christian theology and pagan philosophy. The Church has had to brace herself to many such wrestlings with the dark angel of truth, but never perhaps in her long history has her grasp of tactics been more sure, never has she more skilfully made use of her adversary's own weight to subdue him to herself, and never has he blessed her more abundantly at the end of the conflict. The strength which seemed to be turned against her, she captured and made her own: the steel of Aristotle's rationalism is welded into the structure of the *Summa*. If she had dealt in a similar temper with Copernicus and Galileo, with the mechanistic philosophers of the Enlightenment, and the Evolutionists in the 19th century— if her strategy in the so-called "conflict" between science and religion had been less defensive and uncertain—we might have been spared many heart-burnings. To-day, her dealings with the psychology of the unconscious and with Existentialist philosophy show a return to her mediæval form; and it is not without significance that this renewed Christian aggressiveness was ushered in by a Thomist revival.

There is, of course, also the human and historic panorama of those astonishing centuries—a spectacle none the less moving and impressive in itself because it has sometimes been over-romanticized: the founding of the grammar schools and the great universities; the gathering of scholars from all corners of Europe to hear famous masters lecture in a language that all Europe could understand; the disputes and rivalries of the Faculties; the songs and the torchlight along the banks of the Seine; the tragedy of Abelard; Sigier of Brabant fleeing from condemnation to die at the hands of a crazy clerk; Aquinas seeing in ecstasy "that which makes all my writings seem but straw;" Dante visiting Paris and Bologna in his exile, and gathering the great doctors of all the rival schools to dance together like the circling stars in the shouting and splendour of the *Paradiso*.

The veil that interposes itself between us and the philosophers of the Middle Ages is not a very thick one; the questions which interested them were not quite the questions which consciously interest us, and their method of argument is one which we no longer use. For this reason, they sometimes seem alien and obscure. With Dr. Curtis's book before us, we can see better just what the great problems were which challenged the mediæval thinkers, and how the mediæval habit of thought gradually disposed itself towards that change which we call "the modern outlook"; and for his lucid guidance I, for one, am grateful.

DOROTHY L. SAYERS.

AUTHOR'S PREFACE

THIS book is a simple introduction to the history of the philosophy of the Middle Ages. It is intended not only for undergraduates who are studying this subject as part of their degree course, but also for students in university extension classes and members of a wider public who have hitherto been deterred by the scarcity of English translations of the works of mediæval philosophers and of commentaries upon them. In order to make this study accessible to all types of reader, especially those who have little knowledge of languages other than their own, all quotations from mediæval writers have been given in translations. With the exception of a few unavoidable cases where no English works exist, the Suggestions for Further Reading have been limited to such books as are available in English.

Many years' experience in the teaching of the history of mediæval philosophy has shown the author the difficulty students find in picturing the sequence of mediæval thinkers. It is hoped that the simple chronological chart will assist the reader in this process. The technical terms employed by mediæval thinkers have often led modern students into the belief that the Middle Ages were concerned with philosophical problems which are of no significance at the present day. The author has been sparing in his use of such terms, and where he has employed them, has endeavoured to illustrate their meaning. At the same time, he has tried to relate the problems of mediæval philosophy to ideas which either preceded or succeeded them. Brief biographical details have been given of the principal thinkers. The intention is to present the outstanding philosophers as human beings and not merely as minds. Since the development of Scholastic philosophy would not have taken place but for the educational facilities that were available, a very brief sketch of the mediæval schools and universities has been included.

Limitations of space have necessarily restricted the treatment accorded to individual thinkers, but the importance of the Thomistic system and its influence upon after ages has seemed to warrant fuller attention being given to the work of St. Thomas Aquinas than to other systems of thought. It is hoped that this small book will be for many the prelude to a more detailed study of mediæval philosophy or of the thought of particular philosophers.

The author would like to express his thanks to Miss Dorothy L. Sayers for her kindness in contributing the Foreword, and for the valuable assistance she gave after reading the book in proof.

S. J. C.

Leeds, October, 1949.

INTRODUCTION

THE revival of interest in mediæval philosophy is one of the most striking tendencies of the philosophical thought of the present century. It is not so long ago that most histories of philosophy passed over the whole of the Middle Ages with a few brief notes as though it was agreed that philosophical speculation entered upon a long period of inactivity and slumber after the closure of the schools of Athens and did not awaken until Descartes and Bacon opened up new fields to the inquiring mind.

The early 19th century regarded mediæval philosophy much in the same light as an earlier generation had looked upon Gothic architecture, and even Newman was surprised to find that in the Western Church the study of St. Thomas Aquinas had so languished that other systems of thought were occupying a more prominent place. This attitude has completely changed. The discovery that the human spirit did not (as if it ever could) enjoy a "dogmatic slumber" over so many centuries is but the last of a series of changes in the attitude of the modern world to the Middle Ages. Beginning with an interest in the life and activities, the literature, art and building of the Middle Ages, modern thought inevitably reached the point when it was realized that mediæval philosophers and theologians might, after all, have something to say which was not merely restricted to their own age, but which would stand for all time.

The revival began on the Continent and may be considered to have started in 1836, when Victor Cousin published his *Introduction aux ouvrages inédits d'Abelard*. This work was followed by a series of studies by Rousselot, Remusat and others, and eventually by the classic work of Hauréau, *Histoire de la philosophie scolastique*. The latter, although in many ways defective from the standards of modern scholarship, remained for a number of years the most important contribution to the history of mediæval philosophy.

The modern critical study of mediæval thought dates from about 1880 and was ushered in by the works of Baeumker, Ehrle and Denifle. Since then, most European countries and America have made important contributions; and although the scientific study of mediæval philosophy is still in its infancy, what has already been accomplished constitutes a considerable body of literature.

For practical purposes, the historian considers the Middle Ages as commencing with the fall of the Western Empire in 476 and as concluding in the latter part of the 15th century. The discovery of America in 1492 forms a convenient dividing point between the mediæval and modern worlds. It is more difficult to assign the exact limits of mediæval philosophy. The teaching of Greek philosophy continued until 529, when an edict of Justinian closed the schools of Athens and forced the last band of pagan philosophers to seek a less congenial home at the court of Persia. In the West, the Christian thinkers of the 5th and 6th centuries continue in many respects the traditions of the Graeco-Roman civilization, and mediæval thought does not assume its characteristic form until the period of the Carolingians. At the other end of the period, a thinker such as Nicholas of Cusa has been claimed by moderns and mediævalists alike. There are, however, three thinkers, St. Augustine, the Pseudo-Dionysius and Boethius, who, although they have a very close affinity with the ancient world, yet, because of their influence upon later thought, cannot be ignored by the historian of mediæval philosophy. During the earlier Middle Ages, Augustinian philosophy and theology were predominant throughout the greater part of the Western Church and proved formidable opponents to the revived Aristotelianism of the 13th century. Although the labours of Albert of Cologne and the genius of St. Thomas Aquinas secured the final triumph of Aristotelianism, the Scholastic philosophy of the later period still owed much to St. Augustine. The Pseudo-Dionysius is not only the Father of Mediæval Mysticism, but his writings had a most important influence in shaping both orthodox and unorthodox systems of thought. Finally, the logical commentaries of Boethius served as the occasion for the outbreak of the controversy over the problems of universals which loomed so large in the early Middle Ages.

For these reasons, a brief survey of the thought of St. Augustine, the Pseudo-Dionysius and Boethius forms a necessary prelude to the study of mediæval philosophy.

CHAPTER I

THE PRECURSORS OF MEDIÆVAL PHILOSOPHY: ST. AUGUSTINE, THE PSEUDO-DIONYSIUS AND BOETHIUS

ST. AUGUSTINE (354–430), forms an essential link between Greek and mediæval thought. In one important respect he differed from the majority of early Christian teachers. Unlike them, he did not despise classical learning but considered that he was justified in "spoiling the Egyptians," that is, in making use of whatever in Greek philosophy was true and in agreement with the Christian faith.

Augustine drew his inspiration, as regards his philosophy, from Plato. He mentions Aristotle only three times in his voluminous writings and seems to have known him merely as a logician. He admired the dialectic of Aristotle and used the method in the interpretation of the Scriptures. This reacted upon the early Middle Ages and served to strengthen the reputation of Aristotle as a logician. It was, however, the metaphysics of the Neo-Platonists, whom he identified with the Platonists, which had the greatest influence upon him. He knew but little Greek, so that his knowledge of Plato's thought was obtained through the translations of Marius Victorinus, the leading Neo-Platonist of that period. He may also have read a fragment of the *Timaeus* in Latin translation. In the *Confessions*, Augustine relates that it was the Platonists (Neo-Platonists) who led him to one of the turning points of his life. Hence, it was the Christianized Platonism of Augustine which had so remarkable an influence upon mediæval thought.

Augustine was familiar with Stoicism, Epicureanism and Scepticism as represented by contemporary writers. He was also a student of Cicero, and it was from the latter and not from the original that he obtained his knowledge of early Greek philosophy. He describes how the reading of Cicero's *Hortensius*, a treatise not now extant, aroused in him a love of philosophy. "But this book altered my affections and turned my prayers to Thyself, O Lord; and made me have other purposes and desires. . . . For with Thee is wisdom. But the love of wisdom is in Greek called 'philosophy,' with which that book inflamed me. . . . I was delighted with that exhortation, so far only, that I was thereby strongly roused, and kindled, and inflamed to love and seek and obtain and hold and embrace not this or that sect, but wisdom itself, whatever it were."[1]

The search for wisdom is a leading characteristic of Augustine's teaching. He identifies wisdom with happiness. Hence, at bottom, his philosophy is practical; it is the search for the supreme good of the human soul. All men desire happiness but they are not agreed upon what constitutes it. The supreme object of desire must be a permanent good, independent of the vicissitudes of fortune, for to love what may be lost or can perish results not in happiness but in a state of constant fear and anxiety. As all earthly goods are perishable, they should not be the supreme object of our desire. God alone is permanent, changeless and eternal. He alone is the supreme object of desire, and the possession of God is the indispensable condition of perfect happiness. To possess God is to possess the highest good, but knowledge of God is a necessary prerequisite. "I desire to know God and the soul," he once wrote. "Nothing more? Nothing at all."

It is easy to exaggerate the Augustinian intellectualism, but to do so is to misunderstand Augustine. Knowledge of the Supreme Good is an indispensable stage, but only a stage, in the acquisition of perfect happiness which can only consist in the possession of God. The true philosopher must also be a lover of God. Through love, enlightened by reason, man reaches his final end. To achieve it, man not only must know the end but must in a sense become that end. This can only be brought about by love, for it is a characteristic of love that it produces an assimilation of the lover to the object of his love. In loving God, man becomes like God. Hence we find in Augustine's thought a perfect blend of intellectualism and mysticism. The true philosopher not only seeks to know the Eternal Truth, God, but he loves God and thereby becomes assimilated to Him.

Augustine regards the existence of God as so self-evident as scarcely to need proof in the strict sense of the term, but he admits that there are a few individuals so hardened in sin as to deny God's

[1] *Confessions*, III. 4.

existence. One of his main arguments for the existence of God anticipates the *Cogito ergo sum* of Descartes. Prior to his knowledge that God exists, man has incontrovertible proof of his own existence. "We both are and know that we are, and delight in our being and our knowledge of it. . . . What if you are deceived? For if I am deceived, I am. For he who is not, cannot be deceived, and if I am deceived, by this same token I am." Augustine then argues that the certitude of self-knowledge provides three aspects on which the argument for God's existence can be built. These are, being, life and knowledge. Of two objects, that is the higher in the scale of existence which presupposes the other. An object, such as a stone, can exist without the added perfections of life or knowledge, but a living creature presupposes the fact of being. An object can be alive without being capable of knowing, as in the case of a plant, but a knowing subject presupposes both life and being. Knowledge, then, is the highest of these three aspects, since its possession implies the other two. At its lowest level, knowledge involves the power to perceive through the senses. Rational knowledge is superior to sense perception. Is there anything superior to reason? Since an examination of human nature shows that reason is man's highest power, any faculty superior to reason must be sought outside human nature.

Augustine, however, realizes that to discover a principle superior to the highest principle of human nature is not necessarily to find God. He must also show that such a principle can be none other than God. Can we therefore find in the intelligence itself something that points the way to a higher principle? Among the truths grasped by human intelligence, there are some that are unique in being eternally and necessarily true. When I enunciate such a proposition as 5 plus 7 is equal to 12, I do not intend that 5 and 7 ought to amount, or have in the past amounted, to 12. I am stating an eternal truth of which the characteristics are necessity, eternity and immutability. Such characteristics cannot be derived from sense-experience, for the objects of the sense world are continually changing, coming into and passing out of being. Nor does my individual intelligence confer these characteristics, for the eternal truths are grasped universally by every intelligence. They are not reached by a process of reasoning, but at a certain stage of thought are immediately present to intelligence and constitute the axioms or basic principles of all our knowledge and conduct.

Such truths, then, point the way to the existence of an Eternal Truth, necessary and unchanging, which is God. In other words, there are certain truths which cannot be accounted for by sensible objects nor by the nature of mind itself, but which demand a reality transcending the individual intelligence, a reality which is itself eternal, self-subsistent and unchangeable. This reality is God, the original Truth which lightens every man coming into the world.

Augustine, influenced by Platonism, tends to regard the soul as constituting pre-eminently the human being. Soul is a "rational substance created to govern a body." Body and soul are separately existing substances and by their union bring about the human being. Hence, "man is a rational soul making use of a body." The soul is the principle which confers life on the body. It is simple, immaterial, non-quantitative and non-extended, and is also immortal. As a spiritual substance, it is not located in any particular part of the body but permeates the body as a whole as a vital presence. It acts as an intermediary between the body which it animates and the Divine Ideas which animate it. The body, which is material and extended, is incapable of participation in the Divine Ideas. The latter are spiritual and of the same nature as the soul. Hence the body participates indirectly in the Divine Ideas only through the medium of the soul, for without such a participation it could not have existence.

Augustine hovers between two opposing theories concerning the origin of the soul. Traducianism stated that the soul of the child was derived from the soul of the parents. Augustine was anxious to maintain the doctrine of Original Sin against Pelagius, who had denied it. Hence, he seems at times to favour Traducianism as offering an explanation of the transmission of sin. Usually, however, he adopts the theory of Creationism, which teaches that the soul is infused into the body by a creative act of God.

Augustine's theory of knowledge presents certain difficulties. He believes that sensible experience cannot account for our universal ideas. Any doctrine, such as Aristotle's, which finds the origin of ideas in a process of abstraction from sense experience finds no favour in his eyes. He also rejects the Platonic doctrine of Reminiscence, which implies the previous existence of the soul. We must look upwards towards the Truth which is God, Who teaches and illumines the mind. The eye cannot see without light and the same holds in a spiritual manner concerning the soul. Without an internal light, the soul is blind. God is the internal light within us Who illumines the darkness of our minds.

This doctrine is usually known as the theory of Divine Illumination. Augustine calls God the "Secret Teacher of the soul," the "Sun of the soul" and the "Light of the intellect in which we see the eternal truths."

Many divergent interpretations of this doctrine have been given. Some thinkers have tended to minimize the difference between St. Augustine and St. Thomas Aquinas and to give to Divine Illumination a rôle approximate to that of the Active Intellect of later Scholasticism. Such a view ignores the considerable differences between the thought of the 5th and the 13th centuries, and neglects the influence of Neo-Platonism in shaping Augustine's philosophy.

St. Augustine's theory of Divine Illumination is developed most fully in the dialogue *De Magistro*, a treatise which, strange to say, has received little attention from English students. The dialogue is based on an actual conversation that occurred between Augustine and his son Adeodatus.[1] The object of the *De Magistro* is an inquiry into the origin of our ideas, and in the course of the discussion Augustine expounds his views on teaching method. He emphasizes that the common assumption of an interchange of ideas between teacher and pupil is quite false. What actually occurs is an interchange of words, and the function of language is not to produce ideas in the mind but to stimulate and awaken those that are already there. The true teacher of the soul is the Divine Word, Christ, the secret teacher of the soul. The metaphor of Divine Illumination does not refer to any supernatural process, and Augustine uses the

[1] Adeodatus was a natural son of Augustine born in the period before his conversion and Baptism. In the *Confessions* (IV. 2), he wrote, "In those years [from nineteen to twenty-eight] I had one—not in that which is called lawful marriage, but whom I had found out in a wayward passion, void of understanding; yet, but one, remaining faithful even to her." In another passage (IV. 6), Augustine refers to the writing of the *De Magistro*. Speaking of his Baptism, he says, "We joined with us the boy Adeodatus born after the flesh of my sin. Excellently hadst Thou made him. He was not quite fifteen, and in wit surpassed many grave and learned men. I confess unto Thee Thy gifts. There is a book of ours entitled *The Master*; it is a dialogue between him and me. Thou knowest, that all there ascribed to the person conversing with me were his ideas, in his sixteenth year. Much besides, and yet more admirable I found in him. That talent struck awe into me. And Who but Thou could be the work-master of such a son? Soon didst Thou take his life from earth; and I now remember him without anxiety, fearing nothing for his childhood and youth or his whole self." This passage fixes the date of the composition of the *De Magistro* as 389. The treatise is again mentioned in the *Retractions* (I. 2). "At the same time I wrote a book entitled *De Magistro*. In it is disputed and sought and found that there is no master who teaches man. (One is your Master, Christ.) This book begins, What do we seem to you to seek to do when we speak."

words, *natura* and *naturalis ordo* to emphasize this. Nor does God take the place of man's intellect and think for him. Man is a being naturally constituted so that his mind will be receptive of the Divine Light. Moreover, the human mind is illuminated directly by God; there is no intermediary. (*Nulla natura interposita.*) The universal truths with which our thought is concerned are none other than the Divine Ideas. Augustine employs a variety of terms to describe them—ideas, forms, species, thoughts and laws.

How does the mind see the Divine Ideas? The view that we see them as they exist in the Divine Essence misrepresents Augustine. The ideas have a twofold existence. From one point of view, they are the ideas of God in the light of which all things were created. In the Divine Mind, they exist as exemplars, or patterns, but in the world they have another mode of being. As the idea of the table exists first in the mind of the artisan and later in the material object he fashions, so the world is permeated with the Divine Ideas which are the cause of being to all the objects of the sensible world. To speak of nature as being impregnated with the Divine Ideas is another way of saying that the universe is intelligible for a mind capable of knowing it as such. The material universe cannot enter into a spiritual and superior substance such as mind. On the other hand, because the mind is superior to the body, it can transcend the materializing conditions under which the objects of the physical world appear to the senses and see directly the Divine Ideas which permeate them. Mind intuitively seizes the intelligible realities which underlie the individual existences of sense experience and it is on account of the intuition of the Divine Ideas that our concepts are universal and necessary. In modern language, the universe presents certain uniformities, principles and laws which are intuited as universal and necessary by thought. Thus the Divine Illumination becomes the guarantee of the truth of our concepts, which not merely are subjective in their significance but truly apply to the facts of experience.

Augustine's teaching about matter and forms had a considerable influence upon the Middle Ages. It springs from his interpretation of the six days' work of Creation. "In the beginning, God made heaven and earth." Augustine attaches a symbolic meaning to the statement. *In principio* does not mean in the beginning of time. It refers to creation having taken place through the Word of God, in which principle heaven and earth were made. The account in

Genesis is not intended to convey the idea of an act of creation extending over a number of days. The symbolism is used as a concession to the feebleness of our understanding. God created all that exists in one instant, simultaneously. By earth, the physical universe is intended. Heaven means the angelic spirits.

The angels possess a spiritualized matter and on account of this, in their essential nature, they are subject to change. In actuality they are changeless, for their contemplation of the Divine Essence secures this for them. Although, at times, Augustine speaks as if matter could exist without God, yet his real teaching is that God created the earth—*i.e.*, a matter which was absolutely "without form and void." This does not mean that He created matter one day and then on the next proceeded to clothe it with forms. The creation of matter did not precede that of forms in order of time but only in order of causality. It has only a logical priority over form. Voice does not exist apart from the words which are uttered by the voice and which are its form, and yet, in thought, we can trace a logical priority due to voice. Actually, the creation of matter and the forms was simultaneous. One might almost say that God created a matter impregnated with forms.

Matter is without form but it is not mere non-being. Although absolutely indeterminate, it is something. It serves as a substratum or support of forms and is the permanent without which change could not occur. Change means the passing away of one form, its place being taken by another.

How then is matter endowed with forms? Augustine's explanation is based upon his belief in the prior existence of the forms in God as the Divine Ideas or Exemplars. As constituting the Divine Ideas, the forms are eternal and changeless, yet they are destined to become the forms of contingent and perishable things. Thus they possess a twofold mode of existence; they are both ideas in the Divine Mind and also exist as the forms of contingent beings. These two modes of existence are simultaneous. When the artisan produces a table, the latter first exists as an idea in his mind, but when his activity is completed, it comes to dwell in the material object which he has made. The existence of the form in the material object, however, does not interfere with its existence in the mind of the artisan.

According to Augustine, the clothing of matter by the forms constitutes the work pictorially represented by the account of the six days' creation. God's act of creation has a double aspect: He both makes and perfects. The act of making consists in giving being to things; that of perfecting, in endowing them with their proper forms. God created the world through the Word and impressed upon matter a movement which, tending towards Him, is an imitation of that intimate union which exists between the Word and the Father. It is because of the closeness of this union that the Word is described as "the express image of the Father." So, too, matter becomes an imperfect image of the Word and of the ideas which dwell in the Word. It is in this fashion that matter is perfected and endowed with forms.

Another problem arises for Augustine. How can one account for the appearance of new beings, if God's creative act was performed once and for all time? Augustine answers that there are two kinds of creatures: those created in their definite form in the beginning—*e.g.*, the angels, the sky, the stars, the four elements of fire, air, water and earth, and the soul of man, created before entering the body, and those created in germ, as it were, ready for some future process of development. The latter are described by Augustine as existing in their seeds (*rationes causales* or *seminales*). It is in virtue of the existence of *rationes seminales* that matter contains the principle of all future development. Augustine suggests that the *rationes seminales* are humid, akin to water, and contain within themselves an active principle of development. Thus God created everything simultaneously, either in actuality or in their *rationes seminales*. One must be careful not to credit Augustine with views approximate to those of modern Emergent Evolution. He believed in the fixity of species; man begets man and the oak tree produces its kind. The theory of *rationes seminales* is intended to explain the coming into existence of new individuals within the species and not the appearance of new species. The germ is "earmarked" beforehand and can only develop into an individual in its particular species. Thus viewed, the *rationes seminales* guarantee stability in development.

One of the most interesting productions of early Christian philosophic thought is the collection of writings which passed under the name of the works of Dionysius the Areopagite. The collection is not only of interest in itself as a type of synthesis of orthodox Christianity with Neo-Platonism common to certain thinkers of the East in the 5th and 6th centuries, but it is of great importance in its influence upon thinkers of the later Middle Ages. Four important treatises bear the name of the Areopagite: the *Divine Names*, the *Mystical Theology*, the *Heavenly Hierarchy* and the *Earthly* or *Ecclesiastical Hierarchy*. In addition are a number of letters purporting to have been written by him, some to unknown persons such as Caius the Monk (*Epistles*, 1–4), and others to historic persons such as St. John, St. Polycarp and Titus (*Epistles*, 7 to Polycarp, 9 to Titus and 10 to St. John in his exile on the island of Patmos). All these works are products of the same pen, for examination shows that their style is the same, that quotations from others appear in each one and that their teaching is similar.

The first appearance of the works was in 532 or 533, when they were quoted at a conference held at Constantinople and the Catholic bishops raised doubts about their authenticity. Gregory the Great mentions them, and in the 7th century Maximus the Confessor produced a commentary on them. At the Lateran Council of 649, Martin I corrected certain phrases in the text showing that Dionysius was already being regarded as authoritative.

The actual author of the treatises is entirely unknown. He claims to be the companion of St. Paul and Timothy and gives as the date of his treatises A.D. 98. We read in the Acts of the Apostles that after the sermon of St. Paul at Athens, "certain men clave unto him and believed; among the which was Dionysius the Areopagite." With few exceptions this claim was accepted until the 16th century. Since then controversy has raged over the question of authorship, but the general consensus of opinion attributes them to an unknown writer who flourished at the end of the 5th or at the beginning of the 6th century. He was probably a Syrian monk, possibly a bishop. The writings are permeated with Neo-Platonism, and passages can be found in them which bear a marked similarity to certain portions of the works of Plotinus and Proclus. The mediæval world believed in the author's claim. Traditions about the Areopagite grew, and several lives of Dionysius were written. After some years, he was supposed to have left Athens and to have preached in Gaul, where he met a martyr's death near Paris. Hence he became identified with St. Denis, the patron of France, and the Abbey of St. Denis was erected in memory of his martyrdom. His name appears in the Kalendar of the Book of Common Prayer for October 9th and is given as St. Denis, Bishop and Martyr.

Various conjectures have been offered in explanation of his claim to be the genuine Areopagite. The most plausible suggestion is that since the original Areopagite was a member of the judicial council of Athens, a man of education and presumably an adherent of an important school of Greek thought, he did not forsake his philosophic interest on his conversion to Christianity. He would retain those views which he deemed were compatible with the new religion, or, more likely, construct a working synthesis of the two. The 5th and 6th centuries in the East were a period when synthesis was in the air. Such attempts were viewed with suspicion by the Church, which was strongly hostile to Neo-Platonism. If the synthesis of the Pseudo-Areopagite was not to suffer immediate condemnation, this unknown writer would endeavour to obtain for his work the support of a recognized authority, and what authority would carry greater weight than the name of the well-known convert of St. Paul?

The object of the treatise on the *Divine Names* is to discover the way in which the names applied to God in the Scriptures are to be understood. Since man is restricted to knowledge which has been developed from sense-perception, in order to convey to him some idea of the nature of God, Holy Scripture represents the Godhead by means of symbols taken from the world of sense experience. Such symbolism, however, does not give a real insight into the nature of the Divine. It is merely a method by which thought attempts to reach a higher reality, a means through which finite minds can gain some knowledge of the Infinite which in its essence is wholly beyond the scope of human reason.

In this present life, there are two ways in which man can seek knowledge of the Infinite, the affirmative and the negative. The Scriptures lead man along the affirmative path as far as he is able to go, but such conceptions of the Divine Nature they give are to be regarded in the form of metaphor and analogy. In His essential nature, God is above and beyond all beings, sensible and spiritual. Indeed, He is above all the conditions of being as we know it and in His Super-Essence is completely inaccessible to reason. All perfections of creatures can be attributed to God to a superlative degree, but, as the cause always remains superior to the effect, the Supreme Cause can only be described in analogical fashion. When goodness is attributed to God, we do not mean that He is good in the way in which goodness belongs to creatures. The goodness of the creature is an effect of God's causality and is but a faint copy of the super-goodness which belongs to God and which cannot be understood by a finite intelligence.

God is not even being itself, but above all being and all conditions of being. Dionysius expresses this idea through the use of the term Super-Essential. The word "being" indicates an individual existence, and the highest type of individual existence we know is the person. Therefore, by saying that God is Super-Essential, Dionysius implies that the Godhead considered in Itself is super-personal. God is super-personal because He is the Infinite. He is ultimate reality, or, to use a modern term, the Absolute. We cannot even ascribe a personal consciousness to Him. In the state of consciousness, the thinking subject becomes aware of himself as an object of thought, but no such relation as thinker and object of thought can exist in the nature of God. At this level, all such distinctions vanish and Dionysius feels that such consciousness as belongs to the Absolute must be a universal, a super-consciousness.

Thus, the Godhead in Its true nature is super-personal, absolutely undifferentiated and, therefore, wholly inaccessible to human reason. Dionysius, however, is a Christian as well as a Neo-Platonist, and he is compelled to bring his conception of the super-personal Godhead into line with the Christian doctrine of God. He does this by bringing in the distinction between the Differentiated and the Undifferentiated names of God. So far, he had been considering the Divine Nature as It is in Itself—*i.e.*, the Undifferentiated Godhead. He turns now to consider the Godhead in Its relation to us—*i.e.*, the Differentiated Godhead. The Scriptural titles of God are Undifferentiated names in the sense that they apply to the whole nature of the Godhead. They certainly attempt to describe the Godhead, though most inadequately, but it is necessary for the philosopher to avoid the error of thinking that they express real distinctions in God's nature. The Undifferentiated Godhead has no parts, and the names employed by Scripture are symbols that dimly represent something that is true of the Deity as a whole. The Differentiated names are those of Father, Son and Holy Spirit. Such names as Good, Wise and Fair denote the whole Godhead though in an inadequate manner, but the name Father denotes something different from the Son and both of these from that of the Holy Spirit. The whole Divine Nature is good and wise and fair, but there is a distinction between the Father, the Son and the Holy Spirit.

The distinction between the Differentiated and the Undifferentiated names shows clearly the two lines of thought which shaped the teaching of the Pseudo-Dionysius. On the one hand we have elements derived from orthodox Christianity, and on the other those whose source is in the Neo-Platonism of Plotinus and Proclus. The Christian source of his doctrine is freely acknowledged, but Dionysius makes no mention of his borrowing from Neo-Platonic writers. The latter were still viewed with suspicion by the Church, and references which showed his debt to pagan philosophy would have been unwise. The synthesis is incomplete, as one would naturally expect, when the two terms to be synthesized are so unlike, and its superficiality is at once apparent when the diverse statements made by Dionysius are carefully examined. In spite of his Christianity, the Neo-Platonic influence is the more fundamental in shaping his thought. Although this thought is disguised under the terminology of Christianity, yet its leading ideas are non-Christian in origin. We are forced to admit that the Differentiated names represent subjective rather than objective distinctions in God's nature. They express the different aspects under which the Divine Activity appears to us, but they have no roots in the substantial being of God. Though the Persons of the Trinity are differentiated, the same creative energy springs from all alike.

The idea of a stream of energy issuing from the Godhead leads naturally to the consideration of creation. Once more, two opposing views struggle for mastery. On the one hand, Dionysius makes use of the Neo-Platonic idea of Emanation. On the other, he apparently agrees with the orthodox Christian belief that the world is a reality distinct from God and created *ex nihilo* by Him. The term "emanation" is used in a number of senses. The Persons of the Trinity are called emanations since they represent streams of energy proceeding from the undivided Unity. The outgoing stream of energy is also an emanation, and when this undifferentiated stream becomes divided into separate forces, each of the latter receives the same name. Although the use of the expression, due to the ambiguity of such terms as Cause and Create, is not inconsistent with the former statements of Dionysius, yet it is difficult to see how to reconcile it with the Christian belief as expressed in the Creeds. Orthodox Christianity believes in a transcendent God Who is in the world but not of it. The world exists as the result of a free act of creation, but if we take the theory of Emanation seriously, the distinction between the world and God disappears. The created universe flows as inexorably from the nature of the Godhead as the properties of the right-angled triangle are a necessary consequence of its nature, and the world becomes as necessary to God as He is to the world. The idea of a transcendent God does not tie up easily with a thoroughgoing Emanation theory, for it is difficult to see, if the world is the result of an emanation from the Deity, how its substance can be other than that of the Divine Nature. It loses its independent reality and is reduced to a moment in the eternal evolution of the Absolute. An Emanation theory leads to a thinly veiled pantheism, and throughout the writings of the Pseudo-Dionysius this trend of pantheistic thought can be discerned. As Bishop Westcott remarked, "It must be frankly admitted that they bear the impress not only of a particular age and school, but also of a particular man which is not wholly of a Christian type."[1]

It is, however, only fair to Dionysius to point out that he never irrevocably commits himself. It is possible, as Aquinas does, to read him in an orthodox sense, but other thinkers, such as Erigena, have developed the Neo-Platonic aspect and have experienced the same difficulty in accommodating their views to Christian dogma. It would be a grave misrepresentation of the facts to term Dionysius a pantheist. There is most certainly an element in his teaching which lends itself to development on pantheistic lines, but while asserting the immanence of God, Dionysius also teaches His transcendence. His view, to use a term which has become popular of late, is "panentheism" rather than pantheism. Inconsistencies in his synthesis are due to the difficulty in fusing Neo-Platonism and its Emanation theory with Christianity which holds most strongly to the idea of creation *ex nihilo*.

The greater part of the long fourth chapter of the *Divine Names* is concerned with the discussion of the origin and nature of evil. There is little originality in the treatment, for nowhere is the debt of Dionysius to Neo-Platonic thought more clearly revealed. It is generally acknowledged that sections 18 to 34 of this chapter are based upon a fragment of Proclus. Although lacking in originality, this chapter is extremely important because of the influence it exerted upon subsequent thinkers. With the teaching of Augustine,

---

[1] WESTCOTT, B. F., *Essays in the History of Religious Thought in the West* (Macmillan: 1891), p. 189.

it was responsible for the general attitude of Scholasticism towards the problem of evil, and in particular, it helped to shape not only the doctrine of Aquinas, but also his method of dealing with the topic in the *Summa contra Gentiles*.

The discussion opens with a consideration of the good. God, as the Supreme Good of the universe, extends His goodness to all creatures, so that all being shares in the good, but there are manifestly different grades of perfection in the universe dependent upon the extent to which individual creatures participate in the good and the beautiful. So fundamental is the notion of the good, that in the Divine Nature it takes precedence of being, a statement which Aquinas finds difficult to accept without qualification. The discussion of the nature of the good leads directly to the problem of evil, and Dionysius concludes that evil must be some kind of non-being. "All creatures in so far as they have being are good and come from the good, and in so far as they are deprived of the good, neither are they good nor have they being."[1] It is impossible to find anything that is totally evil, for such a being would cease to exist. Even in the most depraved beings there must be some spark, however faint, of the good. The essence of evil lies in the privation of good.

In his long and rambling discourse on the nature and origin of evil, Dionysius repeats himself at wearisome length, constantly reiterating his position that evil is a weakness and a deficiency of good. There is much in his account to which modern writers would object. Dionysius and other writers of his type too easily minimize the dire effects of evil and sin. To deny its reality and to assert, as he does, that it is a necessary ingredient of the universe, perhaps even adding to the whole by its contrast with the good, just as the dark shadows of a painting help to throw into greater relief the high lights, is extremely unconvincing to a world that has experienced the positive evils associated with two world wars. Social workers, clergy and doctors would all register a protest against any attempt to minimize the awful reality of sin and suffering. Metaphysical speculations of this kind seem to have little in common with the experience of those in daily contact with the positive results of sin and disease. Dionysius shows himself more the Neo-Platonic philosopher and less the Christian in his treatment of evil. There is little indication in his account of the Christian view of sin as a

[1] *Divine Names*, IV. 20.

wilful act of rebellion against the tender love of a Heavenly Father, an act which inflicts a deadly wound upon the individual soul and cuts it off from the influence of Divine Grace. The consequences of human sin, the agony of the Passion and the awful sufferings of Calvary seem to have no place in this system of thought.

One of the most important conceptions of the Areopagite, and perhaps the most fruitful as regards his influence on later thought, is that of an hierarchy. For Dionysius, the universe presents a scale of being and perfection extending from matter, which is the mere potentiality of being, and rising by gradual steps to God, Who is beyond all being as we know it. Man occupies an intermediate position in the scale of being. Below him are the animals, plants and the varied range of non-living substances. He shares the nature of the material because of his possession of a body, but, on the other hand, through his power of reason, he forms a link with the purely spiritual existences, the angels. This scale of being is such that any intermediate member partakes of the nature both of that which is below and of that which is above it.

The title, hierarchy, is applicable in a more special sense to the Heavenly Hierarchy, represented by the descending orders of angels, and to the earthly copy of the heavenly type, the Ecclesiastical Hierarchy of the Church. The leading idea is as follows. Each species of finite existences, so far as it is able, mirrors the beauty and perfections of the Creator, reflecting, as it were, the Divine Light. The function of both hierarchies is assimilation to God, and each individual rank endeavours to accomplish this purpose by the triple activity of purifying, illuminating and perfecting those in the grade beneath it. Of all created beings, the angels participate most freely in and are nearest to the Divine Nature. In the same way, the highest order of angels, being placed nearest to God, receives boundless treasures of illumination, knowledge and grace, which in turn it transmits to the second order. The third order is illuminated by the second and in its turn illuminates the souls of men.

The members of the Heavenly Hierarchy are all called angels because of their ministering office, but, strictly speaking, this title is only applied to members of the third and lowest order of intelligences. The highest order consists of those intelligences which participate most completely in the Divine Illumination, thrones, cherubim and seraphim. In the second order are powers, dominions and virtues, and in the third angels, archangels and principalities.

The conception of the angelic hierarchies made a tremendous appeal to later mediæval thinkers. Its influence may be seen in the last book of St. Bernard's treatise *On Consideration* or the *Paradiso* of Dante. Thus in Canto X, Dionysius appears among the twelve spirits who surround Dante and Beatrice. "Next look upon that taper's light, which, in the flesh below, saw deepest into the angelic nature and its ministry." Again, in Canto XXVIII, Pope Gregory explains the orders of the Heavenly Hierarchy, saying, "These orders all gaze upward, and downward have such conquering might that toward God all are drawn and draw." He concludes, "And Dionysius with such yearning set himself to contemplate these orders that he named them and distinguished them as I." As a philosophical doctrine, the teaching of Dionysius was adopted by Aquinas, and his elaboration of it earned for him the title of the Angelic Doctor.

Each rank in the Heavenly Hierarchy has its own proper work. The highest order, in the closest union with God, receives a direct revelation of His nature. The seraphim represent most fully the Divine Love and know most completely because they love most. The cherubim, whose special function is that of illumination, and the thrones, receive directly the Divine Illumination. Each rank, while striving with the whole of its nature towards perfect assimilation with God, receives and passes on what it has received to those below it. The highest order, purified, illuminated and perfected directly by God, purifies, illuminates and perfects the order next below it. The third hierarchy is most connected with human affairs. The angels and archangels guide both nations and individuals and bear messages from God to man.

In a truly Platonic spirit, Dionysius regards the Ecclesiastical Hierarchy as an earthly copy of the heavenly archetype. The end of each hierarchy is the same, namely, assimilation to the Divine and the imparting to inferior members of the results of this assimilation. The Ecclesiastical Hierachy consists of three ranks, bishops, priests and deacons. The function of the bishop is that of perfecting; of the priest, illumination; and of the deacon, purification. The Ecclesiastical Hierarchy leads men from preoccupation with material things to the contemplation of the Divine by means of sensible symbols. These symbolic acts or Sacraments possess a twofold power. To the uninitiated, they are sensible rites and ceremonies, but to the initiated, they show the way to the truths of the intelligible world. Dionysius names amongst these symbolic rites Baptism, Confirmation, the Eucharist, Ordination and Prayer for the Departed.

As the function of the members of the hierarchy is to purify, illuminate and perfect, so the initiated fall into three groups corresponding to the three stages of assimilation. The lowest, consisting of those who are being purified, are committed to the care of the deacons who prepare them for the reception of Baptism. The priests take charge of the baptized, who are in the stage of being illuminated and who partake of the Eucharist. The highest grade consists of those who are being perfected and are given to the charge of the bishop. They consist of members of religious orders who have taken vows of service and devotion to God.

We have already seen that any affirmation made about the nature of God is true only in an analogical sense. Analogy does, however, provide a definite knowledge of God, but such knowledge is very inadequate. It is but a step leading to a more excellent method of knowing. In the upward journey of the soul to God, the negative path of Unknowing should be pursued in preference to the affirmative path. It is possible to grasp more fully the nature of God by realizing what He is not, than by endeavouring to attribute to Him qualities drawn by analogy from the sensible world. In making use of the affirmative path, man is not employing the highest powers that he is able to exercise. Intelligence, though the characteristic human power, is not the highest which is possible to man. In the initial step, man employs discursive reason and, through meditation, makes use of symbols drawn from sense-experience in order to frame intellectual conceptions which can be applied to God in a metaphorical way. But there comes a time when he can take a further step. He throws aside what is now useless to him and, leaving meditation, he enters upon the higher and more difficult art of contemplation. The paradox of mysticism is that the highest knowledge is something which is not knowledge at all. Extremes meet and the most perfect knowledge consists in Unknowing (*Agnosia*). In an act of perfect knowledge, the soul becomes in some sense like the things it knows, for "knowledge unites the knower and the objects of knowledge."

Even in the highest flights of intuition, the soul never achieves

this complete identity. Always, the distinction between the knowing subject and the object known exists and is only partially
bridged in the living act of knowledge. To reach *Agnosia*, the soul
must become Godlike, completely assimilated to the Divine, and
then, in this supreme moment, like is known by like. This mystical
union of the soul with God is an ecstatic union attended by raptures
of knowledge and transports of love. The mystic allows himself to
be passively illumined by the Divine Rays, and as the bodily eye
is blinded by excess of light, so the eye of the soul is darkened by
the glory proceeding from the vision of God. Hence the paradoxical
conception of the Divine Darkness which is the state of the soul in
the presence of excessive light. Dionysius speaks as though the
mystical vision of God was possible to man whilst living upon this
earth. Aquinas, whilst conceding this possibility, severely restricts
the authenticated cases of the Beatific Vision in the present life
to those of Moses and St. Paul.

The last of the precursors of mediæval philosophy is Boethius,
who was born between 470 and 475. He came of a noble family.
His father was consul in 487, and his grandfather, who had been
executed by Valentinian III, was the praefect of the Praetorian
Guard. Boethius mourned the decay of the Western Empire and
the period of anarchy which had followed its collapse. He hailed
the accession of Theodoric the Ostro-Goth, as king of Italy, as the
promise of the restoration of peace and security. He quickly
gained the friendship of the new king and was appointed administrator of the public revenues. One of his first undertakings was the
reform of the coinage of Italy, and later, he relaxed the regulations
for the support of the army in order to provide food for the starving
population. Boethius seems to have been a very efficient administrator but he made many enemies because of the austerity of his
character. In his later years, Theodoric developed into a jealous
and suspicious tyrant who firmly believed that his Roman officials
were conspiring to bring Italy under the rule of Constantinople.
Boethius was accused of treason by his enemies and his suspicious
master committed him to prison. It was during his imprisonment
that he wrote his famous *Consolation of Philosophy*, which Alfred
the Great translated into Anglo-Saxon. After lingering for some
time in prison, Boethius was executed in 525.

Boethius was an accomplished Greek scholar and his ambition
was to translate the works of the Greek philosophers into Latin so

that they could be read by the Italians of his day. He planned an extensive programme. His intention was to start with the works of Aristotle and then proceed to the *Dialogues* of Plato. It is uncertain how much of this programme he was able to carry out. If he completed the task, the translations have not come down to us. It is certain, however, that he translated the logical writings of Aristotle known as the *Organon*, but his versions of the *Prior and Posterior Analytics*, the *Topics* and the *Sophistical Refutations* seem to have been lost and not rediscovered until the latter part of the 12th century. We also have some of his commentaries on Aristotle's *Logic* and on the *Isagoge* of Porphyry. The latter was written by Porphyry, the pupil of Plotinus, and was intended to be an introduction to Aristotle's treatise *On the Categories*.

Boethius was also the author of several original treatises—*e.g.*, *On Unity and the One*, and *On Arithmetic, Geometry and Music*. Certain theological treatises have been attributed to him, of which the most important are those *On the Trinity* and *Against the Heresies of Nestorius and Eutyches*.[1] These were accepted as genuine by the Middle Ages, which regarded Boethius as a devout Christian and even as a martyr for the Catholic Faith put to death by an Arian King. German critics of the early 19th century raised doubts concerning the theological treatises and even about his belief in Christianity. It was urged that in the *Consolation of Philosophy* there is no direct reference to Christianity. On the other hand, there is no evidence in his other writings to show that he was not a Christian. Thus, F. D. Maurice, writing in the middle of the 19th century, excludes the theological treatises from the genuine works of Boethius.[2]

The modern attitude towards the theological treatises represents agreement with the mediæval tradition. This is due to the discovery by Alfred Holder of a fragment at the end of a 10th-century manuscript of Cassiodorus, the friend and kinsman of Boethius and the secretary and chief minister of Theodoric. The fragment is presumed to be part of a memorandum written by Cassiodorus

---

[1] Nestorius taught that in Christ there are two Natures and two Persons, and Eutyches the opposite error, that there was but one Nature and one Person in Christ. The Catholics maintained the doctrine of two Natures, human and Divine, in the one Person.

[2] "There is not a single element in his scientific teaching which is not derived from teachers of the old world, or from teachers who were adverse rather than friendly to Christianity."—MAURICE, F. D., *Mediaeval Philosophy* (Richard Griffin: 1857), p. 16.

and it was translated and published with a commentary by the German scholar Hermann Usener in 1877. The second paragraph states categorically that Boethius wrote the book *De Trinitate* and also a treatise in refutation of the errors of Nestorius.

The influence of Boethius on after ages was exerted in four main directions:

(*a*) The *Consolation of Philosophy* has been one of the most popular works of all ages. During the mediæval period, it was probably more widely read than any other philosophical work and was translated into most European languages.[1]

(*b*) In his treatise *On Arithmetic* he defined the subject of the study and its relations to geometry, astronomy and music.

To these four studies Boethius gave the name of the Quadrivium. "This then is that Quadrivium in which those must travel whose mind being raised above the senses, is brought to the heights of intelligence." The remaining studies, the Trivium, consisted of grammar, rhetoric and dialectic or logic. This classification of studies was afterwards elaborated by Cassiodorus and Isidore of Seville, who were responsible for the idea of the Seven Liberal Arts. The subjects of the Trivium were studied in the mediæval grammar schools whilst those of the Quadrivium furnished the curriculum of the universities. The latter formed an introduction to the higher philosophic studies and to theology.[1]

[1] "To go no further than our own land for a few of the famous names that are associated with the book: King Alfred valued it so highly that he laid upon himself the task of translating the *Consolation* for the instruction and edification of his people, or rather of paraphrasing and interpreting it, for he did not keep by any means closely to his text; Geoffrey Chaucer, besides showing in his poetry many marks of Boethius's powerful influence, made a prose translation of his greatest work; Sir Thomas More . . . valued the *Consolation of Philosophy*, commended it to his children's study and evidently had it in mind when he named the book he wrote during his own imprisonment, *A Dialogue of Comfort against Tribulation*; Queen Elizabeth felt the book's spell and made her own translation it; and a writer so rarely carried away by enthusiasm as Edward Gibbon has called the work 'a golden volume not unworthy of the leisure of Plato or Tully'."—BARRETT, HELEN M., *Boethius* (C.U.P.: 1940), p. 2.

[1] "The grammar schools of the later Middle Ages were thought of as feeders for the universities, and therefore the curriculum was designed as an introduction to university studies. Theology was considered the queen of studies to which philosophy served as an introduction. The studies which led to the supreme study of theology were known generally as the Seven Liberal Arts. The arts (or sciences) were termed liberal from *liber*, free, and constituted the course of study suitable for the freeman as contrasted with the practical and mechanical arts which were learned and practised by slaves in the classical period. The conception of the Liberal Arts takes us back to Greece, at least as far as Plato, and passed over to

(c) The works of Boethius furnished St. Thomas Aquinas with two celebrated definitions which became authoritative in the mediæval schools.

One is the definition of eternity from Book V, para. 6, of the *Consolation of Philosophy*; "Eternity is the whole and perfect possession of unlimited life all at once (*Aeternitas igitur est interminabilis vitae tota simul et perfecta possessio*)."

The other is the definition of a person given in the treatise against Eutyches and Nestorius, "A person is an individual substance of a rational nature (*Reperta personae est definitio: naturae rationalis individua substantia*)."

(d) Last, but not least in importance, is the paragraph in Boethius's *Commentary on the Isagoge of Porphyry*, which set the main philosophical problem for the next six hundred years.

In his *Commentary*, Boethius started by considering the right order which should be followed in the study of logic. He traced briefly the relations between the different treatises of Aristotle and showed why the categories should have priority. The primary distinction in the categories is that between substance and accident. Therefore, it is necessary for the student to know something about the nature of the two. Before these primary distinctions are studied it is also necessary to understand the laws of logical division. This need is satisfied by Porphyry, whose introduction provides a suitable text book for the beginner. Boethius then proceeded to comment upon the *Isagoge* paragraph by paragraph. In the course of his *Commentary* occurs the oft-quoted passage, "What does Porphyry mean by saying that he merely touches and passes over certain points which older philosophers had discussed at great length? He means this: he omits the question whether general and species have

---

Rome with other aspects of Greek thought. The idea was given more definite form by the late Latin writers, Augustine and Martianus Capella, in the 5th century, and Boethius and Cassiodorus in the 6th. The latter two were responsible for fixing the number of the arts as seven, no doubt due to Prov. ix. 1, 'Wisdom builded her house; she has hewn out her seven pillars.' The division into the Trivium and Quadrivium was completed by Isidore of Seville, 570–636. His *Etymologiae* was widely known to the early Middle Ages. That the Seven Liberal Arts were known quite early in England is evident from the works of Alcuin of York."—CURTIS, S. J., *History of Education in Great Britain* (University Tutorial Press: 1948), p. 20.

B

an actual subsistence, or dwell in the mind and intellect alone; whether they be corporeal or incorporeal; and whether they are separate or joined to the things which our senses perceive. On these matters, seeing that the disputation was a deep one, he promised to be silent."

The successors of Boethius saw that he had but lightly touched upon the problem, and hence this passage served as the stimulus to the controversy about the nature of universals which occupied so much space in the first period of mediæval philosophy.

Suggestions for Further Reading

A Monument to St. Augustine (Sheed and Ward: 1934). This book was first published in 1930 to commemorate the 15th centenary of St. Augustine's death. It consists of a number of essays by present-day experts who present different aspects of his life and work. The reader will find the following essays of great value in understanding Augustine's philosophy:

"The Philosophy of St. Augustine," by M. C. D'Arcy, S.J.

"St. Augustine and St. Thomas Aquinas," by Jacques Maritain.

"The Mysticism of St. Augustine," by E. I. Watkin.

Rolt, C. E., *Dionysius the Areopagite on the Divine Names and the Mystical Theology* (S.P.C.K.: 1920). This is an English translation of the two most important works of the Pseudo-Dionysius. It has an excellent introduction. The complete works of Dionysius are obtainable in the French translation of Mgr. Darboy (A. Tralin: Paris, 1932). Mgr. Darboy accepts the claim of the Pseudo-Dionysius to be the convert of St. Paul and in the long introduction gives a detailed account of the influence of these writings upon later philosophy.

Barrett, Helen M., *Boethius—Some Aspects of his Times and Work* (C.U.P.: 1940). This is the only available account of Boethius in English. An English translation by Adrian Fortescue of the *Consolation of Philosophy* was published by Burns, Oates and Washbourne in 1925. Other English translations are that in the Loeb Classical Library (with Latin text), edited by Stewart and Rand, and a tranlation by W. V. Cooper in the Temple Classics (Dent). An English translation of the *Commentary on the Isagoge of Porphyry* is given in *Selections from Medieval Philosophers*, vol. I, by R. McKeon (Charles Scribner's Sons: 1930).

CHAPTER II

JOHN THE SCOT, AN ORIGINAL THINKER OF THE 9th CENTURY

With the close of the Patristic period, no really original thinker appeared until the 9th century. What little philosophic thinking existed was concentrated on the collection on facts[1] and on premature attempts to deal with the problems brought to the notice of the early Middle Ages through Boethius's *Commentary on the Isagoge*. There are several reasons for the tardy rebirth of speculative thought. The collapse of the Western Empire resulted in the disintegration of the existing social order, which in turn produced a decay of classical learning. Only in the monasteries of Ireland and Northern Britain did the ancient culture continue for a time to flourish, and when the Carolingians set about the revival of education in Western Europe, it was to these distant outposts of civilization that they turned for their scholars. The insecurity which followed the downfall of the Empire was not favourable to the growth of philosophy. The Church, too, had little time left for philosophy during these years. The energies of the Western Church were directed to Christianizing the barbarians whilst the Eastern Church was torn asunder by theological disputes. No sooner had the new barbarian rulers achieved some kind of good order and stability in their dominions, than they began to struggle amongst themselves, and internal strife opened up an opportunity for the ravages of fresh hosts of invaders, the Vikings in the West and the Saracens in the East.

The result was that philosophy had to make a fresh start with very little upon which to build. Suddenly, at the very height of the Viking invasions, there appeared the remarkable figure of John the Scot, a Greek scholar and a daring and original thinker who developed a systematic philosophy showing strong Neo-Platonic influences. Very little that is authentic is known about his life,

[1] The age of the encyclopædists—*e.g.*, Isidore of Seville.

though the legends clustered about his name are numerous enough. He has been claimed as a native of Ireland, Scotland and England. The first is the most probable and the title, Scotus, suggests that he was a member of the Scoti who inhabited Northern Ireland at that time. This hypothesis would also account for his knowledge of Greek, since classical studies flourished in Ireland long after they had disappeared from the Continent. We are on fairly safe ground in assuming that he was born between the years 800 and 815 and that some time before 847 he appeared at the court of Charles the Bald. According to tradition, he was head of the Palace school and was on most intimate terms with the king. We do not know how long he resided in France or the date of his death. William of Malmesbury, writing in the early years of the 12th century, asserts that he was invited by Alfred the Great to England and taught for some years at the Abbey of Malmesbury where, some time after 877, he met a tragic death, being stabbed by the pens of his pupils.[1]

John the Scot is frequently referred to as Erigena though the reason for this cognomen is a matter of uncertainty. In the title to his translation of the works of the Pseudo-Dionysius, he is styled Jerugena. Although De Wulf thinks that Eriugena is the more accurate rendering of his name,[2] general usage sanctions the spelling Erigena. The name may possibly be derived from either a Greek or a Celtic term denoting that he came from Ireland, the island of the saints.

Two main influences can be traced in the works of Erigena. Prior to 851, he was influenced by Latin writers, in particular St. Augustine. Bett stresses the Augustinian influence[3] but this should not lead us to underestimate that of the Neo-Platonists, which became most marked in the works written after 851. The latter was mainly due to the Pseudo-Dionysius. In 827, the Byzantine Emperor, Michael the Stammerer, sent to Louis I a copy of the manuscript of Dionysius. The gift was received with great ceremony at the Abbey of St. Denis by Abbot Hilduin. Its arrival, we are told, was heralded by an outburst of miracles and nineteen sick

---

[1] The evidence for John's residence at Malmesbury is discussed at length by R. L. Poole in his *Illustrations of the History of Medieval Thought and Learning* (S.P.C.K.: 1920), pp. 273–85.
[2] DE WULF, *History of Medieval Philosophy*, 3rd edition (Longmans, Green: 1909), p. 167.
[3] BETT, H., *Johannes Scotus Erigena* (C.U.P.: 1925), p. 157.

people of the neighbourhood were healed of their complaints. Hilduin was unable to read the Greek text and the manuscript remained in the Abbey until, at the request of Charles the Bald, Erigena undertook the task of translation. This was probably in 851 and gives an explanation of the influence of Dionysius in the works written after that date. Pope Nicholas I complained that the translations had not been sent to him for approval and claimed that Erigena was responsible for a number of heretical statements.

Although we know so little about Erigena's life, contemporary references show that he took a leading part in the controversies of his day. The first was the dispute over the meaning of predestination. Gottschalk, an earnest student of the works of Augustine, wrote a treatise in which he asserted the doctrine of predestination in all its severity. His denial of human free will and responsibility alarmed Hincmar, Archbishop of Rheims, who sought a scholar able to combat these opinions. His choice fell upon Erigena, who agreed to write a treatise on predestination to support the orthodox belief. Erigena published his tract in 851, but the arguments he employed to defend the orthodox cause were almost as abhorent to Catholics as those of Gottschalk. The storm reached its climax in 855 when the Synod of Valence was summoned to consider the matter, and nineteen propositions selected from the works of Erigena were condemned.

Another controversy in which Erigena played a leading part was that concerned with the doctrine of the Eucharist. In 831, Paschasius Radbertus wrote a treatise on the Eucharist in which he asserted the doctrine known later as Transubstantiation. He was opposed by Ratramnus who in turn wrote a treatise, *Concerning the Body and Blood of the Lord*, in which he affirmed a Real Presence in the Eucharist but denied that it was a corporeal one. Erigena's contribution to the controversy is not now extant. The work that has frequently been attributed to him is probably the original treatise of Ratramnus which was condemned in 1050 at the Council of Vercelli. Erigena seems to have gone a step further than Ratramnus, for if we are to believe the assertion of Hincmar, he denied the Real Presence and taught that the Eucharist was nothing more than a memorial of Christ's Death and Passion. According to Bett, the treatise of Ratramnus was carefully studied by Cranmer and Ridley and was the basis of the doctrine expressed in the Book of Common Prayer.

Erigena's most important work was the *Division of Nature* (*De Divisione Naturae*), which was probably written between 865 and 870 when the influence of Dionysius upon his thought was at its height. The book is cast into the form of a dialogue between a master and a disciple. Its alternative title, περι φυσεως μερισμοῦ clearly indicates the Greek influence. Erigena commences by stating that the general name for the totality of things is φυσις or, nature. The first and most fundamental division of nature is that into those things which are (*ea quae sunt*) and those things which are not (*ea quae non sunt*). By existing things, he means all that is capable of comprehension by the senses or the intellect. What is beyond the grasp of sense or intellect is non-existent, non-being. He describes five distinct ways in which we can speak of an object as non-being. In the first place, all that which, because of the excellence of its nature, is beyond the grasp of sense or intellect, is truly non-being. Thus, in this meaning, God and matter are non-being because in their essential nature they are beyond the grasp of our minds. The essences or true natures of things fall into the same category. They are inaccessible to knowledge, "for the true essence of all is He alone Who truly is." Erigena emphatically declares that the essential natures are hidden from us. We can only know the accidental qualities perceived by the senses, but the underlying substance is for ever unknowable. His conclusion is that since we cannot know the essences of things, as far as we are concerned, they do not exist. The student of modern philosophy will note the superficial resemblance to the *noumena* of Kant and the Idealism of Berkeley.

The second mode of non-being is applicable to all those things which cannot be understood by means of a knowledge of those objects which are inferior to them in the order of nature. "To affirm the lower is to deny the higher and to deny the lower is to affirm the higher." Erigena's own illustration is that the nature of the angel cannot be understood through a knowledge of the nature of man. By affirming that a man is mortal, one denies that he is an angel.

All potential existence is likewise non-being. The acorn is potentially the oak but one cannot speak of the oak as actually existing in the acorn.

Only those things which are grasped by the intellect have true being. The objects of the physical world which come into existence through generation and are subject to change, growth or decay, have an incomplete being. They are merely forms of matter existing in space and time and are thus only appearance, in contrast with the eternal realities of the intelligible sphere.

The last mode of non-being is concerned with human nature alone. Man was created in the image of God, and if through sin he loses this likeness he truly ceases to be.

Erigena now proceeds to unfold his well-known fourfold division of nature. "It seems to me that we must hold that there is a division of nature through four differences into four species. The first is that which creates and is not created; the second is that which is created and creates; the third that which is created but does not create, and the fourth that which neither creates nor is created. Of these four, two in turn seem to be opposed, for the third is opposed to the first and the fourth to the second."

The first and fourth of these divisions refer to God as the uncreated origin of all things and as their final end, respectively. The second represents the world of ideas or exemplars which are the primordial causes of things, and the third the effects of the primordial causes—*i.e.*, the objects existing in space and time in the sensible world.

Erigena presents the conception of an impersonal God, the Absolute, the Infinite and the Eternal. One can easily see in this the doctrine of Dionysius. God is totally beyond the reach of the human intellect and can be known only indirectly through His effects in the visible world—*i.e.*, by Theophany, a term the meaning of which will be discussed later. Any positive quality we ascribe to God can be true only in a figurative sense. The same predicate can be affirmed and denied of God. The affirmation is only metaphorically true but the denial is literally true. Hence the superiority of negative over affirmative theology.

At this point, the disciple raises an objection. "I think we ought first to consider why the holy father and theologian, Dionysius, taught that these names, I mean Being, Goodness, Truth, Justice, Wisdom and others of this kind, which seem not only Divine but the most Divine of all attributes, apply only to the Divine Substance and Being in a figurative way—*i.e.*, metaphorically transferred from the creature to the Creator." The master replies that all the terms employed by human thought in framing a conception of the Deity are drawn from our limited and finite experience and can have no literal application to the Eternal and Infinite. God is not merely Good but is Super-Good. It is in this way that the same quality can both be affirmed and denied, of the Absolute. "For whoever says that He is Super-Essential says not what He is but what He is not. He declares that His Being is not being but above and beyond all being (*plusquam essentiam*)." In the view of Erigena, God is the Absolute of Whom nothing can be truly affirmed beyond the fact that He exists. Hence it is not possible to know His essential nature and the most real knowledge consists in unknowing. Even God does not know His essence, for in order to know Himself, He must first define Himself. All definition implies the idea of genus, species and difference. God, however, can be in no genus or species and is therefore indefinable. If He could be defined, He would not be the Absolute. Such is the doctrine of the Divine Ignorance, which is an infinite and incomprehensible knowledge surpassing all knowledge.

God is ἄναρχος *i.e.*, without beginning or cause—but He is the Cause of all beings. "He is, therefore, beginning, means and end. Beginning because all things are from Him and participate in His essence; means, because in Him and through Him all things subsist and are moved; and end, because all things are moved to Him."

Erigena quaintly derives the name of God (θεος) from the verb θεω, I run. He says, "Although the Divine Nature is described by many names such as Goodness, Being, Truth and others of this kind, yet Scripture employs most frequently the Divine name of God. The etymology of this name is derived from the Greek, either from the verb θεωρῶ which means I see, or from the verb θεω, which means I run, or, more probably, since the same meaning is implied in both, it comes from both. Thus from the verb θεωρῶ, we get θεος, which means seeing. He is, indeed, all things that exist, for He sees them in Himself, while He sees nothing outside Himself, because there is nothing outside Himself. If we derive it from θεω, then θεος means running. He, indeed, runs through all things and in no way stands still but fills all things by his running. . . . It is not other in God to run through all things than to see all, since both by seeing and by running, all things come to be." Hence the conclusion that God is the essence of all that exists. "He is the essence of all things. For because there is no material good beside Him, all that is called good is good because of participation in the One Supreme Good. Thus, everything which is said to exist, exists, not in itself, but through participation in His truly existing nature."

Although God in His essence is unknowable to us, yet He may be known and contemplated in all things. This revelation of God through creation is what Erigena intends by the term Theophany taken in its widest sense. Not only men, but angels and the redeemed are dependent on revelation for their knowledge of God. But, "In my Father's house are many mansions." As the receptive powers of different individuals vary so greatly, there are different grades of revelation to suit different individuals. The generality of mankind is able to receive only the lower and more obvious manifestations of the Divine. The higher forms are received by holy souls, purged and illuminated through a devout life.

In its narrower meaning, Theophany, in the words of Maximus the Confessor, has a twofold aspect. On the part of God, it is a revelation of Himself to rational beings in such measure as they can understand. Such a condescension on the part of God demands a corresponding elevation of the soul to Him through a life of contemplation and good works. In contemplating the objects of the visible world, we are contemplating God revealed in His effects. This is the meaning of the saying that God is all things in all things (*Deus omnia in omnibus*).

At the final consummation of all things, everything will be absorbed into the Divine Nature. Iron which is rendered molten by fire loses its qualities as iron and becomes like fire. Yet the substance of the iron is not destroyed and it still retains its individual existence. Exactly the same thing will occur in the general consummation; all things will be absorbed into God but they will still retain their individuality. Thus God is the beginning and end of all things. He is their fount and origin and, ultimately, all will return to Him. This is the completion of the world cycle. As the One became the Many by descending into the physical world, yet without ceasing to be one, so at the last, each inferior will pass into its superior and finally into God, the Many becoming the One, without prejudice to its being many. The final return of all things to God is called the *Adunatio*. "And this is the end of all things visible and invisible, for all visible things pass into intelligible and all intelligibles into God in a wonderful and ineffable union, but the union is not accompanied, as we have often insisted, by any confusion or destruction of essences or substances."

To prevent misunderstanding, Erigena employs a large number of analogies. Thus, many individuals constitute one species, many species, one genus and many genera, one essence. In the monad, all numbers, and in the point, all lines, implicitly exist. Many musical notes combine to form one tune without prejudice to their individual existence. A crowd can assemble to watch the same spectacle and each individual can see the same objects at exactly the same time. Many lamps burning in one room blend into a single illumination.

A parallel difficulty arises for Erigena in his doctrine of Creation, which involves the reverse process, the One entering into multiplicity whilst preserving the Divine Unity. Erigena conforms to the Catholic belief by stating that the world was created by God *ex nihilo*, but it is the particular twist that he gives to the latter phrase that is distinctive of his thought. Nothing should not be interpreted as the negation of being. In creating the world from nothing, God has really created it out of Himself, for the Super-Essence transcends all ordinary beings to such an extent that in reality they may be regarded as nothing. "And so He makes all things from nothing—*i.e.*, from His Super-Essence He creates essences, from His Super-Life and from His Super-Intelligence He makes life and intelligences. From the negation of all things which are and are not, He produces the affirmation of all things which are and are not."

Another way of stating the process of creation is to say that the Divine Essence enters into Theophanies. That which was nothing because it is beyond all being, enters into an existence conditioned by space and time. God creates Himself in the world by means of the primordial causes. The second division of nature, created and creating, is God considered as containing, within Himself the primordial causes.

Scripture tells us that in the beginning God made heaven and earth. These signify the intelligible and the sensible worlds respectively. Here we can see the influence of Augustine. Before creating the world, God created the primordial causes in His Son. They are the eternal ideas or exemplars in the likeness of which all things were made. Created in the Word, they are perfected and diffused by the Holy Spirit.

The objects of the visible world derive their reality because of their participation in the primordial causes. Erigena gives a list of the primordial causes and starts with the most general idea, that of goodness, which following Dionysius he puts prior to being. In descending order, they are, being, life, wisdom, truth, intelligence, reason, virtue, justice, health, greatness, omnipotence, eternity, peace and all the powers and grounds created at one and the same time by the Father in the Son and which apply to all creation. Whatever has being, is wise or is intelligent, is so by virtue of its participation in being, wisdom or intelligence.

As created in the Son, the primordial causes are one and the same and entirely beyond the grasp of finite minds. When they issue forth in Theophanies, they are divided, multiplied and exhibit degrees of perfection. The multiplicity and grading of the primordial causes exist in our minds only.

Erigena's teaching about the nature of evil was not considered as satisfactory by the ecclesiastical authorities. Following Augustine and the Pseudo-Dionysius, he regarded evil as the privation of a good which should by rights be present. Sin originated in the irrational tendencies of human free-will, but it is caused by the abuse, not the use, of freedom. The individual desires what appears to him as a good (desire is *sub specie boni*), but the senses are misled by what seems to them to be good and the taint spreads to the intellect which becomes contaminated and falls into sin. Evil, however, is only temporary and it will disappear in the final consummation of all things. Although it appears in a part of the universe as a defect, yet if we consider the totality, in some way it contributes to the beauty and perfection of the whole. "True reason does not fear to declare that what in parts of the universe seems evil, dishonesty, wretchedness, misery and retribution, to those who are unable to see the whole at one time, yet when contemplating the whole, just as regarding the whole of a beautiful picture, it is neither retribution, nor misery, nor wretchedness, nor dishonesty nor sin." The Neo-Platonic trend of this doctrine sufficiently obvious to call for no further comment beyond the fact that it was not acceptable to the majority of Christians who had such a profound horror of sin and evil that they could not agree that evil could possibly contribute to the greater beauty and perfection of the universe.

Was Erigena a pantheist? Many passages from his works, if

taken literally and apart from their context, seem to suggest the affirmative. He was certainly regarded as a pantheist by later ages, and certain unorthodox thinkers developed his philosophy along pantheistic lines. Wicksteed warns us, "The peculiar phraseology he uses may well mislead the novice into attributing to him still more startling views than he actually held."[1] In another work, Wicksteed frankly avers his pantheism.[2] W. Turner also agrees.[3] In the earlier editions of his *History of Medieval Philosophy*, De Wulf emphasized Erigena's pantheism, but in the latest edition (1934) he modified his opinion. He shows that some statements of the *De Divisione Naturae* stress the monist and pantheist point of view, whilst others make a distinction between God and creatures. The problem is to discover which really represent Erigena's thought. De Wulf concludes, "The two lines of thought can be reconciled. The Scot is not a monist (Gilson and Cappuyns have established this beyond doubt), for he believes that the substance of God and that of creatures are not identical."[4]

Other writers, however, champion his orthodoxy. Erdmann writes, "The accusation of pantheism which has been made against Erigena's doctrine of evil is justified only in so far as the latter really avoids dualism more than the opposite extreme."[5] R. L. Poole[6] thinks that the judgment of pantheism is premature and Bett[7] indignantly denies the charge.

We have already met a parallel case in the writings of the Pseudo-Dionysius. Like the latter, Erigena has tried to synthesize two entirely different conceptions, the Absolute of philosophical speculation and the dogmatic truths of Catholic theology. Each position is held with a tenacity which makes real fusion impossible, and the consequence is inconsistency of statement. We have to judge Erigena against the background of his age. Many expressions which seem in our eyes to involve pantheism probably did not suggest the same to him and to readers of his generation. Yet it cannot be denied that at times he comes perilously near to pantheism, and some of his successors developed systems of thought in

---

[1] WICKSTEED, P., *Dante and Aquinas* (Dent: 1913), p. 37.
[2] *Id. Reactions between Dogma and Philosophy* (Constable: 1926), p. 46.
[3] TURNER, W., *History of Philosophy*, p. 251.
[4] *Cf.* DE WULF, *History of Medieval Philosophy*, 3rd edition, pp. 169–70, and 6th edition, p. 138.
[5] ERDMANN, *History of Philosophy*, vol. i, p. 298.
[6] *op cit.*, pp. 67–8.
[7] *op. cit.*, p. 90.

which no attempt was made to reconcile philosophy with orthodox theology.

In spite of ecclesiastical censures, Erigena influenced later thought in many ways. Orthodox philosophy owed him a considerable debt, and Abelard, Gilbert de la Porrée, Simon of Tournai and Nicholas of Cusa borrow ideas from his writings and even adopt his terminology. No Scholastic, however, bases his teaching upon the doctrine of the *De Divisione Naturae*. Erigena was also a considerable influence in the development of mediæval mysticism. He himself can be classed as a mystic and his translation of the works of Dionysius was the source from which some of the greatest mediæval mystics drew their inspiration.

The works of Erigena were known to the Arabian and Jewish thinkers, Avicenna, Averroes, Avicebron and Maimonides, and they may have been a potent factor in the development of the Albigensian heresy which is known to have been affected by Arabian and Jewish thought. Sir Frederick Pollock traces his influence through Maimonides to Spinoza.

Erigena's more immediate influence was upon Amalric of Bene, who was born in the neighbourhood of Chartres in the latter part of the 12th century and taught at Paris in the early years of the 13th century. His views were condemned by the University of Paris and this judgment was upheld by Pope Innocent III. None of his works escaped destruction, and we are dependent for information about his teaching upon certain remarks of the chronicler Martin of Poland and Cardinal Henry of Ostia. The latter derived his facts from Odo Tusculanus, the episcopal chancellor of Paris who compiled a list of Amalric's errors. Both authorities ascribe Amalric's views to Erigena.

The teaching of Amalric spread rapidly and there are records of certain of his followers being burnt at Champeaux and Amiens at the beginning of the 13th century. Amalric taught that God is the being of all things and supported this opinion by a quotation from the *De Divisione Naturae* in which the master asks, "Do you deny that the Creator and creature are one?" The disciple replies, "I cannot easily deny it. To oppose such a conclusion seems to me to be ridiculous." Amalric also believed that each individual man is a member of God in the same sense that Christ was. His followers put this teaching into practice and claimed that, as man and God

were identical, no individual could commit sin and that in the near
future every man would become the Holy Ghost.

Many writers have claimed that Erigena was responsible for the
errors of David of Dinant.[1] Scarcely anything is known about the
life of this philosopher; even his place of birth is uncertain. It has
been assigned to Dinant in Brittany and Dinant near Liège in
Belgium, the latter being the more probable. When his views were
condemned at Paris in 1210, a decree was issued ordering the
exhumation of the body of Amalric. As no mention was made of
David, it may be assumed that he was still alive at this time. His
principal work was the *Quaternuli*, or the *De Tomis, id est, De
Divisionibus*. The alternative title has suggested that he was
inspired by the teaching of Erigena, and De Wulf asserted this in
the 3rd edition of his *History of Medieval Philosophy*.[2] An ex-
haustive study of his teaching and its origins was made by G.
Théry[3] who denies the direct influence of Erigena upon his thought.
This has led De Wulf to modify his previous assertion, and in the
6th edition of his *History* (1934, Vol. I, p. 245) he agrees that the
similarity of the titles of the two works is no decisive proof that
the doctrines of the *De Tomis* were derived from the *De Divisione
Naturae*. Nevertheless, he adds, "But the Extreme Realism of
John the Scot and his vague descriptions of the Theophanies must
have led David to take this path." It has also been claimed that
David was influenced by Neo-Platonic thought coming to him via
the Pseudo-Dionysius and Alexander of Aphrodisias, the great
3rd-century commentator on the works of Aristotle. Théry could
find no trace of the Neo-Platonic influence in the fragments
preserved to us of David's treatise. The belief in the influence of
Alexander of Aphrodisias rested upon certain remarks of Albert
the Great, who failed to distinguish between two different Greek
writers, Alexander of Aphrodisias and Alexander the disciple of
Xenophon who taught a definitely materialistic doctrine. It was
the latter with whose views David was acquainted. Nevertheless,
De Wulf is reasonable in maintaining that these facts do not rule
out an indirect influence of Erigena, though David's chief masters

---

[1] *e.g.*, BETT, *op. cit.*, p. 178. "The little that we know of his teaching all seems
to show that it was a reckless development of Erigena's doctrine."

[2] *op. cit.*, p. 222. "The very title of his work . . . suggests the influence which
Scotus Eriugena's writings must have had in shaping David's pantheism."

[3] *See* THÉRY, G., *David de Dinant* (Bibliothèque Thomiste-Le Saulchoir: Kain,
Belgium, 1925).

were Aristotle himself and Alexander. David may also have been influenced by the *Fons Vitae* of the Arabian philosopher, Avencebrol, which was widely studied at this time.

The decree of 1210, which ordered David's books to be burnt along with those of Amalric, appears to have been strictly observed. All our knowledge of his doctrine is based on the criticisms of Albert the Great and certain quotations given by Nicholas of Cusa. By grouping the various quotations, Théry has succeeded in reconstructing the main lines of the *De Tomis*. From these, we find that David taught a very gross type of materialism. He identified God and matter and formally divided substances into God, soul and matter, but considered that, in essence, all three were the same. God is the one and only reality. "It is clear," he says, "that there is only one substance, not only in all bodies but also in all souls. This substance is none other than God." The crudeness of David's doctrine provoked very strong opposition from Albert and Thomas. Contrary to their usual custom, the former described it as "completely asinine (*omnino asinium*)," and the latter applies the term "most stupidly (*stultissime*)" to his attempt to identify God with matter.

David's work has, therefore, achieved a notoriety which it does not merit. If the revived Aristotelianism of the 13th century was to be regarded favourably, it was necessary to demonstrate that the teaching of Aristotle lent support to neither materialism nor pantheism. Hence the pains taken by Albert to show that David's opinions have no foundation in the philosophy of Aristotle.

SUGGESTIONS FOR FURTHER READING

The most complete English account of the philosophy of John the Scot is that of H. Bett, *Johannes Scotus Erigena: A Study in Medieval Philosophy* (C.U.P.: 1925).

Bett does not agree with the charge of pantheism frequently brought against Erigena. Chapter V, "The Influence of Erigena upon Later Times," is important. Bett suggests connections between the thought of Erigena and that of Spinoza and Hegel in modern times.

The translation of a long extract from the *Division of Nature*, book iv, is given in the first volume of McKeon's *Selections*.

CHAPTER III

THE UNIVERSALS CONTROVERSY: ABELARD

THE problem of the universal is one that is always with philosophy but it takes different forms at different periods. Broadly speaking, it is concerned with the relation between our universal conceptions and the external world which we come to know by means of them. How far, for example, does thought give a true account of the external world? Are those uniformities which we know as scientific laws actually in the objects themselves, or are they the modes in which our mind thinks in order to understand the behaviour of things? Naturally, the mediæval mind had not reached this stage of analysis. The thinkers of the early Middle Ages approached the problem through a consideration of the meaning of class names —*i.e.*, the names of species or genera such as man, horse, oak, animal, etc., the common nouns of English grammar, and of names of qualities such as justice, freedom, equality, etc., the abstract names of the grammar book. The question put was, what is involved when we say of a given individual that he is a man? Does it mean that he participates in some higher reality, human nature or humanity, which exists as a something distinct from the individual men who make up the human species? Or is humanity a quality that exists only in the individuals in which the quality is exemplified? Is the common nature in which all individual men share a purely mental conception due to the experienced resemblances between all members of the species? Or does the name merely cover a classification of convenience which has no foundation in fact? Is justice something which has an existence apart from just men and just actions, or is it the quality inherent in men and actions in virtue of which we call them just?

Such were the problems which confronted the early mediæval thinkers when they tried to construct philosophy afresh with only a slender assistance from the philosophical thinking of the classical world. Such names, those of classes and abstract qualities, were known to them as universals, and before they could advance to the deeper problems of the relation of our thought to reality, they had to settle the meaning of the term from a purely logical standpoint. The problem was presented to the Middle Ages in the form in which it appeared in Boethius's *Commentary on the Isagoge*. This was, however, only the occasion for the start of the controversy. The problem of universals is so fundamental to philosophy that it must have arisen for the mediæval thinkers sooner or later. They would certainly have come into contact with it as soon as the works of Plato and Aristotle were available to them.

The problem admits of four possible types of answer.

(1) The simplest is that given by the doctrine known as Extreme Realism, and, as might have been expected, it was the first in the field. This view asserts that mental conceptions such as goodness, justice and equality have a real existence apart from the particular objects of the sense world which exhibit these qualities. The latter possess reality only in so far as they share in the independently existing ideas.

The ancient form of the doctrine is familiar to readers of the Platonic *Dialogues* and is usually known as the doctrine of the Forms or Ideas. Platonic Realism was criticized by Aristotle on the ground that experience presents us with a world of individual things which are the most real relative to us. He, however, admitted that universals are most real in themselves since we can know the world only by means of them. This view at once raises the problem how universal conceptions are applicable to a world of individuals. The earlier Christian thinkers, such as St. Augustine, adopted Platonic Realism with the important modification that they regarded the ideas as exemplars in the Divine Mind after the pattern of which the world was fashioned. Early mediæval thinkers, influenced by the writings of Augustine and the Pseudo-Dionysius, were Extreme Realists. Thus, Erigena and St. Anselm, though in many ways diverse in their opinions, fall into this class.

(2) The answer given by Moderate Realism developed somewhat later. This was the position defended by Albert the Great and St. Thomas Aquinas. In Greek philosophy it represents the view held by Aristotle. The Moderate Realist, whilst conceding that individuals are both prior in knowledge and most real to us, teach that universals are most real in themselves. The individual can be known only in terms of universals. The paradox is solved

by means of the doctrine of Abstraction. The universal has no existence apart from the individual things in which it is realized—*e.g.*, horse nature is to be found only in individual horses, and justice exists only as realized in just men and just actions. The mind, however, has the power of abstracting the universal from the individuals in which it is realized, and of considering it apart from the individualizing conditions of the sensible world. The full statement of Moderate Realism depended upon the progress of psychological analysis and therefore the view was fairly late in development.

(3) The position which represents the final development in mediæval thought is Conceptualism. The Conceptualist admits the validity of universal conceptions as mental facts and attributes their formation to the synthetic activity of mind. The nature of the latter is such that we are obliged to think by means of universals, but we can never know if there is any reality outside the mind corresponding to such conceptions. William of Ockham and his followers were the mediæval representatives of this view, whilst in modern times, Kantianism is the most complete exposition of Conceptualism.

(4) The last possible answer is that known as Nominalism, which is the opposite to Extreme Realism. It is entirely a modern development and was never held by any mediæval thinker. Hobbes and the Mills are typical Nominalists. According to this view, all external reality is individual and therefore any representation of it must be individual. The mind apprehends individuals through individual sense impressions and represents them by individual mental images. Because groups of individuals seem to resemble each other in certain qualities, we classify the individuals under a common name. The name alone is the universal since it can be attributed to all members of the group.

The so-called Nominalists of the Middle Ages were really protesting against Extreme Realism. They had not defined their own position and were probably unable to do so, but they may be regarded as feeling their way towards Moderate Realism. They may most suitably be described as Anti-Realists.

In this sketch of the history of the controversy, we need hardly consider seriously the statement of Fredegis in the 8th century, that since, during the incidence of the Plagues, Egypt was covered with darkness so thick that it could be felt with the hand, darkness must be an existent thing. The first definite philosophical teaching (if we omit the Platonic Realism of Erigena) was that given by Remi of Auxerre (841–908). He taught that the reality of the individual is due to its participation in a higher reality, that of the species, and, in turn, the reality of the species depends upon its participation in the genus. Thus, the reality of Socrates is due to the fact that he is a member of the human species, and the reality of humanity, the species, is due to participation in the genus animal. Remi was not a Realist in the Platonic sense. For Plato, the universal forms had a real existence in the super-sensible world, but Remi believed that universals are immanent in the sense world —*i.e.*, humanity exists in the human species as such.

Odo of Tournai (died 1113) applied Extreme Realism to certain theological controversies. It seemed to him that it provided an excellent explanation of the doctrine of Original Sin. Since all men form one substance, one reality, when our first parents tasted the forbidden fruit, they not only sinned, but the whole human substance was tainted by the fall. Hence, all future generations were affected by their sin and it is in this way that original sin is transmitted. He was not so happy in the next application of his Realism. Since the substance of the newly born child is that of the species, God has not created a new substance when the infant comes into the world, but has merely brought into existence a new property of the already existing substance. Thus, all men are one in substance and the differences between individuals are due to accidental qualities. From this it is quite easy to see that the logical outcome of this form of Extreme Realism would be Pantheism.

Such statements naturally produced a storm of protest, and the form the objections took was governed by the alternatives given in the *Isagoge*. Are the universals real existences or do they merely exist as ideas of the mind (*nudis intellectibus*)? The opponents of Extreme Realism denied the first alternative and, according to the rules of the logical game, as it was then played, they affirmed the second. They knew from experience that the objects given to us through the senses are all individuals, and they agreed also that the mind has the power of framing universal ideas, but they had no means of bringing these facts together. They did not, even if they could, intend to teach either Nominalism or Conceptualism, since they had not reached the stage of psychological analysis in which such doctrines would have had any meaning for them. As mentioned above, the most satisfactory way of classifying these thinkers is to call them Anti-Realists and to note that they foreshadow the position of Moderate Realism.

Eric of Auxerre (841–76), the predecessor of Remi, had already shown dissatisfaction with the prevailing Realist tradition, but it was left to Roscelin (*c.* 1050–1120) to define the Anti-Realist position more clearly. His works are not now extant. We possess only one letter of his written to Abelard, and therefore his views have to be collected from scattered references in the works of Anselm, Abelard and John of Salisbury. From these we gather that Roscelin started from the fact that experience presents a world in which individuals alone exist. He declared that the universals are mere sounds, breathings of the voice (*voces* or *flatus vocis*). To understand what was in his mind in using such terms, it is necessary to consider his teaching in the light of the alternatives presented in the *Isagoge*. Many writers have credited him with being a Nominalist or Conceptualist, but there is no evidence in the fragments of his works that are accessible to us, which suggests that he denied the existence of something that corresponds to the word which to our minds functions as a symbol of the universal. Hence, when he states that the colour of a horse does not exist apart from the horse of which it is a quality, he is actually asserting the view of the Moderate Realist, but his lack of the necessary psychological knowledge prevents him from defining his doctrine accurately. He has affirmed the existence of individuals and that there are no such things as universals existing in isolation from the individuals, but he has not grasped the important fact that the universal is exemplified in the individual, nor is he able to explain how, from sense experiences, the mind forms mental conceptions which are symbolized by the word. Until the problem had been considered from the standpoint of psychology as well as from that of logic, such an advance was not possible.

It was Roscelin's application of his Anti-Realist theory to theological problems that produced trouble for him. Orthodox Christianity taught that the Godhead was one in substance (*una res*), but Roscelin argued that since individuals alone exist, the three Divine Persons must be three distinct and independent beings. Otherwise, all three must have become incarnate and have suffered death upon the Cross. Hence, the Persons of the Trinity should be regarded as three distinct Beings, equal in majesty and glory but possessing one will and omnipotence. This opinion of Roscelin is usually known as tritheism, and was strongly opposed by St. Anselm, who wrote a treatise attacking the doctrine from which a good deal of our information about Roscelin's statements has been obtained. Roscelin was summoned before the Council of Soissons in 1092 and his doctrines were condemned. He recanted in order to avoid excommunication.

In the 12th century, Extreme Realism flourished in the school of Chartres, where the influence of Plato's *Timaeus* was very pronounced. The school was founded by Fulbert in 990, and for nearly two centuries it produced a line of well-known thinkers who rivalled in fame the teachers of the schools of Paris. Fulbert had been a pupil of the famous Gerbert, the outstanding scholar of that period who was elevated to the Papacy under the title of Sylvester II. Fulbert himself was a man of wide culture. Apart from his theological studies, he was interested in mathematics and he must have possessed a most attractive personality for his pupils proudly referred to him as "our Socrates." Fulbert's ablest student was Berengar of Tours, who like Roscelin could not resist the temptation to apply his dialectic to theological matters. In his case, the field in which he chose to exercise his talents was the meaning of the Sacrament of the Lord's Supper. By this time, the doctrine of Transubstantiation was widely accepted, and when Berengar taught that the Eucharist was a bare memorial of Christ's Death and Passion (an interesting fore-shadowing of the doctrine of Zwingli), he was summoned to Rome and chose to recant rather than suffer the penalty of excommunication. Another pupil of Fulbert was Lanfranc, who became Abbot of Bec and, later, Archbishop of Canterbury. His contributions to philosophy were very slight and he shines rather as a statesman and administrator than as a speculative thinker.

The tendency to apply dialectic to the doctrines of the Church provoked a reaction which is seen to a certain extent in Lanfranc but which is far more pronounced in Peter Damian (1007–72). He was the author of a work *On Divine Omnipotence*, in which he claimed that God, by an arbitrary fiat of His Will, could, if He wished, make past events not to have been. To the reply that such would be in opposition to the Law of Contradiction, that the same quality cannot both belong and not belong to a thing in the same sense and at the same time, Peter answered that such logical rules applied only to things which fall within the field of human experience. God is not bound by any such invariable laws. In the words of the Psalmist, He does whatever pleases Him.

After Fulbert's death in 1029, we have little information about the progress of the school of Chartres until the appearance of Bernard of Chartres (died about 1130). Most of our information regarding the school is derived from John of Salisbury, who describes Bernard as "the most perfect Platonist of our time (*perfectissimus inter Platonicos saeculi nostri*)." According to Bernard, being can be arranged in three categories: the Supreme and Eternal Reality which is God; matter, which arose from nothing through the creative act of God; and ideas, which are the eternal exemplars in the Divine Mind and through which the individuals of the finite world are ever present to Him. Bernard's work was continued by Theodoric of Chartres (died about 1155), whose pupil was John of Salisbury. William of Conches (1080–1154) was also a follower of Bernard and became tutor to the young Henry II of England. William developed the pantheistic tendency which was always latent in the teaching of Chartres. He was strongly influenced by Neo-Platonism, and in his attempt to reconcile that philosophy with Christianity, he at one time identified the Holy Spirit with the World Soul of the Neo-Platonists.

Another pupil of Bernard was Gilbert, Bishop of Poitiers, generally known as Gilbert de la Porrée (1076–1154). Gilbert was an ardent Anti-Realist. He, too, fell into trouble by the application of his ideas to theology. At this time, the different books of Aristotle's *Organon* in Latin translation, possibly the versions made by Boethius, were beginning to appear in Western Europe. In his book *On the Six Principles*, Gilbert shows his knowledge of the categories of Aristotle which it is the business of his treatise to explain. Gilbert's book became one of the standard treatises on logic. It was studied in the universities, was commented upon by Albert the Great and quoted by St. Thomas. Gilbert applied his Anti-Realist views to the interpretation of the doctrine of the Trinity. He was brought to trial at the Council of Rheims where his implacable opponent, St. Bernard, failed to secure the verdict of heresy. John of Salisbury gives a detailed account of the proceedings of the Council which does not add to the reputation of St. Bernard. As R. L. Poole puts it, "It is also necessary to bear in mind that the latter [Gilbert] would in all probability never have attracted hostile notice, had not the party of tradition first tasted blood in the person of Abailard. Ignorance, prejudice, an incapacity for criticism, coupled the two men together; and Gilbert suffered from the tail of the storm which had overwhelmed Abailard."

The outstanding personality in the Universals controversy was Peter Abelard (1079-1142). From the autobiographical sketch, *The History of my Misfortunes* (*Historia calamitatum mearum*), we learn much about the details of Abelard's life and about contemporary thinkers. Abelard was born at Palais, near Nantes. He tells us, "I came from a country of which the soil is light and the temper of the inhabitants is light; and I had a wonderful facility for acquiring knowledge. My father had some taste for letters before he became a soldier. He wanted all his boys to be scholars before they adopted the military profession. Me, his eldest born, he was specially careful to educate. But I soon abandoned the privilege of my seniority to my brothers, leaving them to follow Mars and casting myself into the lap of Minerva. And since I preferred dialectical reasoning to all other writings of philosophy, I changed other weapons for these, and abandoned the trophies of war for the conflicts of argument. So, travelling through different provinces wherever I heard that the study of this art of disputation was flourishing, I exercised it myself as I journied and I became a rival of the Peripatetics."[1]

Eventually, Abelard came to Paris, attracted by the fame of William of Champeaux, the best-known teacher of his age. He listened to William for a time and then began to dispute with the master. He disagreed so thoroughly with William's teaching that he resolved to set up a rival school. "Hence my misfortunes began. Presuming on my talents, youth as I was, I aspired to the government of schools and I fixed upon Melun, the seat of a royal palace, as the place in which I would exhibit my powers." William did his utmost to prevent Abelard from opening his school but the latter had powerful patrons. Abelard's eloquence soon had the effect of attracting most of William's pupils to him.

Over-study seems to have affected his health, and after a slight breakdown, he returned to Brittany to recuperate. Several years

[1] Peripatetic was the name given to the followers of Aristotle, since, according to tradition, that philosopher lectured to and discussed with his pupils whilst walking to and fro in the long corridors of his school, the Lyceum.

later, he came back to Paris and renewed his contest with William, who was now archdeacon of that city. The dispute was on the subject of universals. William was a strong Realist, and Abelard records, "By most patent arguments, I compelled William of Champeaux to change his opinion; yea, to abandon it." The change of view, however, did not save William's reputation. "Those who had most adhered to our Master and who had formerly most denounced my doctrine, now fled to my school." The rivalry grew so intense and bitter that Abelard deemed it wise to retire from Paris to Melun and William entered a monastery. This was the signal for Abelard to return to Paris, but as soon as he heard that Abelard had resumed his teaching, William came out of the monastery to renew the contest. At this point, Abelard was recalled to Brittany to be present when his mother took the vow. When he came back to Paris, he found that William was now a bishop.

Abelard now attached himself to the school of Anselm of Laon but he was soon dissatisfied. He wrote, "If anyone came to him in uncertainty of mind to discuss with him any problem, he returned more uncertain. He was a wonderful man in the eyes of those who listened to him, but he was nought in the sight of those who asked him questions. He had a wonderful practice of words but it was a practice that was contemptible in sense and empty of reason. When he kindled a fire, he filled his house with smoke. That great tree of his attracted one by its leaves when it was seen from afar off; but when one came near and looked carefully at it, one found that it bore no fruit."

Abelard was soon engaged in dispute with Anselm. On one occasion the latter referred contemptuously to theologians who merely copied other commentators but never tried themselves to deal at first hand with a text. Abelard knew that this gibe was aimed at him, and when his fellow-students dared him to comment on the text of Ezekiel, he accepted the challenge. Only a handful of students attended his opening lecture. They went away and told others with the consequence that the rest of his lectures were crowded. The course was so successful that Abelard was requested to put his commentary into writing. Anselm tried to hinder this and Abelard had to return to Paris to finish it. The result was that he became as well known as a theologian as he had previously been as a logician.

Whilst he was in Paris, Abelard was introduced to Fulbert, a canon of Notre-Dame. The latter persuaded Abelard to become a tutor to his niece, Héloïse. Although Héloïse was much younger, Abelard fell passionately in love with her. He tells us that at this period he neglected his studies and lectures and that his only compositions were love songs. The amour was discovered and the lovers fled to Brittany, where Héloïse bore a son who died quite early. Fulbert enforced a marriage but Abelard insisted that the fact of the marriage should be kept a secret. Although at this time celibacy was not universal for clerics, yet marriage was a certain bar to the career of any priest who wished to succeed as a public teacher of philosophy or theology. Abelard returned to his lodgings and Héloïse went back to live in her uncle's house. Fulbert, probably anxious for the good character of his niece, divulged the fact of the marriage. Héloïse immediately denied that a marriage had taken place. She undoubtedly had Abelard's career in mind. Abelard placed her in a convent so as to be safe from Fulbert. The latter plotted revenge. He hired a gang of ruffians to break into Abelard's lodgings whilst he was asleep. Abelard was frightfully mutilated and left for dead, but his amazing constitution preserved his life. Overwhelmed with shame and misery, he retired to the monastery of St. Denis where he eventually took up his studies again and, in answer to many requests, he began once more to write and to lecture. Héloïse sought refuge in the convent of Argenteuil.

Whilst at St. Denis, Abelard wrote an *Introduction to Theology* in which his teaching upon the Trinity had serious repercussions. Two of his enemies, pupils of William and Anselm, accused him of heresy. He was summoned to answer at the Council of Soissons, and although he defended himself very ably, his book was condemned and ordered to be burnt. Abelard returned to St. Denis, but here he soon stirred up trouble for himself. He pointed out that the patron saint of the monastery, St. Denis of France, was not the same as Dionysius the Areopagite, the convert of St. Paul. This roused such hostility that he was forced to take refuge in the domains of Count Theobald. Here, in the woods, he constructed an oratory of rough timber and for a time lived the life of a hermit. His retreat did not remain a secret for long and soon crowds of students flocked to him. The wooden oratory was replaced by a stone building and dedicated to the Paraclete. His troubles, however, were not at an end. In order to escape the persecution of his enemies, he accepted the Abbey of St. Gildas in Brittany. Whilst he was abbot, the convent of Argenteuil, of which Héloïse had become prioress, was dissolved. Abelard obtained permission to hand over the Paraclete to her as a convent of which she was the first prioress. His enemies sought him out in his retreat in Brittany and he was forced to retire. It was during this dark period that he wrote the history of his misfortunes which by chance came into the hands of Héloïse. She was fired with indignation against his persecutors and wrote the first of her famous letters, which was the beginning of a correspondence that has appealed to the romantic susceptibilities of later ages.

Eventually, Abelard found his way back to Paris and for a time his school of St. Geneviève was crowded with students. He also resumed his writing, and it is to this period that the famous *Sic et Non* belongs. This work is a theological treatise but it is important for the historian of philosophy because of the influence its form of exposition had upon the Scholastics of the following century. In the Prologue, Abelard stated that the words of holy men seem often to be not only diverse but even contradictory. This diversity of opinion should not lead us to judge them and accuse them of inconsistency, since the world is ordained to be judged by them. We have to bear in mind that they were inspired by the Holy Spirit when they wrote and we are not. Yet their statements are frequently puzzling to us. One reason is that they varied their statements to provide variety so that we should not be wearied by constant repetition of the same words. Abelard then stated his aim in writing the treatise. "These things premised, we have thought it good to collect the different statements of the Holy Fathers, as they have occurred to our memory, containing some problem which they appear to raise because of their lack of agreement, so that the reader may be stimulated to greater energy in the inquiry after truth, and may be made more acute in the pursuit of it."

The method employed in the first chapter is typical of the whole work. The topic of the chapter is whether faith is to be supported by reason, and Abelard introduces evidence from various sources, the Apostles and Apostolic Fathers, Church councils, decrees of Popes and the teaching of recognized doctors of the Church. The quotations are conflicting and contradictory on this important question but they are all gathered from those whom the Church recognized as reliable authorities. The treatise contains 158 questions or problems each of which is dealt with on similar lines. Abelard had no quarrel with the teaching of the Church, and it was not his aim to undermine confidence in her by setting forth the contradictory statements of her most authoritative teachers. He believed that the contradictions were capable of reconciliation and that the scholar would obtain a better understanding of the problems discussed by studying their pros and cons and coming to a reasoned, deliberate decision than by merely accepting the statements of authority. Abelard's trouble was that he was in advance of his age and his intentions were misunderstood, especially by his enemies. His method was not an original invention of his. In fact most of his texts were borrowed from Yves of Chartres. The method of setting forth the pros and cons and then the solution was already in use amongst the canonists of the 11th century—e.g., Bernold of Constance and Yves of Chartres. "During the ninth, tenth, and eleventh centuries students of what is technically termed 'Canon Law'—the successive decrees and canons of Church Councils and Popes—had been making collections of these documents; but there had been no uniformity, and the result was an accumulation of various and on some points conflicting material. From the point of view of historical scholarship, and from that of discipline and order, this state of things was very undesirable. During the early years of the twelfth century the study of Canon Law at Bologna was being deepened and extended largely under the influence of Gratian. . . . About 1141 he published the results in his famous *Decretum*, known at first by the more significant title *Concordantia discordantium Canonum*."[1] Gratian dealt with his texts in a way similar to that of Abelard. The importance of Abelard's *Sic et Non* is the influence it had upon the method adopted and perfected by the great Scholastic philosophers of the 13th century.

One of Abelard's enemies, William, Abbot of Thiérry, compiled a list of what he considered heretical statements and sent them to St. Bernard of Clairvaux. St. Bernard does not appear in a favourable light in the controversy which followed. In his treatise *On the Errors of Abelard*, he endeavoured to crush his antagonist

---

[1] MELLONE, S. H., *Western Christian Thought in the Middle Ages* (William Blackwood: 1935), pp. 113–14.

by appeal to authority rather than by meeting him in reasonable argument. Abelard replied most spiritedly and his enemies prevailed on Bernard to take an action which was repugnant to him. Abelard was summoned to answer a charge of heresy at the Council of Sens, 1140. St. Bernard was instructed to press the charge and this he somewhat unwillingly did. Although Abelard was only sixty-one, he had become prematurely aged by his calamities and was unable to defend himself with the brilliant energy of his earlier days. The result was that he was unanimously condemned. Another item against him was his association with his pupil Arnold of Brescia, who was the leader of the popular opposition to the temporal power of the Papacy and who wished to restore the freedom of the city of Rome by re-establishing the Senate and Tribunes of classical days.

Abelard did not wait for sentence to be pronounced but fled from the council and made his appeal to Rome. The Pope upheld Bernard and the verdict of the council, and Abelard, worn out by his struggles and broken in health, sought refuge in the Abbey of Cluny, the abbot of which was the kindly and pious Peter the Venerable. The latter did all he could to bring comfort to the declining years of Abelard. He contrived to effect a temporary reconciliation between Abelard and Bernard, and obtained for him absolution from the Pope. In these last years he wrote his *Confession*, in which without retracting he tried to explain his views. Later, in his *Apology*, he issued his defence and claimed that Bernard had secured his triumph by misrepresenting him. In his last letter to Héloïse, full of tender affection, he expressed the wish that he should be buried in the Paraclete. The end came in 1142. Abelard and Héloïse met for the last time. She carried out his wish, and when she died in 1164, her body was buried beside his in the same grave.

Abelard's contribution to the Universals controversy is contained in two treatises, *Concerning Genera and Species* (*De Generibus et Speciebus*), which was discovered by Victor Cousin in 1836, and the *Glosses on Porphyry*, brought to light by Dr. Bernhard Geyer in 1919. The latter has added to rather than detracted from his philosophical position. For the sake of clarity of exposition the two accounts will be combined.

Before Abelard announces his own view, he discusses three opinions current in his day. The first was the original view of

William of Champeaux which is usually known as the Identity theory. Briefly, it is the view that the universal essence exists in its totality in each member of the species. Thus, the universal essence, humanity, is identical in all the individuals of the human race. The differences between individuals are due to forms which are added to the essence.

Abelard holds this opinion up to ridicule. He argues that if each man constitutes the whole human species, then the latter will be in its totality in Socrates at Rome and in Plato at Athens. Since Socrates contains the whole human essence, he must be wherever the latter is. Therefore, Socrates will be at the same time in both Rome and Athens. The same will apply to Plato. Such a view is manifestly absurd.

Also, since health and sickness belong to the animal, when the whole animal existing in Socrates is sick, it must at the same time be sick in Plato. Further, the species is distinguished from the genus by the addition of differences which mark it off from other species of the same genus. Thus, in the definition of the right-angled triangle, the difference, that of possessing a right angle added to the genus triangle, constitutes it as a particular species of triangle. Abelard points out that, according to William's theory, the difference both rational and irrational can be added to the genus animal with the result that they will co-exist in the same universal, since the species exists wholly in each individual and the genus wholly in each species. The conclusion to be drawn is that the species is merely an accidental modification of the single generic essence. "Certain philosophers, indeed, take the universal thing thus: in things different from each other in form they set up a substance essentially the same; this is the material essence of the individuals in which it is, and it is one in itself and diverse only through the forms of its inferiors. If these forms were taken away, there would be absolutely no difference of things, which are separated from each other only by a diversity of forms, since the matter is in essence absolutely the same. For example . . . in the different individuals of the species man, there is the same substance of man, which is here made Plato through these accidents, there Socrates through those."[1] The conclusion to be drawn is that the species is merely an accidental modification of the single generic

---

[1] "The Glosses of Peter Abelard on Porphyry," trans. R. McKeon, in *Selections from Medieval Philosophers* (Charles Scribner's Sons: 1930), vol. i, pp. 222-3.

essence. Abelard's account of William's first theory shows that it was a variety of Extreme Realism and its logical consequence would be pantheism.

The second opinion reviewed is the Indifference theory of William which he had adopted when ridiculed by Abelard. "There is nothing existing in nature except that which is individual; but this drawn out or expanded in different degrees becomes species and genus and that which is most general. Socrates, in the nature in which he is the subject of sensible observation, is an individual, because there is something belonging to him, the whole of which is never found in another. But the intellect may ignore that which is denoted by the word Socrates and consider only that which is denoted by the word man, namely, a mortal, rational animal: in this sense he is a species. If, again, the intellect overlooks the rationality and mortality and only contemplates what the word animal denotes; in this meaning, he is genus. But if, ignoring all other forms, we consider Socrates in that which denotes substance, here is the highest generality. Socrates, therefore, as an individual, has nothing except that which is peculiar to himself; but as species, he has that which belongs to him indifferently (*indifferenter*) with all men, and as genus he possesses that which belongs to him indifferently with all other animals."[1]

William is asserting that every existing thing is an individual, but in each individual there are specific determinations which belong to it as an individual, and other qualities which are not different from—*i.e.*, shared indifferently by—other members of the species or genus. Whether we call Socrates individual, species or genus depends upon the point of view adopted.

Once more, Abelard ridicules this doctrine. It is inconsistent with the views of the authorities on logic, for neither Porphyry nor Boethius would suggest such an absurdity. "Every individual man, in so far as he is man, is affirmed by this doctrine to be a species; whence it may be truly stated of Socrates, 'This man Socrates is a species.' If Socrates is a species, he will be a universal; if he is a universal, he cannot be an individual. Hence Socrates is not Socrates."[2] This conclusion is denied by the followers of William, who affirm that every universal is a particular and every particular

---

[1] *Ouvrages inédits d'Abélard*, trans. Victor Cousin (Paris, Imprimerie Royale: 1836), p. 518.
[2] *ibid.*, p. 520.

is a universal. "See how great is their impudence! (*Vide quantae impudentiae sint!*)" exclaims Abelard.[1]

The third doctrine to be criticized is that of Anti-Realism. In Abelard's criticism of this view we see how wide of the mark is the term Nominalism so frequently applied to his own teaching. "Just as a statue consists of brass which is its matter, and of figure which is its form, so species consists of genus which is its matter and of the differences which constitute its form."[2] He points out that the attempt to reduce species and genus to sounds (*voces*) is a vain one. Animal is the genus to which man belongs. How can the word animal be the matter of the word man, seeing it neither comes from it nor is in it?

Abelard then states his own view. "Every individual is a composite of matter and form. Socrates as regards his matter is a man, but as regards his form, he is Socrates. The form, Socraticity, which constitutes Socrates as an individual is nowhere out of Socrates, and in the same way, the human essence which sustains the Socraticity in Socrates, is nowhere except in Socrates. I say, then, that species is not that essence of man only which is in Socrates or which is in any other individual, but the whole united collection of all the different elements which make up this nature. This aggregate, although plural is, however, called by the authorities one species, one universal, and one nature; as a people, although it is formed of many individual men, is called one."[3]

Thus Abelard was definitely opposed to Extreme Realism. "Socraticity does not exist outside Socrates." In nature, the individual alone has a real substantial existence. Up to this point, he is an Anti-Realist, but we have seen that he does not agree with Nominalism. Neither is he a Conceptualist. He is really feeling his way towards Moderate Realism. He definitely affirms that the mind frames universal and abstract ideas. How are they related to the individual substances of the sense world? Abelard replies that the intellect has the power of seizing upon those points in which a number of individuals resemble one another and of ignoring what is proper and peculiar to each individual. This is the power of abstraction. "The conceptions of universals are formed by abstraction. . . . In relation to abstraction it must be

[1] *Ouvrages inédits d'Abélard*, trans. Victor Cousin (Paris, Imprimerie Royale: 1836) p. 521.
[2] *ibid.*, p. 522.
[3] *ibid.*, p. 524.

known that matter and form always subsist mixed together, but the reason of the mind has this power, that it may now consider matter by itself; it may now turn its attention to form alone; it may now conceive both intermingled. The first two processes, of course, are by abstraction; they abstract something from things conjoined that they may consider its very nature. . . . Conceptions of this sort through abstraction seemed perhaps false and vain for this reason, that they perceive the thing otherwise than it is, and therefore to be empty. For if one understands otherwise than the thing is constituted, in such manner that one considers it manifestly in such a nature and property as it does not have, certainly that understanding is empty. But this is not what is done in abstraction. For, when I consider this man only in the nature of substance or of body, and not also of animal or of man or of grammarian, obviously I understand nothing except what is in that nature, but I do not consider all that it has. And when I say that I consider only this one among the qualities the nature has, the *only* refers to the attention alone, not to the mode of subsisting, otherwise the understanding would be empty."[1] Thus, the mind seizes upon the nature which is common to all individual men, and the result of this activity of abstraction is the universal. The common nature, humanity, is the matter, the substratum, for all the individualizing forms which constitute Socrates. In a similar fashion, animality, the genus, is the matter which sustains the specific forms of rationality and mortality.

Abelard has not a sufficient knowledge of the psychology of thinking to indicate in detail how the process of abstraction works, but he has said enough to show that he has envisaged the answer to the problem along the lines of Moderate Realism. Hence, John of Salisbury could say of Abelard and his disciples, "They are my friends (*Amici mei sunt*)." Abelard added a fourth question to the three originally proposed by Boethius. "We may add a fourth question, namely, whether genera and species, so long as they are genera and species, must have some thing subject to them by nomination, or whether, if the things named by them were destroyed, the universal could still consist of the meaning only of the conception, as this noun *rose* when there is not a single rose to which it is common."[2] His answer shows that he dimly grasped

---

[1] "The Glosses of Peter Abelard on Porphyry," pp. 245–6.
[2] *ibid.*, pp. 219–20.

the distinction which St. Thomas was to elaborate later as that between essence and existence. "The following is the solution, that we in no wise hold that universal nouns are, when, their things having been destroyed, they are not predicable of many things inasmuch as they are not common to any things, as for example the name of the rose when there are no longer roses, but it would still, nevertheless, be significative by the understanding, although it would lack nomination; otherwise there would not be the proposition: there is no rose."[1]

Abelard made a most important contribution to moral philosophy in the treatise entitled *Know Thyself* (*Ethica seu Scito Teipsum*). Rashdall described it as "an original treatise on moral philosophy more valuable and interesting, perhaps, than anything which the Middle Ages produced after the recovery of the Nichomachean Ethics of Aristotle."[2]

The *Scito Teipsum* was bitterly attacked by William of Thiérry, who collected in a letter, which he sent to St. Bernard, a number of quotations from the treatise which seemed to him to be heretical. In truth, Abelard's ethical views were much in advance of his age and were opposed to the rather external and legalistic outlook on morality which was a part of the Augustinian tradition. The *Scito Teipsum* was one of his most mature works and was probably written shortly before 1140. The ideas expressed in it mark a definite advance in ethical thought, and for this work alone, Abelard deserves a place amongst the great philosophers.

The accepted view in his days was that Adam's sin had involved the whole human race in his guilt (*culpa*). As a consequence of the Fall, man became powerless to rise again by his own efforts and became dependent on Divine Grace. Sin was a falling away from the good, and to restore the relation between the sinner and God, penance was necessary. Sins were divided into mortal—*i.e.*, grave sins which bring death to the soul unless repentance follows, and venial—*i.e.*, lesser faults which do not separate the sinner from the Grace of God. It was the custom to draw up lists of sins classified according to whether they were mortal or venial, and the appropriate penance for each was suggested. Abelard's innovation consisted in drawing attention to the impossibility of basing one's judgment on the overt action alone without taking into account the

---

[1] "The Glosses of Peter Abelard on Porphyry," p. 254.
[2] H. RASHDALL, *History of the Mediaeval Universities*, vol. i., p. 62.

C

motive which led the agent to perform the particular act. He differentiated between sin and the weakness or defect of human nature, due to the Fall, which rendered the individual liable to temptation and disposed him to sin. "We are, that is, inclined to consent to what we ought not to do, or to leave undone what we ought to do. Consent of this kind we rightly call sin."[1] The weakness of human nature which leads us to desire what is wrong ought not to be called sin. The latter consists in the act of consent, and the person who consents to the evil prompting is equally a sinner with the individual who goes one step further and allows the consent to issue in action. "A man crosses another's garden. At the sight of the delectable fruit his desire is aroused. He does not, however, give way to desire so as to take anything by theft or rapine, although his mind was moved to strong inclination by the thought of the delight of eating. Where there is desire, there, without doubt, will exists. The man desires the eating of that fruit wherein he doubts not that there will be delight. The weakness of nature in this man is compelled to desire the fruit which, without the master's permission, he has no right to take. He conquers the desire, but does not extinguish it. Since, however, he is not enticed into consent, he does not descend to sin."[2]

Previous thinkers, whilst acknowledging that the act of consenting to an evil desire is sinful, had taught that the actual performance of the deed added to the guilt because of the pleasure which accompanies the act. Abelard repudiated this idea. He insisted that the essence of sin lies in the consent which implies a contempt of God and the overt action makes no difference at all. If the pleasure resulting from the action heightened the degree of sin, we should have to maintain the absurd position that all pleasure is sinful. "Sin is not, therefore, increased by the doing of an action: and nothing mars the soul except what is of its own nature, namely, consent. This we affirmed was alone sin, preceding action in will, or subsequent to the performance of the action."[3]

Abelard's insistence upon the motive of the action is an anticipation of Kant. He says, "Whether you actually give alms to a needy person, or charity makes you ready to give, makes no difference to the merit of the deed. The will may be there when the opportunity

[1] J. R. McCallum, *Abailard's Ethics* (Basil Blackwell: 1935), p. 18.
[2] *ibid.*, p. 23.
[3] *ibid.*, p. 28.

is not. . . . God considers not the action, but the spirit of the action. It is the intention, not the deed wherein the merit or praise of the doer consists. Often, indeed, the same action is done from different motives. . . . Two men, for instance, hang a guilty person. The one does it out of zeal for justice; the other in resentment for an earlier enmity. The action of hanging is the same. Both men do what is good and what justice demands. Yet the diversity of their intentions causes the same deed to be done from different motives, in the one case good, in the other bad."[1]

Abelard issues a warning about basing our moral judgment upon the overt action alone. "Men judge of visible, and not of invisible fact. They do not estimate the error, so much as the effect of the action. God alone considers the spirit in which a thing is done, rather than merely what is done."[2] The law is bound to base its penalties to a large extent on the overt act. "Although the evil action has no imitators, or even none who recognize it as wrong, nevertheless, in so far as it is a public act it must, in human society, be chastised more than private guilt, because it can occasion greater mischief, and can be more destructive by the example it sets, than the hidden failing. . . . The greater the social stumbling block, the more stringent must be the social correction, even though the original guilt be relatively light."[3]

Abelard was not satisfied with the traditional view of original sin. Distinguishing between guilt (*culpa*) and punishment (*poena*), he asserted that Adam's descendants do not share his guilt but are liable to the punishment incurred by the first act of disobedience. He pointed out that the term sin can be employed in more than one sense. From a purely external point of view, those who condemned Christ to death or persecuted St. Stephen committed sin, but provided they honestly acted in accordance with the dictates of their conscience, we cannot properly speak of their deeds as sinful. "I feel that, properly speaking, sin is that which can never come about without personal guilt. Not to know God, to have no belief in Him, to do wrongly under a misapprehension—such things can be found in many a life without there being real fault. A man, for example, may not believe in the Gospel or in Christ because he has heard no preacher. . . . What blame is to be

[1] J. R. McCALLUM, *Abailard's Ethics* (Basil Blackwell: 1935), p. 31.
[2] *ibid.*, p. 38.
[3] *ibid.*, p. 40.

attributed to such a man for not believing? . . . The persecutors of Christ and of their own kinsfolk whom they thought ought to be persecuted, may be said to have sinned in action only (*per opera-tionem*). But they would have sinned really and more grievously had they, contrary to their own conscience, permitted their victims to go free."[1] There is no sin save that against conscience. St. Thomas developed, a hundred years later, the same topic along similar lines.

The most prominent theological controversy of the age was on the subject of confession. About the 8th century, public confession, because of the scandal which resulted, had been replaced by private confession to a priest. The latter was not made compulsory until the Lateran decree of 1216, which insisted upon confession once a year and imposed the seal of the confessional. Abelard, writing before the decree was promulgated, was quite free to give his own views. He did not believe that penance was a sacrament and asserted that auricular confession was not necessary for forgiveness. The three necessary parts of penitence are sorrow for the commission of sin, confession and satisfaction. As soon as the individual is truly sorry for his sin and has confessed it to God, he receives God's forgiveness, but true penitence is known by the fruits it produces. Resolve for amendment of life and satisfaction, where it is possible, will follow contrition.

Abelard brings charges against the clergy which remind us of those made by the leaders of the Reformation. He says, "The greed of priests who promise a valueless security leads astray many of the dying. They are told to offer their store of money to purchase the masses, which would never be freely given them. It is well-known that there is a fixed tariff among clerics for this trade. The price for a mass is a penny, and if annual the charge is forty pence."[2] Again, "There exist many inexperienced doctors to whose care it is dangerous or useless to entrust cases of illness. Similarly many priests of the Church may be found, without faith or discretion, who will easily reveal sins confessed to them. Confession to these fellows may be not merely useless but a real danger."[3] It was these abuses which led the Church to tighten up discipline by the Lateran decree of 1216.

[1] J. R. McCullum, *Abailard's Ethics* (Basil Blackwell: 1935), p. 53.
[2] *ibid.*, p. 65.
[3] *ibid.*, p. 78.

For a time, the traditional views about morality prevailed and Abelard's opinions were condemned by the Council of Sens, but nevertheless they bore fruit in the following century. When St. Thomas discussed the subject of mortal sin, he took into account the factor of intention in assessing the degree of guilt.

SUGGESTIONS FOR FURTHER READING

Richard McKeon, in vol. i of the *Selections from Medieval Philosophers* (Charles Scribner's Sons: 1930), gives a translation of "The Glosses of Peter Abelard on Porphyry. This treatise was found and edited by Dr. Bernhard Geyer in 1919. McKeon's selection is taken from this work, which, as he says, "added considerably to Abelard's philosophic stature."

Abailard's Ethics, trans. J. R. McCallum (Basil Blackwell: 1935). This is a translation of the *Scito Teipsum* and it contains a valuable introduction and useful notes.

CARRÉ, M. H., *Realists and Nominalists* (O.U.P.: 1946). Chapter i gives an account of the Neo-Platonic Realism of St. Augustine and is followed by a study of Abelard's position. Chapters iii and iv deal respectively with St. Thomas Aquinas and William of Ockham as regards their attitude towards the problem of universals.

CHAPTER IV

ST. ANSELM OF CANTERBURY

APART from his fame as a philosopher and theologian, St. Anselm is one of the best-known personalities in English mediæval history. He was born at Aosta in 1033 and his parents were members of a noble Lombard family. At the age of fifteen he wished to enter a monastery, but his father was strongly opposed to the idea. Anselm is supposed, for a time, to have led a very worldly life, but from what we know of his character, the tradition is hardly to be trusted. We do know that about the age of twenty, feeling that his relations with his father were incapable of amendment, he left home and travelled to Normandy, attracted by the fame of Lanfranc, then Abbot of Bec. At the age of twenty-seven he entered the monastery of Bec, and when Lanfranc moved to Caen, he became Abbot of Bec in 1078. It was during his primacy at Bec that he wrote his most important philosophical treatises, the *Monologion*, the *Proslogion*, the *Dialogues* and *Meditations*, and his *Homilies*.

When Lanfranc died in 1089, the see of Canterbury remained vacant for four years since William II refused to nominate a successor. In 1093, the king had a serious illness and, believing that he was near to death, he sought to make amends and offered the archbishopric to Anselm. The latter was at first unwilling to accept but he was dragged to the king's bedside and the pastoral staff was thrust into his hands. Anselm had grave doubts about his ability to work with William; he compared himself to a weak old sheep yoked at the plough with a fiery bull. Anselm's doubts were justified, for when William recovered, he turned once more to his accustomed way of life. At this time, the Papal authority was being disputed by Urban II, who had the support of the majority of the Church, and Clement III, the nominee of the Emperor. Anselm was in favour of Urban but the king supported his rival. In 1095, Anselm proposed to visit Rome to receive the pallium from Urban. William refused to recognize the latter's claims, and a council was assembled at Rockingham to decide the question. The barons strongly supported Anselm, although most of the bishops, who were creatures of the king, were in opposition. The king, finding that Anselm had such strong support from the lay nobility, was unable to take further steps, but when, in 1097, Anselm left for Rome, William seized his estates.

After William's death in the New Forest, his brother Henry was chosen as king. One of his first acts was to recall Anselm from the Continent, but unfortunately Anselm and the king were soon engaged in a bitter quarrel. The dispute was on the subject of investiture. As Archbishop of Canterbury, Anselm was not only an ecclesiastic but one of the most important of the king's barons. He was unwilling to receive his investiture at the hands of the king and even refused consecration to a number of bishops who had been chosen by Henry. There is no doubt that Anselm's refusal was dictated by conscientious motives. After his experience with William, he felt that the only effective safeguard against royal tyranny was to insist on the complete independence of the Church. Eventually, the dispute was settled by a compromise similar to that which ended for a time the quarrel between the Empire and the Papacy. It was agreed that bishops should receive the emblems of their spiritual office, the ring and staff, from their ecclesiastical superiors, and then should perform the act of homage to the king for their estates. Worn out by the cares of office and his struggle against the royal power, Anselm died in 1109.

St. Anselm's philosophical position is that of Extreme Realism, but he did not push his views in a pantheistic direction. He was saved from this by the Platonic or Neo-Platonic influence exercised through the works of St. Augustine and the Pseudo-Dionysius. In this he presents a contrast to Erigena, who was primarily a metaphysician, whilst Anselm was a theologian and a moralist. This is not to deny his interest in metaphysics, but in his mind morality occupied the prior position. His interest in philosophy proceeded from a firm conviction that goodness is a contradiction unless it has the support of truth.

Anselm's philosophical outlook shows him as a true successor of St. Augustine, and the phrases *fides quaerens intellectum* and *credo ut intelligam* fully describe his attitude. Faith is prior to reason, and it is when the latter is sustained and assisted by the former that it raises the individual to God. Reason applied to the study of the Scriptures discovers their true meaning, resolves difficulties and apparent contradictions and produces a rational study of revealed truth. For Anselm, the ideal is a perfect faith fully understanding what it believes. Such an ideal cannot be reached in this life; it is completely achieved in the Beatific Vision when the object of faith is presented to the soul directly without the intervention of visible images and symbols.

In the *Monologion*, a soliloquy about the nature of God, St. Anselm analyses the idea of God. In the prologue, he tells us how the treatise came to be written. It was a résumé of his lectures to the brethren at Bec. The monks had asked him to deal with the essence and existence of God in a rational fashion without appealing to the teaching of revealed religion. Although he felt himself to be inadequate for this duty, he could not refuse his pupils, but he hoped that what he did would be confined to the cloisters of Bec. The lectures were transcribed and became known to the outside world. Hence, when he wrote the prologue, Anselm asked his readers to bear in mind the original idea which had inspired the work.

It is important to realize that the *Monologion* was written for professed Christians, otherwise the argument of this treatise and also of the *Proslogion* will be misunderstood. The key to St. Anselm's meditation on the nature of God is the principle of Perfection. God is the Supreme Perfection, Absolute and Infinite Perfection, and from this it follows that He is the Infinite and Absolute Being. With this idea in his mind, Anselm begins his argument with the sensible world, and from the creature, reaches the Creator; from the finite and incomplete beings of this world, he arrives at the idea of an Infinite Perfection.

St. Anselm's reasoning proceeds on the following lines. If we examine the objects of the sensible world, we shall notice that the world is made up of a multiplicity of things all possessing varying grades of perfection and exhibiting different degrees of goodness. Every existing thing is from some point of view good, and all the objects to which the term good is applicable are good because of their participation in the common quality of goodness. An objector might urge that objects are called good for various reasons so that qualities appearing good from one point of view will seem to be evil from another. Thus, a strong active horse is considered good but the same qualities in a thief are called bad. This objection is a consequence of confused thinking. The terms good and bad are employed by us in senses relative to ourselves and our purposes. Good often means useful to us. But from the standpoint of philosophy, strength and efficiency in a robber are qualities that are good in themselves. They are only evil when they are put to evil uses. Objects are good because they participate in goodness to different degrees and in different ways. Goodness in itself is the cause of goodness in things.

Anselm then appeals to a principle which was especially attractive to mediæval thinkers. It was derived from Neo-Platonism and is the axiom that the effect must needs be less perfect than its cause. Goodness in finite things is the effect of Supreme Goodness. If anything superior to goodness can exist, then by the axiom it must derive its goodness from some other source and not from goodness. It would be good because of participation in some other quality than goodness. Such a conclusion is absurd, so that we are forced to assume a supreme good through which all other things receive their goodness. St. Anselm then repeats the same argument for other perfections such as beauty and majesty.

His next step is to show that all these perfections are united in one single essence. The beautiful is good and the good beautiful. If the good and the beautiful were not one and the same essence, one would have, at the same time, one superior or one inferior to the other according as it was the participator or participated in by the other. Hence, all the perfections form one essence, absolutely simple and, at the same time, infinitely rich in perfections. This essence is good and beautiful and true through itself; it depends on no other essence, but all being depends upon it. This Supreme Essence we call God.

Another way of reaching God is through the conception of differing degrees of perfection. The term less perfect has no meaning unless a more perfect exists. Thus the gradation of the universe demands a Supremely Perfect which is God. One cannot envisage a series of degrees of perfection unless there exists an *Ens perfectissimum*. Again, every finite being receives its existence from another—*e.g.*, man begets man. This regression cannot be infinite, and reason demands a First Being existing of Itself and Whose existence provides an explanation of the existence of everything else.

These lines of thought lead to the idea of a Supremely Perfect Being. What are the essential characteristics of such a Being?

He is the source of all the perfections we know and therefore we are correct in attributing to Him all perfections to a supreme and absolute degree. Here, however, an objection must be countered. A Being so superior to the finite objects of experience would seem to have nothing in common with them. Is it legitimate to apply perfections drawn from the world of finite experience to God? How can human language express the perfections of God? Is not the gulf between creature and Creator one of infinite width, and since the Essence of God is inaccessible to finite minds, how can the concepts we form represent Him as He is?

In his reply, St. Anselm anticipates that of St. Thomas to the same problem. Every effect bears some likeness to its cause, and the more perfect the effect, the more fully does it exhibit the likeness. The creature reflects the Creator, and it is through this reflection, vague and imperfect though it is, that we gain some knowledge of God. Such knowledge is acquired by analogy. Of all created beings we know, man is the highest and therefore in his nature most adequately reflects the Divine Essence. Through the study of our own souls we can arrive at a knowledge of God in as far as any finite being can know Him.

God is the meeting place of all positive and absolute perfections, which, although distinguishable on the human level, are not in reality distinct from His Being. It is inaccurate to regard the perfections as attributes or qualities of the Divine. They are to be identified with God's Essence. He is not good or just; He is Goodness and Justice. He does not possess Being; He is Absolute Existence, for in Him essence and existence coincide. God is, therefore, the Supreme Being, the Cause of every being and every perfection. He is the Creator, the Life and the Truth. He is Absolute Goodness and Beauty, Infinite Justice and Wisdom, eternal and unchangeable. In addition, He is an infinite number of other perfections; in fact, He is the Supremely Perfect Being (*Ens perfectissimum*) and a Being than Whom no greater can be conceived (*Ens quo maius cogitari nequit*).

The last phrase leads direct to the celebrated Ontological argument for God's existence which is Anselm's most important contribution to philosophy. The argument is given in the *Proslogion*. Once again, St. Anselm is writing for the faithful who have intimate experience of the truth they believe. The believer, if he is an intelligent person, will wish to feel that his faith is reasonable and can be supported by reasonable argument. The Ontological proof serves this purpose. It is an indirect demonstration of God's existence, defensive in the sense that it is intended to refute the fool who says in his heart, There is no God. From the impossibility of denial of God's existence, St. Anselm seeks to establish it. If we look upon the Ontological argument as a method for convincing the unbeliever, we shall misunderstand it. The argument rests upon the same principle of Perfection which was used in the *Monologion*. It asserts that a being endowed with both perfection and existence is more perfect than a similar being deprived of existence.

The argument is as follows. The analysis of the *Monologion* has shown that God is the Supremely Perfect Being, the most perfect of all possible beings (*Ens quo maius cogitari nequit*). Is it at all reasonable to doubt that He exists? The fool of the Psalms is indeed a fool for he says what he does not understand. His assertion is not only false but contradictory, and cannot even be thought if thinking signifies anything beyond a purely verbal thought. In other words, the proposition, God is not, contains an internal contradiction.

In the *Monologion*, guided by the principle of Perfection, we arrived at the conception of God as the *Ens quo maius cogitari nequit*. If the being endowed with every possible perfection were only imaginary, a being that did not exist outside our thought, then it would not be the *Ens quo maius cogitari nequit*. It would be a simple matter to think of a more perfect being which existed in reality as well as in thought. The latter would be a being more perfect than the *Ens quo maius cogitari nequit*. Such a conclusion is absurd; hence, we cannot logically think of God without thinking of Him as existing. The fool, by denying God's existence, contradicts himself.

Put into syllogistic form, the argument becomes: The idea of God is the idea of the Greatest Conceivable Being (*id quo maius existare nequit*).

To exist in reality as well as in thought is more perfect than to exist only in thought.

Therefore, God, the Greatest Conceivable Being, exists in reality.

How then can we explain the fool's denial, for is not saying in one's heart the same as thinking? St. Anselm then begins to examine the different ways in which an object can be said to be thought. In the first place, it is possible to think a thing without thinking of it as existing in reality. This is not the same as thinking of it as non-existent. We can think of an object without concerning ourselves with the question of its existence. Thus, an artist who has conceived in his mind the plan of a picture which he has not yet painted may be said to have the picture in his mind but he certainly is not thinking of it as existing. If, when he has completed the picture, he thinks it again, he represents it in an entirely different way as something which has actual existence (*intelligit esse*).

There are many people who have God in their minds without conceiving Him as existing in reality, without understanding that He is a real Being, in fact, the Most Real Being. This is how the fool thinks. Anselm is concerned to show that God ought not to be thought in this way. We are obliged to think of Him as existing, so that it is contradictory to deny His existence and claim that He only exists as an idea in the mind.

We can also think a thing adequately—*i.e.*, think of it with all the qualities that really belong to it and understanding the words which express our thought—or verbally—i.e., without any true thought or realization of the object denoted by our words. The fool thinks God verbally; in fact, he does not think God at all because he does not understand what is meant by God. His idea is inadequate and vague because it does not correspond to what God really is.

The fool has made an absurd statement but he has not realized how foolish it is. He says the word God, but he does not understand that God is the *Ens quo maius cogitari nequit*. If we really understand the meaning of the word God, we cannot logically deny that He exists. Nobody in his senses could believe that water and fire are identical if he understands the nature of water and fire. But he could say the words that express this absurdity if he pays no attention to the meaning of the words water and fire.

St. Anselm's argument was attacked in his own lifetime by Gaunilon, prior of the monastery of Marmoutiers near Tours. He wrote a treatise, *On Behalf of the Fool* (*Pro Insipiente*), in which he stated that he did not wish as a good Catholic to deny the conclusions of Anselm's argument, but that he was concerned to show the faulty nature of the reasoning employed. Gaunilon was called by Hegel, "the Kant of the ancient world." Certainly his objections are similar to those raised by Kant at a later date but they are far more pertinent. Gaunilon did not realize that Anselm's argument was to strengthen the faith of the believer (*fides quaerens intellectum*), but he regarded it as an attempt to convince the sceptic. Hence, he remarks that one should not conclude that the fool's idea of God is the same as that of the believer. He charges Anselm with not paying sufficient attention to his opponent's state of mind (*non satis attendit cui loquatur*). The fool's conception of God is so different that Anselm's conclusions do not follow from it. The fool has never admitted that he has the idea of the *Ens quo maius cogitari nequit*, and therefore he is not contradicting himself when he says that there is no God.

Moreover, the believer himself cannot possess an adequate idea of God. Anselm should be the first to admit this because he has already shown that the nature of God is incomprehensible to finite minds. The gulf between the Creator and the creature is so immense, that human beings can make no true assertion about God, and if they try to do so, it is impossible to find any contradiction between the subject and the predicate of such an affirmation. In other words, God cannot be a term in a logical judgment.

When one speaks of an object in the sensible world—*e.g.*, a man—it is easy to represent such an object to oneself even in his absence or if he is somebody one has never met. This is possible because of our previous experience of other members of the human species. The idea we form is based upon experience of other men and their characteristics. There is, however, no possible experience of God on which we can build. What meaning can such a phrase as the *Ens quo maius cogitari nequit* have for me? It is nothing more than a sequence of words received by the ear. It is impossible for a finite human mind to frame an adequate idea of God.

Gaunilon's best-known argument is that of the lost island. "Suppose a certain person tells me that somewhere in the ocean there is an island which, because of the difficulty or rather the impossibility of finding what does not exist, is called the Lost Island. He adds that it possesses unthought-of riches and pleasures far exceeding those attributed to the Fortunate Isles, and since it has no owner or inhabitant, it is superior in treasures to all the lands in which men dwell. Let us suppose he tells me this. I shall understand his words quite easily since there is no difficulty in doing so. But suppose he adds by way of conclusion, 'You cannot doubt the real existence of this island so superior to all other lands. You do not deny that the idea is in your mind, and since it is a more excellent thing to exist in reality than in the intelligence only, it follows of necessity that it really does exist. If it did not, then any land which really exists would be more perfect, and therefore, this island already conceived by you as the most perfect, would not be more perfect than any other.' If he wished to persuade me by his argument that this island exists and that its existence cannot be doubted, I should either think that he was joking, or that I was uncertain which of the two of us was the more stupid, myself for believing that he was right, or my informant, if he believed he had proved the existence of this island so certainly without first finding out whether this same perfection is in my mind as an object which really exists without shadow of doubt and not as something false or uncertain."[1]

Gaunilon's contention is that the passage from thought to an existent reality corresponding to the thought is not legitimate.

His objection is similar in form to that of Kant. There is no evidence that Kant was aware of Anselm's argument. He states that he is dealing with the "celebrated demonstration of Descartes," but he is in fact criticizing the form given to the Ontological argument by Leibnitz. Kant's illustration is that the thought of a hundred dollars in my pocket is not the same as the actual possession of that sum of money. Kant failed to realize what the Ontological argument set out to do. Anselm's object was to distinguish between the idea of God and all other ideas. The former case is unique. As Sorley remarks, "Gaunilon's objection . . . comes nearer the point than Kant's does. Anselm had argued that existence must belong to one idea, though to one only, the idea than which nothing greater can be conceived. To say, as Kant does, that the idea of a hundred dollars does not involve their existence, is quite irrelevant, for we can easily conceive greater things than a hundred dollars, and, in a tolerable coinage, any one hundred dollars is not better than any other. On the other hand, Gaunilon's idea of a perfect island was at least the idea of something perfect or complete of its kind. Nothing greater of its kind could be conceived."[2]

[1] GAUNILON, *Liber pro Insipiente*, chapter vi.
[2] SORLEY, W. R., *Moral Values and the Idea of God*, Gifford Lectures of 1914–15, (C.U.P.: 1918), pp. 312–13.

Hegel's criticism is on similar lines. He says, "The unexampled favour and acceptance which attended Kant's criticism of the Ontological proof was undoubtedly due to the illustration which he made use of. To mark the difference between thought and being, he took the instance of a hundred sovereigns, which, for anything it matters to the notion, are the same hundred whether they are real or only possible, though the difference of the two cases is very perceptible in their effect on a man's purse. Nothing can be more obvious than that anything we only think or fancy is not on that account actual; and everybody is aware that a conception . . . is no match for being. . . . Those who like to taunt the philosophic idea with the difference between being and thought, might have admitted that philosophers were not wholly ignorant of the fact. Can there be anything pettier in knowledge than this? Above all, it is well to remember, when we speak of God, that we have an object of another kind than any hundred sovereigns."[1]

In his reply, St. Anselm emphasizes that Gaunilon's criticisms are based upon a neglect of the terms of the original statement. The argument about the lost island is quite beside the point. We are not talking about lost islands but the *Ens quo maius cogitari nequit*. The existence of God is a unique case. No illustration drawn from objects of the finite world can be relevant to the issue. Although in the physical world a gulf is placed between thought and existence, in God we have the meeting of the two.

Anselm also complains that Gaunilon has substituted the phrase "that which is greater than all things" for "that than which nothing greater can be conceived." The conclusions which follow from the one are not necessarily the same as those which can be deduced from the other. Gaunilon has also objected that we cannot form an adequate idea of God. This may be granted but it must also be noted that every inferior good implies a superior. Thus our thought shows a continuous ascent from what is felt to be partial and defective to that which is whole and perfect. This is the meaning of the Scriptures when they say that the invisible things of God are grasped through our experience of the visible.

We shall see that the Ontological argument was rejected by St. Thomas. It was revived in a slightly different form by Descartes and again by Leibnitz, and in the latter form was criticized and rejected by Kant.

[1] *The Logic of Hegel*, trans. by William Wallace (Clarendon Press: 1874) p. 91.

SUGGESTIONS FOR FURTHER READING

Unfortunately there is neither an English translation of St. Anselm's philosophical writings nor any English work dealing with the details of his philosophy.

McKeon in his *Selections from Medieval Philosophers*, vol. i, gives a translation of Anselm's *Dialogue on Truth*.

Anselm's doctrine of God is ably dealt with by C. C. J. Webb in his *Studies in the History of Natural Theology*, chapter ii (Clarendon Press: 1915). The Latin text with a French translation of the *Proslogion*, the criticism of Gaunilon and Anselm's reply has been published by A. Koyré, *Saint Anselme de Cantorbéry—Fides Quaerens Intellectum* (J. Vrin, Paris). Koyré has also made a study of Anselm's philosophy in his *L'idée de Dieu dans la philosophie de saint Anselme* (J. Vrin, Paris: 1923).

CHAPTER V

JOHN OF SALISBURY, THE HISTORIAN OF THE UNIVERSALS CONTROVERSY

No HISTORY of mediæval philosophy would be complete if it omitted John of Salisbury, the outstanding figure of the middle years of the 12th century. John, whose real name was John Little (Johannes Parvus), was born about the year 1115 and came as a young man to pursue his studies at Paris in 1136. He came of Saxon stock, and he refers to his surname in his *Epistles* by describing himself as "little by name, less in skill and least in worth." Very little is known of his early years, but from the time he came to Paris, the autobiographical description in the *Metalogicus* gives full information not only about himself and his studies, but also about the leading personalities of the age and the cultured life of the middle 12th century. The *Metalogicus*, like his other important work, the *Polycraticus*, is dedicated to Thomas Becket, and carries as its alternative name the title *De nugis Curialium et vestigiis Philosophorum* (*Concerning the Vanities of Courtiers and the Traditions of Philosophers*).

John's life falls into three well-marked periods. From 1136 to 1148 he studied in the schools of Chartres and Paris, probably spending the last two years in secretarial work at the Papal court at Rome, where he made numerous friends and acquaintances who stood him in good stead in later years. From 1148 to 1176, he was the politician and man of affairs who played a prominent part in the disputes between Henry II and Archbishop Becket. Finally, he was chosen as Bishop of Chartres where he remained until his death in 1180.

During the first period, John received firsthand experience of the views of the leading protagonists in the Universals controversy. Abelard gave him his early lessons in logic, and after this he spent three years at the school of Chartres, at that time under the direction of William of Conches. It was here that he received a thorough grounding in both the Trivium and the Quadrivium. As mentioned in Chapter III, Chartres at this time was strongly in favour of Extreme Realism and its teaching was characterized by the Platonic tradition and an enthusiasm for Latin studies. The humanistic traditions of the school had a deep influence upon John, both in developing his own Latin style and his knowledge of classical literature and in broadening his outlook upon life. It was during the time he spent at Chartres that he became acquainted with Gilbert de la Porrée.

Shortly after 1140, he returned to Paris to find his old friends of the schools still busily engaged in logic chopping. He wrote, "And so it seemed pleasant to me to revisit my old companions on the Mount, whom I had left and whom dialectic still detained, to confer with them touching old matters of debate; that we might by mutual comparison measure together our several progress. I found them as before, and where they were before; nor did they appear to have reached the goal in unravelling the old questions, nor had they added one jot of a proposition. The aims that once inspired them, inspired them still: they only had progressed in one point, they had unlearned moderation, they knew not modesty; in such wise that one might despair of their recovery. And thus experience taught me a manifest conclusion, that, whereas dialectic furthers other studies, so if it remain by itself it lies bloodless and barren, nor does it quicken the soul to yield fruit of philosophy, except the same conceive from elsewhere."[1]

Whilst at Paris, John found it necessary to support himself by private tutoring. "I received the children of noble persons to instruct, who furnished me with living." He also became acquainted with Adam du Petit Pont. The latter was an Englishman (later Bishop of St. Asaph), who took his name from the Petit Pont which leads from the centre of Paris to the Latin Quarter. John thought highly of Adam's ability as an exponent of Aristotelian logic, but he disliked intensely his mercenary attitude towards teaching and was careful to emphasize, "I was his disciple not for one day."

In 1148, John was present at the Council of Rheims where St. Bernard was urging the condemnation of Gilbert de la Porrée. Evidently he made the acquaintance of St. Bernard, for the latter recommended him to Archbishop Theobald of Canterbury, whose

[1] POOLE, op. cit., pp. 185–6.

secretary he became. This was the beginning of a busy political life for John during which he was frequently employed on diplomatic missions to the Roman court. At this time, the Englishman Adrian IV was Pope, and John obtained from him the authority for Henry II to invade and subjugate Ireland. When Theobald died, John became secretary to his successor, Thomas Becket. During the quarrel between the king and the archbishop, John loyally supported the latter, incurred the royal displeasure and accompanied Becket on his exile. When Becket returned, John was one of the witnesses of his murder in Canterbury Cathedral.

John of Salisbury's importance does not consist in the originality of his philosophical thought. He was not a builder of systems; he was rather a fine scholar, a man of liberal culture whose vast learning was accompanied by good taste and a sound judgment. R. L. Poole sums him up by saying, "John of Salisbury reflects something of all the characteristics of the school of Chartres of which Gilbert de la Porrée was the most famous product, but his training is wider than the school itself. Before he went there he had caught the dialectical enthusiasm from Abailard: afterwards he brought his trained intellect under a new guidance, and his theology breathes the ethical spirit of Hugh of St. Victor. He is thus a critic and a dialectician, a humanist and a divine; and it is the balance of his tastes and acquirements that make him in many respects the fairest type of the learned men of his time."[1]

John's greatest contribution to thought lies in the realm of political philosophy. His *Polycraticus* is intended as a statesman's handbook, and the political theory which it develops owes much to the jurists and canonists of the school of Bologna. The treatise was written in the years 1159–60, a period when, owing to his championship of the rights of the Church, he was out of favour with the king.

The *Polycraticus* is not a formal systematic work on political philosophy. It is somewhat discursive in method and contains a good deal of criticism of the life and manners of courtly society in the 12th century. This criticism may be regarded as clearing the way for a discussion of its central theme, the nature and ordering of the state under a good government. John's thought is characterized by an attempted reconciliation of two lines of

[1] *op. cit.*, p. 175.

thought which do not completely fuse. On the one hand, he teaches a spiritual individualism arising out of his Christian faith, which works out in practice in democratic tendencies, and, on the other, a theory of the social organism which leads to directly opposite conclusions.

The idea of society as an organic whole was a commonplace in mediæval thought about the state, but nowhere has it been worked out in greater detail than in the *Polycraticus*. His view is partly moulded by classical tradition, partly by St. Paul, who in I Cor. xii rebukes the false and unrestrained individualism of the Corinthians and employs the analogy of the human being in whom there are many members but one body. The eye, ear and hand cannot separate themselves from the body or claim independence, for "God hath tempered the body together, having given more abundant honour to that part which lacked, that there should be no schism in the body."

The biological analogy has its uses in modifying a wrong-headed individualism, but mediæval thought regarded it as a full and satisfactory theory of the nature of society. John received further support for his analogy from the late Latin treatise, the *Institutio Traiani*, which has been ascribed to Plutarch. The result is that John's conception is that of a highly functional state more complex and more intricately organized than Plato's Republic. The soul is represented by the Church; the head, the seat of executive power, is the prince; the hands are the soldiers; the feet, the husbandmen and workers; the heart is the senate or councillors of state, and the stomach is represented by the financial administration. Following up this detailed analogy, John quaintly remarks that "an afflicted and discontented people is a manifest sign that the prince has the gout."

The prince's authority does not proceed direct from God. He receives the sword, the symbol of temporal power, from the Church, and in all his dealings with his people, he acts as the servant of the priesthood. Probably, with the dispute between the king and his archbishop in mind, John devotes considerable care in considering the duties and privileges of kingship, and he has the book of Deuteronomy to help him in his task (Deut. xvii. 14–20). If the prince fails to carry out his duties and rule with equity, he is a tyrant, and his subjects not only may, but are, in duty bound, obliged to proceed to his deposition. Any means may be employed to get rid of the tyrant, except the use of poison, which John declares is entirely opposed to the English way of life.

John makes no reference to the tyrant having broken his contract with his subjects, thus freeing them of their obligation to obey him. The theory of a social contract had been stated by Manegold of Lautenbach in the previous century and was to appear again in the thought of St. Thomas Aquinas. The tyrant is harmful to the public good; he has put himself above the Law, and if he is not struck down by the hand of man, he is smitten by God. As C. C. J. Webb points out, in practice, John would prefer to leave the smiting of tyrants to God, than to incite men to this dangerous if righteous duty.

John's analogy of the state and the human body breaks down in connection with tyrannicide. The head can consent to a surgical operation on another part of the body, but if the head is cut off, the body perishes. The destruction of any vital organ of the body, however diseased, is fatal, and if society really were an organic whole, killing the tyrant would be social suicide. Reflection on these lines would have suggested to John that the analogy of the body is a useful illustration but, like other analogies, it cannot be pressed too far.

There is also a definite democratic element in John's theory. The prince is not only chosen by God but he owes his office to "the approbation of the people," and in illustration of this point he quotes the election of Joshua. This combination of what may be termed the democratic and organic ideals of community life raises a problem which is a fundamental one. How are we to discover a type of society that, far from destroying individuality, completes and perfects it? At the present day, very few would have anything to say in defence of the *laissez-faire* individualism of the 19th century. The organic theory of the state is a definite advance on this, and hence Fascism found it comparatively easy to revive the mediæval point of view. The true descendant of the view that John of Salisbury expounds is the totalitarian state, and since it is so much more thoroughgoing in modern practice than it could be in the 12th century, its defects stand out more clearly. Under the social organism theory, individual personality tends to be repressed and restricted. It does not allow for the full development of personality but rather forces individuals, classes, and nations into what is often a permanently inferior position. Of all forms of state organization so far invented, democracy comes closest to the ideal of giving scope for the development of the individual. John was a sincere Christian, and his Christian outlook on life prevented him from pushing the social organism theory to its logical conclusion.

In the *Metalogicus*, John gives his views about the value of dialectic. It is noteworthy that in this treatise the whole of Aristotle's *Organon* is utilized showing that the West had now recovered all the logical writings of Aristotle. John was a firm believer in what we should now call a liberal education. Genuine knowledge is based upon a study of all the subjects of the *Trivium*, undertaken, not in isolation, but in their inter-connection. Logic is a very valuable instrument, but its study divorced from other studies is like giving the sword of Hercules to be wielded by the hand of a pigmy.

In his attitude to the Universals controversy, John continues the teaching of Abelard. To seek the Universals apart from sensible things in which they are realized is to waste one's time (*nihil aget et frustra laborabit*). John adopts the position of Moderate Realism and, for the first time in the Middle Ages, attempts a psychological explanation of the process of abstraction and the formation of the concept. His outlook is still Augustinian but it has been considerably modified by his study of Aristotle.

SUGGESTIONS FOR FURTHER READING

In his *John of Salisbury*, C. C. J. Webb has made a very complete study of John's life and teaching. The student is strongly recommended to read this book, which is published by Methuen.

CHAPTER VI

MEDIÆVAL UNIVERSITIES AND SCHOOLS

THE latter half of the 12th century is memorable for the formation of the great European universities without which the remarkable achievements of the following century could not have been accomplished. It is almost impossible to say exactly when the different universities came into existence, for they were flourishing institutions in most cases before they received official recognition. It is generally agreed that the earliest university was that of Salerno, which remained predominantly a medical school. In northern Italy, at Bologna, there was a most important school of civil law to which, later, a school of canon law was added, and, in 1362, theology. These schools attracted scholars from all parts of Europe and gradually, towards the second half of the 12th century, the University of Bologna came into existence.

The influence of the jurists and canonists of Bologna has already been mentioned in connection with Abelard's *Sic et Non* (Chapter III). Of much more importance for our purpose is the development of the University of Paris. Abelard himself played a prominent part in the events which led to its formation. The schools of Notre-Dame, St. Victor and Sainte Geneviève, which were flourishing in his day, coalesced towards the end of the century into the University of Paris. This union was accomplished some time between 1170 and 1175. The university received its charter from Philip Augustus in 1200 and was recognized by the Pope in 1231, but it was an acknowledged institution long before it received official recognition.

In the 12th century, the word university carried a meaning quite different from that which it bears today. Some have considered a university as an institution which attempts to teach all branches of knowledge, and others, as a union of colleges. In its origin, the term had no connection with schools or with learning. It simply denoted an association, and there were universities of merchants and tailors as well as of scholars. Any community bound by common ties of interest was called a university, and in this sense the documents of the Middle Ages described the association of citizens in a town as a university. The *universitas*, or association of craftsmen, was formed to protect the interests of the craft, and in a similar manner, scholars and teachers formed themselves into associations for their mutual benefit and protection. At Bologna, the wealthy students of law formed a university which was more important than the teachers whom they employed. The University of Paris, on the other hand, was an association of masters, and it was considerably later that the name was applied to the collection of buildings in which the teaching was carried on.

The Middle Ages usually called a university by the name of *studium generale*. Any place of learning, such as Chartres, would be entitled a *studium*, but *studium generale* emphasized two important features. It was open to scholars from all lands, and it was understood that instruction was given in the arts and at least one other faculty. Although each university at some time during the course of its early history received its charter from the king or the Pope, G. G. Coulton reminds us, "The universities rose and attained their great influence by the same natural growth which created trade unions in modern Britain and has made them, in their present power and organisation, almost a fourth estate of the realm. It is true that, by about 1300, lawyers had worked out the theory that papal or imperial licence was necessary for the founding of a university, but even these lawyers had to admit that long custom might count also, and that we might have a university 'by custom' (*ex consuetudine*), as genuine as if it had been a papal or imperial foundation."[1]

The system of academic degrees began in the second half of the 12th century. Masters in the schools served a long apprenticeship as students and were naturally jealous of any newcomer who presumed to teach without having undergone this lengthy preparation. This explains the opposition of men like William of Champeaux and Anselm of Laon to Abelard.[2] The masters, therefore, imitated the merchants and craftsmen, and formed associations which to all intents and purposes were guilds of

[1] COULTON, G. G., *Medieval Panorama* (C.U.P.: 1938), p. 395.
[2] It was unlawful for a student to teach without permission of a master and this was one of the accusations brought against Abelard at the Council of Soissons.

learning. Just as the craftsman could not practise until he had been recognized by his guild and the standards of his work approved, so the intending master had to possess the licence of his universitas before he could teach. In its origin, the degree was a licence to teach issued by the masters of the university.

The graduate was a master or a doctor in the subject he taught, and these titles indicated his profession rather than a lifelong distinction. Later, the differentiation between actual teachers and those who had retired from teaching was indicated by the title of *non-regentes* and contrasted with the *regentes*, who had charge of schools. In this way the degree began to be a title rather than the indication of a profession. The bachelor was originally an aspirant to knighthood, but the term was adopted by the universities to signify a person who was no longer a student though he was not yet recognized as a teacher. It was a definite step or degree towards the higher title of master and doctor.

The University of Paris may be regarded as the mother of our own Universities of Oxford and Cambridge. Dr. Rashdall believed that Oxford owed its beginning to the quarrel between Henry II and Archbishop Becket when English clergy in France were ordered to return home. This theory has been disputed, since there is evidence that schools at Oxford existed at least as early as 1133, when Robert Pullus began to lecture on the Bible. In 1149, Vacarius arrived from Bologna, established himself at Oxford, gave a course of lectures on Roman law and published an account of the *Code and Digest* of Justinian. It is not known at what time the schools of Oxford coalesced into a university, but it is quite certain that a *studium generale* was in existence by 1185.

The origin of Cambridge has been traced to a migration of Oxford scholars in 1209, caused by a quarrel between them and the townsfolk. It is possible that schools were already in existence at Cambridge, but in 1231 there is documentary evidence of an organized *studium generale* in that town. Both Oxford and Cambridge took Paris as their model, though in their respective organizations they introduced certain modifications.

At Paris, the universitas of scholars was organized into four Nations, Picards, Gauls, Normands, and English. At the outbreak of the Hundred Years War, the English withdrew and were replaced by the Germans. A similar organization existed at Oxford and Cambridge. At Oxford, scholars who came from north of the Trent belonged to the Northern Nation and the remainder to the Southern Nation. Scotsmen were allocated to the Northern and Irishmen to the Southern Nation. When the University of St. Andrews was founded in 1411, the students were divided into Nations according to the district from which they came. Fife, Lothian, Angus, and Alban. The last comprised all students not in the first three.

At all the universities, disputes and fights between the Nations and between students and townsfolk were of common occurrence. Thus, in 1261 a riot broke out at Cambridge between Northerners and Southerners in the course of which the townsfolk took part, and it resulted in the burning of buildings and the destruction of manuscripts. One of the chief differences between Paris and the English universities consisted in the position occupied by the chancellor. At Paris, the rector was the head of the Nations and from the beginning was in constant conflict with the chancellor who represented the bishop and claimed authority over the university. Eventually the rector became the head of the university and the function of the chancellor was restricted to that of issuing the licence to teach on conditions prescribed by the masters. Oxford and Cambridge were at some distance from the nearest cathedral city so that they developed in independence of episcopal control. The first mention of a chancellor occurs in the legatine ordinance of 1214 when Robert Grosseteste was named as Chancellor of the University of Oxford. Since the chancellor was not only the representative of the bishop but also head of the masters' guild, there could be no dispute between him and the masters as took place at Paris. Hence the office of rector was not found at the English universities.

Another important distinction lies in the way that the collegiate system developed. At one time it was supposed to be peculiar to England but colleges also existed at Paris and continued until they were abolished by the French Revolution. In the early days of the universities scholars lived in what lodgings they could find and the masters taught in hired rooms. The exorbitant rents charged by the townsfolk were a constant source of dispute. The custom began at Paris of scholars living together in houses which they hired for themselves. It was usual to elect one member of the house who would be responsible for the rest. He was known as the master, but at first it was not obligatory for him to be an M.A. These hostels or *hospitia* came under the control of the university authorities. Frequently the hostel was the gift of some public spirited benefactor who endowed a house for poor scholars. One of the most famous of these "houses of scholars" was founded at Paris by Robert de Sorbon. In a similar way, William of Durham endowed a hostel at Oxford in 1249 which became known as Great University Hall. About 1280, it became University College. Sir John Balliol was another benefactor. In his raids across the Border, he inflicted great damage upon the churches at Tynemouth and Durham, and part of the penance enjoined by the Bishop of Durham in 1263 was to provide lodging for poor students at Oxford. Tradition has it that in true Scottish spirit he limited his gift to the sum of twopence. In 1282 his widow, Devorguilla, the Lady of Galloway, added endowments to the hostel and so paved the way to its becoming Balliol College.

Quite early, the University of Paris assumed control of its colleges. Many of them had only an intermittent existence and often fell into decay through lack of funds. The English universities experienced greater difficulty in exercising adequate control over their colleges. At first the lines of development were similar to those at Paris. Some hostels disappeared in later ages but others received further endowments, became recognized as legal corporations and eventually became colleges. The monastic houses of the regulars, and, later, the convents of the mendicants, also provided hostels for their members.

The transition from hostel to college is well illustrated by the foundation of Walter de Merton. In 1264, he provided a "House of the Scholars of Merton," but, unlike the earlier hostels, it was governed by an elaborate set of statutes regulating the corporate life of the fellows. The latter were seculars and were, at first, relatives of the founder. Further statutes had by 1274 converted Merton from an endowed hall into a self-governing college with its warden, its dean to safeguard the morals of the fellows and three bursars to look after the fabric and the financial side of the college. A similar development took place at Cambridge, where Peterhouse, founded in 1284, modelled its statutes on those of Merton.

Space forbids the mention of other foundations except two of special interest and importance. William of Wykeham, Bishop of Winchester, founded New College at Oxford in 1379 and

Winchester College in 1382. The latter was a collegiate school designed on a larger scale than any previous ones and was directly associated with New College. From Winchester, scholars were to go to the sister foundation at Oxford to study arts, law, and philosophy. Wykeham's foundation was called New College to distinguish it from Merton, which had always been known as "The College." As Winchester surpassed previous schools in the magnificence of its foundation, so in New College the buildings were on a scale which entitles Wykeham to the name of the creator of English collegiate architecture.

Wykeham introduced the principle of college tutorial instruction which eventually resulted in the major part of the teaching being given in the colleges and so lessened the control of the university over them. When Henry VI founded Eton College in 1440 and King's College, Cambridge, in 1441, he followed Wykeham's example. Eton became the feeder for King's as Winchester had been for New College. The royal foundations were on a still grander scale, and not only did Henry extend the principle of college tutorial instruction, but he also obtained a Papal Bull withdrawing the college to a large extent from the jurisdiction of the chancellor of the university.

In its academic organization, the mediæval, like the modern university, was divided into faculties. Originally the word faculty simply meant the capacity to teach a subject or group of subjects, but later it was used to denote the body of authorized teachers of those subjects within the university. In the Middle Ages, the recognized faculties were arts, theology, law, and medicine, though every university need not necessarily possess all these faculties. It is characteristic of the Italian universities that they aimed at giving a purely professional education for law or medicine. The University of Paris emphasized the advantages of a liberal education for all its students and the training of their minds became its primary object.

Every student was attached to a master. Robert de Courçon decreed in 1215, "*nullus sit scolaris qui certum magistrum non habeat.*" Just as the apprentice to a craft had to win his title of mastercraftsman, so the young student was regarded as an apprentice for the mastership in his faculty. As soon as he gained this coveted prize, he was permitted to teach in his own university and in any others. Freedom to teach in any university was one of the most characteristic features of mediæval times.

Before he became a master, the student had to achieve the grade of bachelor. The first step consisted of a preliminary test known as Responsions to discover his fitness to proceed with his studies. He was then obliged to present himself before a board of examiners consisting of three—later four—masters of his faculty who satisfied themselves that he had fulfilled the conditions of residence and had attended the requisite classes. If his studies were deemed adequate, he was admitted to determine.

The disputation known as Determination took place at Paris in one of the schools of the Vicus Stramineus (Straw Street), so called because for the sake of warmth, the floors of the examination halls were strewn with straw. It was held before an audience consisting of masters, fellow students and even the public. There were instances where passers-by were dragged in to form an audience.

The period of study for the licence was fixed by Robert de Courçon as six years and the candidate had to have attained the age of twenty. After the licence followed the inception, the corporate act whereby the guild of masters accepted the newcomer as one of themselves. The usual course in arts was at first about four and a half years; two years for the B.A.; another two years for the licence followed by the inception a few months later. The tendency towards an early baccalaureate developed. In modern times, on the Continent, the baccalaureate disappeared or became equivalent to matriculation. Whilst he was a bachelor, although he continued to study under a master, the scholar was allowed to take a limited part in the teaching of the university. In England, the necessity for residence to qualify for the master's degree was discontinued. Many Masters of Arts did not proceed any further but left the university to teach in schools. The professors continued their studies further. A similar rule applied to the other faculties, but in the faculty of theology the course was much more exacting.

Teaching in the university took two forms, the lecture (*lectio*), and the disputation. The former consisted in the explanation of a text-book in the classroom. Thus St. Thomas lectured on the *Sentences* of Peter Lombard and afterwards committed his lectures to writing as his *Commentary on the Sentences*.[1]

---

[1] Peter the Lombard, the Master of the Sentences (d. 1164), wrote a work entitled the *Four Books of Sentences* (*Quatuor Libri Sententiarum*). The book may be regarded as a development of the idea expressed in Abelard's *Sic et Non*. Peter chose certain topics (*distinctiones*) concerning which he collected the opinions of the Scriptures, the Fathers and Doctors of the Church and added sufficient of his own

The disputations were of two kinds, the ordinary disputations (*disputationes ordinariae*) which, if published, bore the title *Quaestiones Disputatae*, and the special disputations (*disputationes quodlibetales*) generally held twice a year in Advent and Lent. The procedure of the ordinary disputation was as follows. On the first day, the master being in the chair, the bachelor under his direction undertook to deal with arguments and difficulties raised by the scholars who were present. The master, on the following day, grouped the arguments and objections, and then, in the *sed contra*, announced what his own view was likely to be. He then proceeded to establish his own view (*determinatio magistralis*) and finally answered each objection in turn. This procedure can be checked by examination of any of St. Thomas's *quaestiones disputatae*, and gives the clue to the actual plan he adopted in writing his *Summa Theologica*.

The *quodlibeta* dealt with any problem that happened to be proposed. These problems might be entirely unrelated, but in the collections of the *quodlibeta* of great masters like St. Thomas, Scotus and William of Ockham, they were reduced to some sort of order. In the writings of St. Thomas one can easily find examples of all these types of teaching, his lectures on the various works of Aristotle, the *Quaestiones Disputatae* and the *Quaestiones Quodlibetales*.

The two great events which changed the life and activities of the universities were the coming of the mendicant Orders and the infiltration of the complete Aristotelian corpus. The latter will be considered in the chapter dealing with the Arabian philosophy and its impact upon Western thought.

When they originated, although the Dominicans were more interested in intellectual matters than the Franciscans, yet events soon brought both Orders into close relations with the universities and philosophy. The introduction of the Aristotelian corpus and the works of other pagan philosophers presented them with the problem of assimilating this teaching, if possible, with Christian

---

to bind the whole together in a systematic form. The Lombard's conclusions were not always taken for granted, and writers like John of Cornwall (1175) and Walter of St. Victor accused him of heresy. The *Sentences* became a text-book at the universities and most masters commented on them. Certain of these commentaries, such as those of St. Thomas, Duns Scotus and William of Ockham, have come down to us. They were often products of their earlier years and are useful in showing how their views developed with age and experience.

traditions. This appeared to them as an absolute necessity in order to preserve Christian civilization. Though this was not always consciously realized, especially amongst the Franciscans, the outstanding leaders of 13th-century thought showed remarkable foresight and statesmanship in their decision.

The Dominicans were the first in the field but they received a very uncertain welcome from the secular clergy and the monks. Although the universities were to a large extent ecclesiastical foundations, they were closely bound up with the secular clergy and the monasteries who viewed the newcomers with a good deal of suspicion which later passed into active hostility.

The Dominicans came to Paris about 1217 and were followed a little later by the Franciscans. Both Orders put forward their claims to chairs of theology in the university but they did not receive either sympathy or encouragement. In 1229, what was a fortunate event for the mendicant Orders occurred. A quarrel broke out between a number of drunken students belonging to the Picard Nation and an innkeeper of the Bourg de St. Marcel. The brawl developed to serious dimensions and certain citizens of Paris were roughly handled. The provost of the city intervened and several students were killed by his archers. The masters supported the students and complained to the bishop and Queen Blanche, the regent. Their complaints passed unheeded, and, to aggravate matters, the populace and the police attacked and ill-treated some members of the university who had had no part in the original dispute. The masters immediately refused to teach and migrated to Angers, Orleans and Rheims. The English king, Henry III, ready to profit by the misfortunes of his neighbours, invited the scholars and masters to England. Quite a number of the English Nation responded and the refugees flocked to Oxford and, to a lesser extent, to Cambridge. Among them was William of Durham, who played such an important part in the development of Oxford University.

Meanwhile, the schools of Paris were almost emptied of students and masters. As the chairs became vacant, the mendicant Orders successfully pressed their claims. The first chair fell to the Dominicans in 1229. In 1231, the Franciscans secured a chair and the Dominicans an additional one. The first Dominican professors were Roland of Cremona and John of St. Gilles, and the first Franciscan was the able Scholastic, Alexander of Hales. Some time between 1233 and 1238, the Franciscans secured a second chair which was held by John of La Rochelle.

Eventually, the Pope, Gregory IX, considered it was time to interfere and the Bull of 1231 reconstituted the university and laid down rules for its management. The friars were now firmly established in the university but the opposition of the secular clergy grew more bitter. Matters came to a head in 1252 when the faculty of theology denied the right of the religious Orders to occupy a chair. The following year, another quarrel arose between the university and the civic authorities and the masters once more refused to teach. The university authorities complained to the Pope, Innocent IV, and brought to his notice their longstanding grievance against the mendicant Orders. Innocent supported the secular clergy, but his policy was entirely reversed by his successor, Alexander IV. The Dominicans were restored to their chairs and all restrictions about their numbers were withdrawn. The seculars refused to obey the decree and were promptly excommunicated. One of their leaders was William, Bishop of St. Amour, who wrote a pamphlet in 1255 bitterly attacking the religious Orders under the title *De Periculis Novissimorum Temporum*. St. Thomas Aquinas replied to it in his *Contra Impugnantes Dei Cultum*.

As a counter blow to the mendicant Orders, the secular clergy resolved to found a secular college. Their schemes came to fruition in 1253, when Robert de Sorbon founded his hostels for poor students. The latter lived a common life subject to rules and were known as the Poor Masters of the Sorbonne (*pauperes magistri de Sorbona*). Robert de Sorbon was the author of the *De Conscientia*, a treatise in which the Last Judgment was compared to the ordeal undergone by the candidate for his master's degree.

Alexander replied to the challenge of the seculars by calling upon St. Louis to exercise the royal power. William of St. Amour was expelled and his treatise condemned, and in 1256, the university authorities submitted to the Pope. They agreed to accept as masters in theology a representative from each of the two Orders. The representatives nominated were St. Thomas Aquinas and St. Bonaventure.

The Dominicans appeared at Oxford in 1220 and the Franciscans five years later. The Benedictines had long been established in Oxford, and the Dominicans precipitated a quarrel by their ambitious plans which annoyed both the seculars and the older monastic Orders. They aimed at acquiring great influence within the university without submitting to its jurisdiction. They met with considerable opposition and at one time the Archbishop of Canterbury put them under sentence of excommunication and was only induced to withdraw it through the mediation of Edward II. The struggle was soon renewed and the university was involved in a law suit which rendered it practically bankrupt. It was only rescued from its financial difficulties by a generous grant from the Convocations of Canterbury and York. The controversy came to an end in 1320 through the usual English custom of compromise. The Franciscans profited by the unpopularity of the Dominicans and, through the outstanding ability of Robert Grosseteste, Roger Bacon, and above all, Duns Scotus, gained an ascendency at Oxford. At Cambridge, the Dominicans had greater success but they produced no outstanding teachers at that university.

Throughout the 13th century, the University of Paris was unique amongst all other institutions of similar rank. The great Popes of that period took it under their special care and protection. They looked upon it not as the university of a capital city nor even of France itself. For them, it was the centre of culture and learning for the whole of Catholic Christendom. Naturally they were chiefly interested in the studies of the faculty of theology, which owing to their support quite overshadowed the faculty of arts. The University of Paris drew its students from all parts of Europe so that it was cosmopolitan in character. After the close of the century its prestige began to decline. The Hundred Years War withdrew practically the whole of the English Nation, and these numbers were not compensated by the entrance of the Germans. The Great Schism added to its difficulties by introducing divisions amongst its masters. The great plague of the 14th century, known in England as the Black Death, took a heavy toll of its members. Hitherto, the University of Paris had successfully maintained its independence against king and Pope, but as a result of its decline in numbers and prestige, it became more and more a French university and was able to offer less resistance to royal attacks on its privileges. Finally, in 1446, Charles VI deprived it of its independence and handed it over to the jurisdiction of the French parliament.

As Paris declined, so the prestige of Oxford grew, so that in the 14th century it became the centre of intellectual advance. This

D

had several very important consequences. At Oxford, the Franciscans had become much more influential than the Dominicans. Also, theological studies never reached the position of importance that they did at Paris. The practical outlook of the English race was responsible for a growing interest in mathematics and natural science. Roger Bacon described Oxford "as the one place in Western Europe where the mathematical sciences were completely taught." In this the Oxford thinkers owed much to the Arabians. When Thomism was gaining its triumphs at Paris, the empiricism of Bacon and Ockham was paving the way for the typical English outlook that became so prominent in the 17th and 18th centuries.

During the 15th century, Oxford, for a time, lost its eminence. We have to remember that John Wyclif (1320–84) was one of Oxford's most influential teachers in the latter part of the 14th century. Although in 1382 he was banished from the university, his influence lived on, and in 1412 it became necessary to compel every Oxford master to take an oath repudiating Lollardry. Oxford was fast gaining a reputation as a centre of heretical teaching. Cambridge was largely untouched by Wyclif's doctrines, with the result that during the 15th century it was favoured by king and Church and gained from the loss in popularity incurred by Oxford.

The grammar schools formed with the universities an essential link in the educational scheme of the Middle Ages. Until recent years, little attention was given to the numerous schools which existed before the Reformation. As Dr. Hastings Rashdall remarked, "Even those who have realised the fact that the Universities were founded in the 12th century, and have been quite alive to the importance and the brilliancy of the great intellectual Renaissance out of which the University movement grew, have often been little in advance of the 'general reader' with regard to what would now be called the primary and secondary schools of the Middle Ages. It has been supposed that the Universities were created in the Middle Ages, but that for the grammar schools this country had to wait till the enlightened days of the Reformation and its equally youthful prodigy, King Edward VI."[1]

[1] RASHDALL, HASTINGS: *Essay on the Origin of Grammar Schools in the History of Harrow School* (Edward Arnold: 1898), p. 11.

The 19th century had vague ideas that all education worthy of the name was carried on in the monasteries. It is quite true that during the two hundred years after the collapse of the Western Empire, what remained of learning and culture was to be found in the monasteries, but this statement requires qualification. It is accurate as regards those countries like England and France where the barbarian invaders disrupted the ancient civilization, but it does not apply to Italy, where the grammar schools of Imperial days continued with certain modifications due to Christian influences. Once the Dark Ages had passed, the monasteries played a diminishing part in the promotion of general education. They had their schools for their own inmates at which outsiders were sometimes allowed to attend, and in certain cases they supported a grammar school in a neighbouring town, but even then, the school was in charge of secular clergy or laymen.

In England and France, the schools may be classified either according to the type of teaching given in them or in regard to the institutions to which they were attached or from which they sprang. From the latter standpoint, there were schools in connection with monasteries, cathedrals and collegiate churches, hospitals, and craft guilds, and, in the later Middle Ages, numerous schools originated from chantries. Foster Watson claims that the earliest chantry foundation in England is that of Lady Berkeley, who in 1348 founded what was later known as the Grammar School of Lady Margaret at Wotton-under-Edge. There were, however, numerous chantry schools founded more than half a century before this date. Appleby Grammar School, for example, originated from two distinct chantry bequests in 1286 and 1331. One type of school which failed to develop in England was the so-called Palace school. If we may believe Asser, Alfred the Great attempted something of the kind but this school does not seem to have lasted after his death. On the Continent, the most famous was the school which developed in the court of Charles the Great and which was directed by Alcuin of York. Erigena is supposed to have been the head of the Palace school of Charles the Bald and Rhabanus Maurus was another famous scholar connected with it. A similar type of school was founded by Otto III and is associated with the name of Gerbert, the most celebrated scholar and man of letters of the 10th century.

If the kind of instruction given in the schools is considered, they can conveniently be divided into two types: Latin schools, which included what were later known as grammar schools, and many of the song schools; and, secondly, the vernacular schools, which taught reading and writing, and corresponded roughly to primary schools. The writer has claimed that the number of the latter has been grossly underestimated, and notwithstanding the fact that many perished in the troublous days of the Reformation, a sufficient number was able to carry on until the work of the philanthropic societies of the 18th century brought about a revival.[1]

The song schools trained boys to take part in singing the services of the Church, but it is the grammar school which is the most important type from our point of view. As is well known, all university lectures and disputations were carried on in Latin and all available texts were written in that language. Where, then, did the university entrant receive his training in Latin? The answer is that it was supplied by the grammar schools. The latter received boys from the age of seven upwards and insisted that they should be able to read and write before they entered. These accomplishments were obtained at a vernacular school which often served the purpose of a preparatory school for the grammar school. Hence we have the educational ladder of the Middle Ages: the primary school or, as it was later, the petty school; the grammar school, and finally, the university.

Although the actual title of grammar school was not used until fairly late in the Middle Ages, the early schools of England and France were to all intents and purposes grammar schools. The original name for the grammar schools of the Empire was *ludus literarius*, and it is noteworthy that Asser tells us that Alfred the Great sent his younger son to a grammar school, *ludis literariae disciplinae*. The term "grammar school" in English seems to have first appeared in the 14th century and rapidly became the usual designation. A. F. Leach has made out a good case for the existence of a grammar school connected with the Cathedral of Canterbury (the ancestor of the present King's School, refounded by Henry VIII) soon after the landing of Augustine, and the school attached to York Minster (now St. Peter's, York) was founded early in the 7th century. It is undisputed fact that both

---

[1] For a discussion of this point see S. J. CURTIS, *History of Education in Britain* (U.T.P.: 1948), pp. 8-10.

schools were flourishing in the time of Archbishop Theodore of Tarsus and Alcuin of York.

Schools of the same type existed in France, and in Paris in the 13th century forty-two schoolmasters and twenty-one schoolmistresses were licensed by the ecclesiastical authorities.

In England, although some of the grammar schools charged fees, many became to be known as "free grammar schools." The exact meaning of the title has been in dispute but it is now generally accepted that it means exactly what it says. A free grammar school was one in which all the pupils or a specified number were taught freely. This did not exclude payments for registration, subscriptions for supplying fuel, light and cleaning utensils or for the provision of cocks used in the popular sport of cock-fighting. There was one characteristic development of the grammar school in England. In some schools, the provisions of the founder admitted only children of the neighbourhood as free scholars, and those who came from other places (foreigners) were charged fees. Often the number of foreigners was limited, so many being assigned to the master's and the rest to the usher's (assistant's) class. Such schools developed later into large day schools such as St. Paul's.

Other schools welcomed pupils from all parts of the country. Once the scholars had been gathered together, provision had to be made for their board for which fees were charged. Thus these developed into large boarding schools, the most famous amongst them later being called Great Schools, or public schools—*i.e.*, schools whose pupils were not confined to a particular district. There was always a tendency for the schoolmaster to charge fees to augment the income derived from the endowment of the school. The ecclesiastical authorities repeatedly used their power to condemn this practice. Thus Pope Alexander III "ordered the schoolmasters that whenever fit and well-bred men wished to teach grammar schools they [the French bishops] should allow them to do so without any charge, lest learning, which ought to be given gratis to all, should seem to have a price set on its head."[1] This was aimed at such people as the Chancellor of Paris, who used to exact the sum of one mark, a large amount in those days. The Lateran Council of 1179 extended this principle to all countries and it was re-asserted at the next Council in 1215.

[1] LEACH, A. F., *The Schools of Mediaeval England* (Methuen: 1915), p. 132.

The early schools catered for pupils of very different grades of attainment. Thus Alcuin's account of the school taught by Albert at York shows that there was no differentiation of function and that the same master undertook the teaching of all the subjects of the Trivium and Quadrivium.

As the universities developed, the subjects of the Quadrivium became part of their curriculum and the grammar schools confined themselves to the Trivium as a preparation for entrance to the university. Certain schools, such as Winchester College and Eton College, were expressly designed by their founders to act as feeders for definite colleges at the older universities. In practice, although the grammar schools tended to concentrate on the study of Latin grammar, many of them gave attention to the two other subjects of the Trivium, rhetoric and dialectic. William Fitzstephen, writing at some time between 1174 and 1179, gives an interesting account of the schools of London. "In London, the three principal churches have famous schools privileged and of ancient dignity, though sometimes through personal favour to someone noted as a philosopher more schools are allowed. On feast days the Masters celebrate assemblies at the churches, arrayed in festive garb. The scholars hold disputations, some argumentatively, others by way of question and answer. . . . Some dispute merely for show, as they do at collections [examinations: cf. end-of-term examinations at Oxford which are called collections]; others for the truth which is the grace of perfection. The sophists and those in training in sophistry are pronounced happy because of the mass and volume of their words; others play upon words. Those learning rhetoric with rhetorical speeches speak to the point with a view to persuasion, being careful to observe the precepts of their art, and to leave out nothing that belongs to it." Thus we see that at the original school speech days, the speeches were really the work of the scholars.

The main business of the grammar school was to give a grounding in the grammar and syntax of the Latin language. Because of the scarcity of manuscripts, the teaching was largely oral. The teacher read from his manuscript and dictated notes to the pupils. The usual grammar text was the *Ars Minor* of Donatus, a teacher who flourished at Rome in the 4th century and had St. Jerome as his pupil. He also produced the *Ars Maior*, which was studied in some of the universities. The use of Donatus was so widespread both in England and on the Continent that the term Donat was employed to describe any elementary book whatever its subject. An alternative used in some schools was the *Institutio de Arte Grammatica* by Priscian, a Byzantine grammarian of the 6th century. This book not only gave the rudiments of grammar and syntax but included a large number of quotations from classical authors to illustrate the rules. In the 12th century the versified grammar of Alexander of Villa Dei was popular. It contained illustrations from the Vulgate and from colloquial Latin. How far Latin literature was studied in the English schools is open to question. Alcuin's catalogue of the books in the library of York Minster shows that the opportunity of studying classical literature existed. De Wulf gives an account of the authors available in Continental schools,[1] though once again the evidence as to the extent they were used is difficult to obtain.

Controversy has raged about the actual social class for which the grammar schools catered. The evidence seems to show that it was mainly what we should now call the middle class. Undoubtedly a few children of the nobility attended the grammar schools but the usual custom was to educate them at home. A few sons of villeins also found their way to the grammar schools. It must be remembered that the divisions between the different social classes were more rigid than in later days, and the gentry were opposed to the inclusion of children of villeins in any great numbers. No villein was allowed to send his son to school without permission of the lord of the manor, and there are many accounts of fines being inflicted for breaches of this rule. It was not until 1406 that the Statute of Artificers proclaimed that "every man or woman of what state or condition that he be, shall be free to set their son or daughter to take learning at any school that pleaseth them within the realm."

Throughout the Middle Ages the Church exercised a rigid control over the schools. Not only were the schoolmasters in orders, sometimes minor orders, and the religious instruction given supervised by the representatives of the bishop, but no schoolmaster was allowed to keep a school unless he possessed a licence to do so issued by the bishop or his chancellor.[2] There are numerous

---

[1] DE WULF, *op. cit.*, vol. i, pp. 59–62

[2] In early days, the bishop was also a schoolmaster but when his duties increased, he delegated the function of teaching to an official who was frequently called the Scholasticas in continental dioceses. This title was rarely used in England, the name of Master of the Schools (*Magister scolarum*) being adopted instead. The *Magister scolarum* was the bishop's chancellor, but as his duties also increased, he

accounts of schoolmasters who tried to evade the law and kept unlicensed schools, thereby implying, that whatever it is now, in those days the keeping of a school could be a lucrative occupation. A. F. Leach records that in the 14th century there was a whole succession of unlicensed schoolmasters in the district of Beverley, Yorkshire.

SUGGESTIONS FOR FURTHER READING

The standard work on the mediæval universities is Dr. Rashdall's *The Universities of Europe in the Middle Ages* (O.U.P.: 1936). Attention has already been drawn to the fact that his account of the origin of Oxford University is generally rejected. The original work was published in 1895, but the 2nd edition, 1936 (reprinted 1942), has been re-edited by F. M. Powicke and A. B. Emden, and contains much additional material in the way of notes and corrections. Leach's criticism of Rashdall's theory of the origin of the University of Oxford has been reprinted in appendix I, vol. iii.

RAIT, R. S., *Life in the Mediaeval University* (C.U.P.: 1912), is a very useful account of student life at that period.

MAXWELL LYTE, H. C., *A History of the University of Oxford* (Macmillan: 1886), is a detailed account of Oxford before 1530.

CURTIS, S. J., *History of Education in Great Britain* (U.T.P.: 1948), contains chapters on the schools of mediæval England, the English universities and the founding and development of the Scottish universities and burgh schools.

LEACH, A. F., *The Schools of Mediaeval England* (Methuen: 1915), is a very valuable contribution to our knowledge of the ancient grammar schools.

WATSON, FOSTER, *The Old Grammar Schools* (C.U.P.: 1916), is a good short description of the founding of the grammar schools, their life and curriculum.

---

delegated the teaching of the grammar school to a schoolmaster and confined himself to teaching in the cathedral theological school and granting licences to teach. As we have already seen, the Chancellor of Paris was the representative of the bishop and should not be confused with the chancellor of an English University.

CHAPTER VII

ARABIAN PHILOSOPHY: THE CONTROVERSY
CONCERNING THE INTELLECT

IF the foundation of the schools and the universities was one cause
of the intellectual achievement of the 13th century, the introduction
of the Aristotelian corpus in the West provided the stimulus which
led to the development of the great scholastic syntheses.[1] The
history of the Aristotelian manuscripts after the philosopher's death
is a romance in itself, and it has been ably described by R. Shute
in his *History of the Aristotelian Writings* (Clarendon Press: 1888).
Like that of Plato, Aristotle's teaching was of two types. The more
popular instruction was through the medium of the dialogue.
Practically the whole of the Aristotelian dialogues was destroyed,
probably when the library of Alexandria was burnt by the Saracens.
The fragment on the constitution of Athens shows that Aristotle
was almost as great a dramatic artist as Plato.

What are now termed the works of Aristotle are, in the strict
sense, not his at all. They consist mainly of notes made by Theophrastus, Aristotle's pupil and successor in the Lyceum. What
became of them? However much or little credence we give to the
story that Theophrastus bequeathed them to Neleus, that they
were left in a damp cellar at Skepsis, where they remained for-
gotten for over a century until discovered by Apellicon who
pieced them together, repaired the damage done by damp and
worms and then proceeded to edit them—the fact is that Western
Europe at the commencement of the Middle Ages knew very little
about Aristotle and only possessed a few fragments of his logical
works. The translations of Boethius and the recovery of the
Organon have already been described.

The metaphysical and other works of Aristotle first reached
the West in Arabic translations. Before the time of Mohammed,
the Arabs did not exist as a nation. They were a loose confedera-
tion of tribes differing in degree of civilization, customs, and

religion, but within a century of the Prophet's death, a great change
had taken place. They had coalesced into a nation and had torn
some of its fairest provinces from the East Roman Empire. As
soon as the first wave of fanaticism had passed, the Arabs began to
absorb certain elements of Greek culture.

The contact of the Arabs with Greek thought may be said to
have commenced in 750 when the Abbasside caliphs invited Syrian
scholars to Bagdad. Most of the chief works of Greek philosophy
had by this time been translated into Syriac and the new arrivals
began to make Arabic versions from their own Syriac translations.

In 832, Al Mamoun established a school of translators at Bagdad
in which most of the works of Aristotle were translated. Plato was
not well known to the Arabs but they received a flood of works
imbued with Neo-Platonism. For example, there appeared a
treatise which was known as the *Theology* of Aristotle. This work
because of its alleged authorship carried great weight. It was
really the substance of *Enneads* 4 to 6 of Plotinus: hence, the Arabs
did not hesitate to combine such doctrines as the Emanation theory
with Aristotelianism.

The Arabs regarded philosophy as a completed science. Aristotle had achieved a final system and all that was left to do was to
interpret the master. Yet, in spite of this, they did not produce a
faithful commentary. In the first place, it is impossible to confine
the creative impulses of human beings even when the restriction
is self-imposed. Hence, the Arabs were forced by this fact of
human nature to add to Aristotle's meaning, even though at
times they were not aware that they were doing so. Thus we
find amongst the greater Arabian thinkers a good deal that is
original. Secondly, they read Aristotle through Arabic translations
of Syriac versions, and in the double process of translation, the
original text became considerably modified. Their commentaries
show that they did not always distinguish between genuine works
of Aristotle and certain Neo-Platonic productions ascribed to
him.

There was always an attempt, as among the Catholics of the
West, to reconcile philosophy and religion, but this task was much
more difficult for the Arabs. Mahommedan orthodoxy was far
more suspicious of philosophy than Catholicism and soon became
so hostile that the philosophers were persecuted.

Arabian philosophy was marked by the attempt to bridge the

gulf between God as pure actuality and matter as pure potentiality. It was here that Neo-Platonism with its doctrine of Emanation assisted them, and between the two extremes of God and
matter, they were able to insert a number of intermediate celestial
intelligences. This theory, since it was drawn from the pseudo-
Aristotelian theology, was not thought to be incongruous.

The Arabians were also anxious to show how through philosophy
the individual seeker after God may rise to union with Him. For
them, God was no longer above *nous*, or intelligence, but was pure
intellect, knowing Himself and all other things in Himself.[12] We
must be careful, however, to realize that the Arabian thinkers were
not pantheists. They consistently clung to a belief in a transcendent
God.[13]

One of the most far-reaching effects of the Arabian tendency to
combine Neo-Platonism with Aristotelianism is seen in the attempts
of various Arabian thinkers to interpret the doctrine of Active and
Passive Intellect. Aristotle's somewhat vague and hesitating
description in the *De Anima* offered an opportunity to the Arabs
which they were not slow to seize. In the third book of the *De
Anima*, Aristotle had been considering the intellect as though it
were a complete unity; then suddenly he tells us, "But since in the
whole of nature, to something which serves as matter for each kind
(and this is potentially all the members of the kind) there corresponds something else which is the cause or agent because it makes
them all, the two being related to one another as art to its material,
of necessity these differences must also be found in the soul. And
to the one intellect which answers to this description because it
becomes all things, corresponds the other because it makes all
things, like a sort of definite quality such as light. For in a manner,
light, too, converts colours which are potential into actual colours.
And it is this intellect which is separable and impassive and unmixed, being in its essential nature an activity.

"For that which acts is always superior to that which is acted
upon, the cause or principle to the matter. Now actual knowledge
is identical with the thing known, but potential knowledge is
prior in time in the individual; and yet not universally prior in
time.

"But this intellect has no intermittence in its thought. It is,
however, only when separated that it is its true self, and this, its
essential nature, alone is immortal and eternal. But we do not

remember because this is impassive, while the intellect which can be effected is perishable and without this does not think at all."[1]

There is little doubt what Aristotle has in mind in this chapter. He realized that all thinking involves the two moments of the creative activity of the knowing subject and the apprehension of the independent truth of the thing known. Sense perception presents a parallel process. On the side of receptivity, sense receives the sensible forms through the action of the sense organs. But there is also an element of synthesis, whereby the sensation complex thus obtained is built up into the perception of the concrete object. The process is more marked in the case of thought. If either side of the question is ignored, the process of knowledge remains unexplained.

If the mind were a *tabula rasa*, it would vanish to zero. To be, the mind must do something. All thinking implies, as Kant realized in a later age, the synthetic activity of mind. On the other hand, if we ignore the side of receptivity, each man's knowledge would dissolve into the arbitrary creation of his own intelligence and the world of objective truth would vanish. Knowledge implies that there is something to know and that the object is known in independence of the act of cognition—i.e., truth is found and not made. Room must be found in the mind for both moments of spontaneity and receptivity, and the doctrine of Active and Passive Intellect is an attempt to do this.

It is tempting to discuss the relation between the human active intellect and the active intellect of God as described in the *Metaphysics*, and also the varying interpretations placed on Aristotle's doctrine by Theophrastus and the Greek commentators, Alexander of Aphrodisias, Themistius and Simplicius. All space permits us to say is that Aristotle left a number of formidable problems for after ages to solve.

Four main interpretations are possible:

(1) Active and Passive Intellects are only two phases of the one intellect. It may be said that Aristotle never intended to make such a clear-cut distinction as some of his commentators have understood. Such evidence as we possess, however, seems to contradict this opinion.

[1] *De Anima*, III. 5, trans. R. D. Hicks (C.U.P.: 1907).

(2) Active Intellect is impersonal and separate from the individual soul; either it is a world intellect or is identical with the Active Intellect of God. This interpretation was adopted by Alexander of Aphrodisias and by the earlier Arabian thinkers.

(3) Active Intellect forms part of the human soul but is separate from the body and the sense faculties because it does not make use of a bodily organ. This was the view of Albert the Great and St. Thomas Aquinas.

(4) In addition, there was the doctrine of Averroes, who not only maintained the unity of the Active Intellect but also declared the Passive (Possible) Intellect to be one in all men.

There is also the further problem of what becomes of the Active Intellect after death. Does it leave the body to join some world intellect or the intellect of God, or is the individual soul immortal and does it preserve its individuality after death?

The consequence of the blending of Aristotelianism with Neo-Platonism is seen in the works of Al Kindi (about 873), an encyclopædic writer who produced 265 treatises. He mentions four species of intellect, three of which are within the soul and one which comes from without. These are (a) Potential or Passive Intellect, (b) Intellect in Act—i.e., the soul in the process of obtaining knowledge, (c) Acquired Intellect—i.e., the act of thought having taken place, and (d) Active Intellect, which comes from outside.

The next important thinker was Alfarabi (d. about 950). Once again he blends Aristotelianism with Neo-Platonism and tries to fit his psychology into a metaphysical scheme of the universe. Between God and matter, he inserts a hierarchy of intelligible principles. The three highest are wholly incorporeal and consist, in descending order, of God, the intelligences of the heavenly spheres and Active Intellect. The three lower, soul, form and matter, are likewise incorporeal but are related to body. Like Al Kindi, he recognizes four species of intellect. The Possible Intellect is in the soul and receives intelligible ideas through the efficient agency of Active Intellect, which comes from outside the soul and is impersonal. Thus we arrive at the Intellect in Act. The next advance is the Acquired Intellect (intellectus adeptus) by which the thinker attains union with Active Intellect. In this perfected activity he reaches the grade of the prophet. Only those who have achieved this union persist after death. Alfarabi is not decided on the question of personal immortality and he gives no hint of union with any higher principle such as God.

Avicenna (980–1037), a highly original thinker and probably the greatest of the Arabian philosophers, exercised a great influence upon subsequent thought both among the Arabs and in the Christian West. He was also a theologian and a physician. As a commentator, he was more faithful than any other Arab philosopher, and the Neo-Platonist influence in his works is less marked. Avicenna evolved a very elaborate and consistent theory of the universe and his hierarchy of separate celestial substances is found in Averroes, Maimonides and Dante.

From the very start we see his divergence from Neo-Platonism; God the first principle is not above intelligence as in Plotinus. He is Intelligence. Then follow the nine intelligences of the celestial spheres. First we have the *primum mobile*, the unmoved sphere that encircles the universe, and then the sphere of the fixed stars. Arab philosophy was always closely allied to Arab astronomy and this is nowhere more clearly seen than in Avicenna.

Thus we find that from God there also follow the seven planetary spheres. There is no multiplicity in God, the First Being, but there is a threefold distinction in the first caused being. This triple division is consequent on the fact that it knows itself as possible through itself, and knows itself as necessary through the First Being. It also knows the First Being. From the fact that the first caused being knows the First Being, follows the intelligence which comes next in descending order; from the fact that the first caused being knows itself as necessary through the First Being, follows the existence of a soul which is that of the limiting sphere; from the fact that it knows itself as possible through itself, follows the existence of the body of the limiting sphere. This mode of emanation repeats itself as we descend the planetary scale. Thus from the intelligence of Saturn, the first caused being, in so far as it knows God, follows the intelligence of the sphere of Jupiter; from the same intelligence in so far as it knows itself, follows the soul and body of the sphere of Saturn. This process continues until we reach the sphere of the moon whose emanation is Active Intellect. We now come to a stop, for there is no necessity, according to Avicenna, to continue the process indefinitely. Active Intellect, the last of the pure intelligences, governs our world and from it proceeds, owing to the influence of the movements of the heavenly bodies, the forms which are designed to actuate sublunary matter.

The Christian philosophers, who denied the existence of a separate Active Intellect apart from the eternal Active Intellect of God and the intellects of individual men, accepted this list but omitted Active Intellect. With this exception, Avicenna's hierarchy is the same as that we encounter in the *Paradiso* of Dante. Although there is a Neo-Platonic tinge in this doctrine, yet it is largely a development of the Aristotelian cosmology, and Aquinas is forced to admit that Avicenna is a very faithful interpreter of Aristotle.

Avicenna distinguishes five stages in the speculative understanding in addition to the Active Intellect whose co-operation is necessary for every act of thought. These stages are: the Material Intellect or the absolute potentiality of knowledge, the Possible Intellect endowed with primary truths, the Intellect in Act completely prepared to receive further knowledge, the Acquired Intellect in possession of this further knowledge, and the Holy Spirit, or mystic intuition reserved for favoured souls.

Avicenna approached Scholasticism nearer than any other Arabian thinker. He was a believer in individual immortality and had a very clear sense of human personality. He taught that each man has an intellect which is his own and which is distinct from the universal Active Intellect, but he never explains satisfactorily how the separate Active Intellect is united to the individual human soul.

For Avicenna, the highest act of man is to become united to Active Intellect by means of a moral life and philosophic contemplation. Besides being a philosopher, Avicenna was a statesman and a man of the world and in his life had known misfortune. Hence he attaches great value to the moral and religious life. But there exist the chosen few who do not need philosophic study to win union with Active Intellect. These are the saints and prophets who possess the fifth grade of intellect, the Holy Spirit.

After the time of Avicenna, philosophy in the East was silenced by the champions of orthodoxy and was forced in the 12th century to seek a new home in Spain. Avempace, who lived at Seville and in Morocco where he died in 1138, wrote a book now accessible only through a Hebrew commentary of the 14th century, entitled, the *Regime of the Solitary*.

Averroes (1126–98) really gathers up in his system all the results of previous Arab philosophy. He was univerally known to the Middle Ages as the Commentator. Dante refers to him by this title in the *Divine Comedy*. Averroes produced three commentaries on Aristotle varying in style according to the type of reader that he wished to reach. His aim was merely to interpret Aristotle, but, as has been suggested earlier, it could hardly be expected that a man of his calibre would give us a commentary unsullied by the intrusion of his own views. Moreover, his knowledge of Aristotle, like that of his predecessors, was derived from Arabic translations, and Aquinas, who had access to the Greek original, was able to refute his views by reference to the actual text of Aristotle.

Arab philosophy was mainly known to Catholic Christendom in the form which it received at the hands of Averroes, and his doctrine of the separate intellects began to spread rapidly in the University of Paris. Hence if the fact of human personality was to be demonstrated, it was of the highest importance that Averroes should be answered. Just as it was necessary in the 18th century to find an answer to Hume, so in the 13th a great deal of energy had to be expended in the refutation of Averroes.

It is to Averroes' misinterpretation of Aristotle that Dante refers in the twenty-fifth canto of the *Purgatorio*, where he says, "But how from an animal [the principle of soul] becomes a human being, thou seest not yet; this is that point which made one wiser than thou to err. So that by his teaching, he made the Possible Intellect separate from the soul, because he saw no organ occupied by it."

Averroes, like most of the Arabs, re-interpreted Aristotle's teaching mainly by elaborating those features which were obscure. The function of intellect is to receive forms. Hence it is passive and without form, otherwise, its own form would colour the objects which are known and knowledge would not be of things as they are. But if the Possible Intellect is a mere aptitude for receiving forms, then it is nothing, for a disposition must be a disposition of something. So the intellect must be granted an objective existence and the act of knowledge will take place through the agency of Active Intellect. Since the Active Intellect is separate from man and is unmixed with matter, it must be one, and the idea of number can be applied only to the individuals who partici-pate in it. The human intellect is the subject which receives the form of Active Intellect. As the sun, by bestowing light, enables the eye to see, so Active Intellect illuminates the intelligible idea and enables the human intellect to realize its capacity for knowledge.

Renan tried to modernize this doctrine. He interpreted it to mean, "the universality of the principles of pure reason and the unity of psychological constitution in the human species as a whole."[1] Later, he says, "the immortality of the intellect means the immortality of the human race, and if Aristotle said that the intellect sometimes is thinking, sometimes is not thinking, this must be understood of the species, which will never disappear and which in some corner of the universe exercises its intellectual faculties. A living and a permanent humanity; such seems to be the Averroist doctrine of the unity of the intellect. The immortality of Active Intellect is none other than the eternal rebirth of humanity, the perpetuity of civilization. Reason is constituted as something absolute, independent of individuals, as an integral part of the universe, and humanity, which is but the act of reason, as a necessary and eternal being."[2]

This will not do for a moment. Averroes had not studied at Königsberg. The interpretation is perhaps suggested by Averroes' belief in the eternity of the species. Since the human race as species is eternal, there always has been and must always be an individual man in existence. Moreover, there must always be a philosopher in the human species (*ex necessitate est ut sit aliquis philosophus in specie humana*). For Renan points out, every potentiality must proceed to its realization or it will be in vain. Therefore, at every moment of time and at some point in space, an intelligence contemplates absolute reason. But man through the agency of his speculative reason has this prerogative alone, so that man and the philosopher are equally necessary to the scheme of the universe. This belief, however, that although the individual is mortal, the species is eternal, is no warrant for interpreting the doctrine of the Active Intellect to mean the reason immanent in and common to all men as men. Averroes believed that Active Intellect is a separate substance which has its being distinct from the human intellect altogether.

Averroes drew a distinction between the Possible and the Passive Intellect. The Passive Intellect, for Averroes as for Aristotle, is a part of the individual human soul. It is closely associated with the body and seems to include the higher sense faculties such as imagination. Its function is to know the particular

---

[1] RENAN, E., *Averroes et l'Averroisme* (Michel Levy Frères, Paris: 1861), p. 137.
[2] *ibid.*, pp. 137–8.

and not the universal, and by its operation on particular mental images, it prepares them for the action of Active Intellect by which they are transformed into universal concepts. Being always in close connection with the body, it perishes when the body perishes. It is the possession of Passive Intellect that distinguishes man from the brutes. Aquinas objected that he failed to see that such an intellect is anything better than a sense faculty and this surely cannot distinguish men from animals. Something must be posited to explain intellectual and moral activity and this something must be the same as Averroes' Possible Intellect. Any moral action performed by me is my moral action, and this would not be possible if Averroes' view that the Possible Intellect is separate from my individual soul were true.

Averroes had split the unity of the human intellect and taught that, like the Active Intellect, the Possible Intellect is eternal and forms no part of the individual human soul. Yet though separated, it mediates the action of Active Intellect upon the individual's Passive Intellect. As Active Intellect has for its objects intelligible forms, so the Possible Intellect has as objects the forms of material things. In fact, it is equivalent to the specific human intellect, and Renan's interpretation of Active Intellect might more plausibly be applied to the Possible.

Averroes accepted Aristotle's statement that the Passive (Possible) Intellect is separate in its literal meaning as separate from the individual's soul, whereas Aquinas points out that this really means separate from the body, since it needs no bodily organ with which to function. Averroes believed that if intellect were individual it could not know universals. To know them, it must itself be universal. If the Possible Intellect were not universal, all science, the knowledge of universals, would be impossible. Again, unless the intellect were the same in all men, the process of learning could not be explained. The teacher's intellect being individual would be different from the pupil's; how then could the same knowledge be in both? When Aquinas answered Averroes, he had to face these problems.

Active Intellect has a twofold function: it brings the soul up to a level at which it can perceive the intelligible and then it carries it to a still higher level where it can attain union with the intelligibles themselves. In this intellectual union with Active Intellect, the lower faculties of soul cease to function. This union, Averroes believed, was possible in this present life by means of philosophic contemplation. Few are capable of achieving it, and this particular doctrine presents a parallel to the 5th book of Spinoza's *Ethics*.

Averroes' treatment of the question of immortality brought about the strenuous opposition of the Scholastics. He taught but a semblance of immortality. Although the soul is immortal, it does not possess a personal immortality. This doctrine was repugnant to both Christian and orthodox Mahommedan thought.

This brief survey of Arabian thought on the subject of the Active and Possible Intellects would be incomplete without a reference to Averroes' Jewish contemporary, Moses Maimonides. The latter was born at Cordova in 1135 and died at Old Cairo in 1204. He only became acquainted with the works of Averroes late in life but he expressed great admiration for them.

Maimonides is interesting in another connection. Some thinkers have believed that directly through his own writings and indirectly through later mediæval Jewish writers he inspired much of Spinoza's teaching. His views about the intellect are to be found in his *Guide for the Perplexed*. They are not original, being for the most part derived from Averroes. Like the latter, Maimonides taught that the end of man is to obtain union with Active Intellect through intellectual contemplation. "It has thus been shown that it must be man's aim after having acquired the knowledge of God, to deliver himself up to Him, and to have his heart constantly filled with longing after Him. He accomplishes this generally by seclusion and retirement. . . . I have shown you that the intellect which emanates from God unto us is the link that joins us to God. You have it in your power to strengthen that bond if you choose to do so, or to weaken it gradually till it breaks, if you prefer this."[1]

We have already seen that in 1162 John of Salisbury was able to make full use of the whole of the *Organon*. From this date translations of the whole of Aristotle's works began to filter into Western Europe. Many of them came from Spain and were shaped by the views of Averroes. Hence it is not surprising that at the start of the 13th century the study of Aristotle was roundly condemned by the Church. The first condemnation was at the Council of Sens held at Paris in 1210. The works of Aristotle on natural philosophy were forbidden to be read on pain of excommunication.

---

[1] MAIMONIDES, *Guide for the Perplexed*, trans. M. Friedlander (Routledge: 1919), p. 386.

In 1215, the Papal Legate, Robert de Courçon, renewed the prohibition. It is obvious from these condemnations that Aristotle was suspected of pantheism. It was still, however, permissible to read the *Organon* and the *Ethics*. In 1229, Pope Gregory IX maintained the prohibition as a temporary measure until the works could be examined and a faithful translation made. He charged three masters of Paris, William of Auxerre, Simon of Anthie and Etienne of Provence, to make this revision, but owing to the difficulty of reconciling Aristotle with dogma, this was never done. In spite of the prohibition, Aristotle was read and soon gained a strong foothold in the University of Paris. In 1255, a statute marked the official entry of Aristotle into the faculty of arts, and in 1263 Urban IV recognized the Aristotelian philosophy and permitted it to be studied in the universities.

The raising of the prohibition was due to the work of Albert the Great and St. Thomas Aquinas. Prior to 1200, Augustinian philosophy and theology dominated the schools, but the introduction of Aristotle's works produced a great change. It was Albert who conceived the object of popularizing Aristotle with the Latins, and with this end in view, he organized the plan of incorporating the subject matter of Aristotle with his commentaries and then adding his own observations.

The genius of St. Thomas Aquinas has tended to overshadow the tremendous work accomplished by Albert. It is not too much to say that without Albert the work of Aquinas would not have been possible. It was in 1254 that Alexander IV had utilized Albert to write the treatise *Concerning the Unity of the Intellect* against Averroes. At this time two things had become essential: an exact translation of Aristotle and a critical and literal commentary on his works. The former was accomplished by William of Moerbeke, probably at the request of St. Thomas. The latter was supplied by Albert and to an even greater extent by Aquinas himself.

But the new tendency did not develop without opposition. Quite early it came into conflict with Augustinianism. The Augustinian doctors fell into two groups, separated not so much by differences of doctrine as by the different bodies to which they belonged. The most important amongst the secular clergy were William of Auvergne, Robert Grosseteste, Bishop of Lincoln, Henry of Ghent, Godfrey of Fontaines, and Giles of Rome. The latter almost became a Thomist. Among the Dominicans were to be found Roland of Cremona and Robert Kilwardby, later Archbishop of Canterbury. The latter was directly opposed to Thomism in 1277. The Franciscans were opposed to Thomism and favoured St. Augustine. The most important were Alexander of Hales, John of La Rochelle, St. Bonaventure, Roger Bacon, and, later, Duns Scotus. They regarded St. Thomas as an innovator and looked upon him somewhat in the way that a pious Anglican now regards the Bishop of Birmingham.

Apart from these doctors who represented the orthodox schools were the Latin Averroists, Siger de Brabant and Boethius the Dacian. They claimed to follow Aristotle, but they read him through the eyes of Averroes. It is difficult to ascertain exactly when Averroism arose. Renan's account is very unsatisfactory. There was no official condemnation of Averroism before 1270 but we know that it must have appeared at Paris sometime before that date. Albert's treatise was written in 1256 and this suggests that it was already established by that time. Mandonnet shows that the evidence puts its first appearance about 1250.

The new doctrine rapidly gained ground, and shortly after 1250 we find a very strong party of Averroists in the University of Paris, so strong indeed that the authorities began to regard it as a definite menace to orthodoxy. But it was Albert and St. Thomas who saw most clearly the danger, and so alive were they to the threat that overhung Christendom that they utilized all their learning and all that they had drawn from the newly translated texts of Aristotle to combat Siger de Brabant and his companions. If Averroism had penetrated the West a century earlier, the issue might have been doubtful, but being introduced at the height of the 13th-century Renaissance, and coming face to face with the comprehensive and logical systems of theology formed by the most acute thinkers of that time, the result never really hung in the balance. Until Mandonnet's research appeared, the real leader of the Averroists was almost unknown. Mandonnet showed that the first mention of Siger de Brabant was 27th August 1266 in the ordinance of the Papal Legate, Simon de Brion, which put an end to the quarrels which had distracted the University of Paris.

Siger de Brabant was born about 1235, and within a few years of his coming to the University of Paris he was accepted as the leader of the Picard Nation. From 1266 he appears as the most prominent teacher amongst the Latin Averroists. The year 1270 produced the personal polemic of St. Thomas and Siger which was followed by the first condemnation of Averroism. In a letter of Gilles de Lessines, fifteen propositions summing up the chief doctrines of the Averroists were submitted to Albert the Great. Of these, the first thirteen were condemned by Etienne Tempier, Archbishop of Paris.

The following doctrines were considered erroneous:

(1) The intellect of all men is one and the same.

(2) It is false and erroneous to say that this individual man understands.

(3) The will and choice of each man is determined.

(4) All things which take place in this world are governed by the celestial bodies.

(5) The world is eternal.

(6) There never was a first man.

(7) The soul which is the human form, and constitutes a man as a member of the species, perishes at the death of the body.

(8) The soul which is separated from the body by death does not suffer from material fire.

(9) Free will is a passive potentiality and not an active one and is determined and moved by the appetites.

(10) God does not know individual things.

(11) God knows nothing other than Himself.

(12) Human affairs are not regulated by the Providence of God.

(13) God cannot confer immortality or incorruptibility on anything which by nature is mortal and corruptible.

The condemnation led to a controversy which became so acute that eventually Siger and his followers took the step of seceding from the university and elected their own rector and officials. Since Mandonnet published certain treatises written by Siger,[1] some additional texts have come to light and have been published by Van Steenberghen.[2] The most important of these is the *Questiones de Anima* in the Munich manuscript discovered by Grabmann. If these texts are genuine, they present an entirely

[1] MANDONNET, P., *Siger de Brabant* (Louvain: 1911).
[2] VAN STEENBERGHEN, F., *Siger de Brabant, d'après ses oeuvres inédites* (Louvain: 1931).

different picture from that which has been accepted for some years. Steenberghen believes that they belong to a period later than those published by Mandonnet and show that Siger modified his views and ended up by espousing doctrines little different from those taught by St. Thomas himself.

In a recent work, Van Steenberghen[1] attempts a reconstruction of the situation of the third quarter of the 13th century. He suggests that the title Latin Averroism is a misnomer and has become current because of the opinions first suggested by Renan and later developed by Mandonnet. These opinions are due to a confusion between Avicenna's doctrine of the unity of the Active Intellect and the teaching of Averroes concerning the unity of the Possible Intellect. He asserts that the term "averroista," which was first employed by St. Thomas, denoted at that period a "partisan of the monopsychic heresy," and that we are not entitled without further evidence to extend the scope of its meaning. The so-called Latin Averroism consisted in the acceptance of the unity of the Possible Intellect, and Van Steenberghen thinks it is more correctly described as a "radical Aristotelianism." The teaching of Jean de Jandun in the 14th century was a genuine Latin Averroism for it consisted in the acceptance of the whole body of Averroistic belief.

The authenticity of the *Questiones de Anima* has been challenged by Gilson and Bruno Nardi. The fact that the manuscript bears the name of Siger is no guarantee of its authorship. The mediævals were not as particular about such things as we are. The possessor of a manuscript considered it to be of little value unless he could assign an author to it, and since the subject discussed was that of the intellect, nothing was more natural than to attribute it to Siger, in spite of the fact that the treatise expounds a doctrine quite different from that contained in the other writings of Siger.

Van Steenberghen, however, considers that it represents a change in Siger's views. He gives us a picture of Siger as a zealous Aristotelian who took his philosophical studies very seriously. Speaking of Siger, he writes, "He has an acute belief in the autonomy of human knowledge in its own field and he jealously guards it from all extraneous interference."[2] The traditional Augustinianism of the majority of the members of the faculty of

---

[1] *Siger dans l'histoire de l'aristotelisme* (Louvain: 1942).
[2] VAN STEENBERGHEN, *op. cit.*, p. 669.

arts definitely opposed the realization of a philosophy in its own right and occupying a position independent of theology.

Van Steenberghen is undoubtedly correct in his claim that nobody in the 13th century accepted the views of Averroes *en bloc*. It is impossible in a book of this type to deal with the pros and cons of this problem in detail. For those seeking further information the article by Gilson in the *Bulletin Thomiste* is recommended.[1] The controversy does, however, raise and perhaps help to solve some interesting and important problems. Gilson had already drawn attention to Siger's declaration that the teaching of the Church represents ultimate truth. To philosophize is to seek the views of the philosophers, to endeavour to enter into their minds and ascertain what they were really trying to express rather than an attempt to reach ultimate truth which in the last instance is provided by the articles of faith. Hence what is true in philosophy may be false in theology and vice versa. It is difficult to know whether Siger was sincere in making such a statement or if he thought it merely prudent to do so.

The polemic of Siger and St. Thomas seems to represent two entirely different views concerning the aim of philosophy and the relations between science and theology. St. Thomas proclaimed that the object of studying philosophy was not to know men's opinions but the truth of things. He was convinced that, on the whole, the philosophy of Aristotle was a reasonable system, but he recognized that on certain questions it was at variance with the teaching of the Church. In such cases, he was prepared to modify Aristotle's teaching, to adapt it to his own needs, and if necessary to reject it altogether.

Siger, on the other hand, was concerned to find out what Aristotle really taught, and concluded that on the problem of the intellect the interpretation of Averroes was the correct one. It does not follow, however, that Siger accepted the doctrine of the unity of the intellect as part of his own belief. It is tempting to ascribe something of the spirit of modern scholarship to Siger. However this may be, it seems clear that he was quite honest in his attitude, and when he found certain doctrines in Aristotle which could not be reconciled with the teaching of the Church, he was not afraid to say so and was not prepared to twist Aristotle's meaning to suit his own convenience. Equally with St. Thomas,

[1] Vol. vi (1940–2), pp. 1–22.

he had the courage to stand up for his convictions and did not seek to evade difficulties, however unpalatable they might seem to be.[1]

Thus we have the picture of two honest, courageous thinkers, one opposing the other because each has a different conception of the aim of philosophical study. Added to this, Siger was a secular, and in the university quarrels between seculars and mendicants St. Thomas naturally supported the latter and was bound to be influenced, even if unconsciously, in his judgment. Any opinion issuing from the side of his opponents would call for a more searching scrutiny than if it came from amongst his own party.

There is also the possibility that the ecclesiastical authorities misread Siger's intentions. St. Thomas was too acute a thinker to have been guilty of this himself. Was the condemnation of 1270 really aimed at Siger or at the doctrines of Aristotle? The faculty of arts at Paris, as representing the older tradition, was strenuously opposed to the revived Aristotelianism of Albert and Aquinas. If one could show that the teaching of Aristotle was anti-Christian and at the same time identify it with the doctrine of Averroes, a most damaging blow would be struck at the innovations of St. Thomas. This would explain the anxiety of St. Thomas to dissociate himself from the views of Siger and also the inclusion of certain Thomistic doctrines in the condemnation of 1277.

The view suggested here would also supply an answer to another problem which has caused considerable difficulty to commentators on the *Divine Comedy*. It concerns the reason why Dante not only placed Siger in Paradise but put into the mouth of St. Thomas the eulogistic words, "The one from which thy glance returneth unto me, is the light of a spirit who, in weighty thoughts, him seemed went all too slowly to his death; it is the light eternal of Sigier who, lecturing in the Vicus Stramineus, syllogized truths that brought him into hate."[2] If Siger really was orthodox, there would be every reason for Dante to include so famous an Aristotelian with Aquinas and Albert among the twelve spirits who circled around Beatrice and Dante. A quite trustworthy tradition affirms that Dante had visited Paris. In any case, it is unbelievable that one

[1] I am greatly indebted to Miss Dorothy L. Sayers for drawing my attention to a quotation from a treatise which was obviously written by one of Siger's supporters. "Sciendum quod sententia Philosophi ab his qui eius libros suscipiunt exponendos non est celanda, licet sit contraria veritati." This admirably sums up Siger's attitude.

[2] *Paradiso*, X. 133-8.

usually so well informed would be ignorant of the real facts of a dispute which shook all corners of the intellectual world. Dante's action is his tribute to two outstanding thinkers whom he wished to record as representing an intellectual honesty which was all too scarce in the 13th century, and perhaps is so in the 20th.

However this may be, Siger left Paris shortly after 1277 and went to Spain, where he met his death at some time between 1281 and 1284 at the hands of a demented cleric. The news of the controversies that were dividing the University of Paris reached Rome, and Pope John XXI asked the Archbishop of Paris to inquire into the heresies that were gaining ground so rapidly. The result was the great condemnation of 1277. The Archbishop condemned some 219 propositions representing the teaching of certain masters of the University of Paris. Amongst these may be found all the Averroist views but also some quite orthodox opinions held by Albert and Aquinas. The explanation is that Etienne Tempier was an Augustinian and seized this opportunity of striking a blow against the influence of St. Thomas, whom he regarded as an innovator. Several days later, Robert Kilwardby, Archbishop of Canterbury, held a similar court at Oxford and a like condemnation followed.

Among the propositions condemned were some relating to the teaching of Aquinas on the unity of substantial forms. Two other teachers were seriously affected by the condemnation, Roger Bacon and Giles of Rome. Hauréau and Renan think that Averroism had its principal adherents amongst the Franciscans but Mandonnet quite soundly rejects this view. Bacon's theory of the unity of the Active Intellect may on a *prima facie* view seem to favour Averroism but in reality it had quite a different foundation. It was grounded on the old Augustinian theory of Divine Illumination and was disguised by a terminology borrowed from Aristotle. Giles of Rome strove to defend his Thomist views with great enthusiasm but with such an obvious lack of tact that as a result his university career was for a time curtailed.

The most decisive answer to the Parisian Averroists was that given by St. Thomas in his treatise *De Unitate Intellectus*. In this work he attacks the problem of the Possible Intellect from three points of view. He asks first of all if the Averroist solution is in agreement with the opinion of Aristotle and his commentators. His next step is to show that his own doctrine can be held on rational grounds, and finally he demolishes the arguments of his opponents. He probably realized that Aristotle's teaching on personal immortality, unlike Plato's, was vague and defective, but, as already mentioned, this very vagueness offered itself to diverse interpretations. Averroes may have more nearly expressed the meaning of Aristotle, but Aquinas is truer to the spirit of philosophy when he expands and adapts Aristotle's view to fit in with his most fundamental convictions.

He was not so drastic in dealing with the unity of the Active Intellect. There is nothing seriously at fault in believing that the Active Intellect of God plays a part in the thought processes of each individual, but the fact remains that God does not as a rule act directly upon individuals in this way. He generally works through secondary agents. Thus God could, if He wished, give us our bread directly from heaven but in point of fact we receive it through secondary causes, the farmer, the miller and the baker. Aquinas was not willing to grant the Occasionalism that such a view of Active Intellect implies. If the Active Intellect is thought of as a separate substance, then Aquinas voices his entire disagreement of such a view.

The attacks of Albert and Aquinas drove Averroism underground. It still continued to exist, and at the Reformation it threw up all pretence of orthodoxy and broke into violent opposition to religion.

SUGGESTIONS FOR FURTHER READING

There is very little in English which deals with this particular topic. Maimonides is represented by several translations of his *Guide for the Perplexed*. That of M. Friedlander (Routledge: 1919), is easily accessible. There is also the more recent translation by Leon Roth (Hutchinson: 1948).

In French, *Avicenne*, by Carra de Vaux, in the series " Les Grands Philosophes " (Felix Alcan, Paris: 1900), is a detailed and sympathetic study of the life and teaching of Avicenna. *Siger de Brabant*, by P. Mandonnet (Louvain: 1911), contains the text of Siger's works as known at that date and an account of the condemnations of 1270 and 1277.

The problems that have been raised concerning Siger de Brabant are discussed by Professor Gilson in *Dante the Philosopher* (Sheed and Ward: 1948). The reader should consult Bk. iv. c. iv., *The Symbolism of Siger de Brabant* and *Eclaircissements* iv and v.

CHAPTER VIII

EARLY 13TH-CENTURY THINKERS:
ALEXANDER OF HALES, ROBERT GROSSETESTE AND ALBERT THE GREAT

ALEXANDER OF HALES is described by Gilson as the link connecting the older Augustinian tradition with the newer developments for which St. Bonaventure was responsible. He was born in Gloucestershire about 1180 and studied at Paris, entering the Order of St. Francis about 1231. As we have seen, he was the first Franciscan to hold the chair of theology at the University of Paris. He retired from teaching a few years before his death in 1245 and was succeeded by John of La Rochelle.

His principal work was the *Summa Universae Theologiae*. Roger Bacon questioned its authenticity but modern research does not entirely agree with his judgment. It is now thought that the first part was written by Alexander but in the later sections there is much material taken verbatim from other writers of the period. It has been supposed that these additions were introduced into the original work by certain of Alexander's pupils, but so far it has not been possible to determine exactly what is due to Alexander and what is not.

Alexander's exposition is a development of the method employed by Abelard in the *Sic et Non*, and the form of the *Summa* is obviously inspired by the *Sentences* of Peter Lombard. Alexander was the first mediæval writer to make use of the whole of the Aristotelian corpus, but although he had a high regard for Aristotle, he put him definitely second in authority to the great doctors of the Church, St. Augustine and St. Anselm. Thus one finds in his teaching an attempt to introduce the terminology and thought of Aristotle where it does not conflict with the fundamental doctrines of Augustinianism. At the same time, Alexander borrows from the Arabian thinkers, especially from Avicenna whom he does not hesitate to criticize.

The two main tenets of Alexander which were handed on to his successors in the Franciscan school were the doctrines of the universality of matter and the plurality of substantial forms. For Alexander, God is pure form Who has created the universe which is definitely distinct from His substance. Thus he completely rejects any thought of the world as being an emanation from God. All created things are composites of matter and form, but spiritual and corporeal matter are sharply distinguished. Spiritual matter is not subject to local movement and cannot serve as a basis for substantial change. The objects of the sublunary world are subject to local movement and, because of their corporeal matter, come into being, change, develop and decay. The matter of the heavenly bodies is also corporeal but is of a higher grade, so that it is only affected by the laws of motion.

Although the soul is related to the body as form to matter, it is also a composite of form and intellectual matter. The body, too, is a composite of form and matter, so that body and soul may be considered as two already existing substances. The soul is created directly by God Who allots it to its appropriate body. We shall find this view still further developed by Duns Scotus. The faculties of the soul are grouped under the headings, vegetative, sensitive and intellectual, but Alexander hesitates to affirm that they are identical with its essence.

Having conceded thus much to Aristotle, Alexander then falls back upon the distinction of the intellectual faculties into reason, intellect and intelligence (*ratio, intellectus, intelligentia*). Reason is concerned with the objects of the sensible world; intellect with created spirits; and intelligence with God and the eternal ideas (*rationes aeternae*). He makes use of abstraction as an explanation of the genesis of our ideas which he attributes to the work of Active and Possible Intellect. He also speaks of the Material Intellect, which is perishable and is really a higher sense faculty akin to the imagination. Although Alexander was acquainted with the views of the Arabians on the unity of the intellect, he insists that the Active Intellect is part of the individual human soul. The light of Active Intellect is not sufficient for knowledge of God and of created spirits and it needs the assistance of Divine Illumination. Thus once again Alexander combines the Aristotelian and Augustinian views of knowledge.

Although the Divine Nature in itself is quite simple, yet in created things there exists a distinction between the *quod est* and the *quo est*. Is this an anticipation of the Thomist distinction of essence and existence? It is difficult to answer this question since Alexander's own thought on the subject is not clear, but it is certain that the distinction he draws is not a real but a rational one (*secundum rationem*). It was left to his successor, John of La Rochelle, to formulate the real distinction between essence and existence, a doctrine which was to be characteristic of Thomism. For Alexander, the real distinction is that between matter and form. Also, like most Franciscan thinkers, he subscribes to the doctrine of a plurality of substantial forms in the individual.

The Englishman, Robert Grosseteste, was one of the most remarkable personalities of the 13th century. As Rashdall says, "His writings show a range and versatility rare indeed among mediæval doctors: he was a French poet, an agriculturist, a lawyer, a physician and a preacher: if he can scarcely be called a Greek or Hebrew scholar, he was at least interested in the study of these languages.[1] More recent research has confirmed that Grosseteste possessed a considerable knowledge of Greek and that he was not only the translator of the Nicomachean *Ethics* and the works of the Pseudo-Dionysius, but also of many other Greek texts.

Grosseteste was born in Suffolk about 1175. The tradition that he studied at Paris is without foundation, though he was well acquainted with developments on the Continent. At Oxford, he became well known for his scholarship and soon after 1208 he was appointed Rector of the Oxford schools. The Legatine Ordinance of 1214 officially granted the title of chancellor to the holder of this office. Later Grosseteste was appointed reader in theology at the Franciscan convent, although he himself never entered the order. In 1235 he was elevated to the see of Lincoln, and in spite of being busily engaged in reforming the way of life of the clergy of his diocese, which brought him into conflict with both the cathedral chapter and the king, he still found time to take an active interest in the affairs of the university. When the popular movement against the foreign favourites of Henry III began to develop, Grosseteste quickly identified himself with it. Although modern writers have singled out for attention his public and political life, when he died in 1253 he was recognized by his contemporaries as

[1] RASHDALL, H., *The Universities of Europe in the Middle Ages*, vol. iii (O.U.P.: 1942), p. 241.

the leader of the humanistic and scientific tendencies of the period.

There is no doubt that the influence of Grosseteste and of his pupil Roger Bacon was responsible for the characteristic features of Oxford thought during the next two centuries. Indeed, some writers have suggested that English philosophy with its practical outlook and empirical approach really originated at this period. Gilson emphasizes that the spirit of the school of Chartres, which had been obscured by the growth of theological studies in the new University of Paris, was inherited by the Franciscan school at Oxford. "The work which had been begun by the schools of Chartres did not finish with them. . . . The University of Oxford, which was both less protected and less regulated than that of Paris, continued to develop freely and with strong emphasis, the philosophy both traditional and scientific of the schools of Chartres."[1]

Thus we find that whilst maintaining the tradition of Augustinianism which was characteristic of the Franciscan thinkers as a whole, Grosseteste showed a keen interest in the development of mathematics and natural science. In this latter aspect the fame of Roger Bacon has tended to overshadow the brilliance of his master. "His teaching on cosmography and astronomy in regard to the formation of the universe and the movements of planets and comets; his projected reform of the calendar; his works on perspective, on colours and the rainbow, on the tides, and on heat and acoustics, reveal Robert as one of the most remarkable men of science of this age. Mathematical reasoning is the dialectical method *par excellence*; mathematics alone can give an explanation of physical phenomena, and he himself applies geometry to the study of optics. Roger Bacon, the pupil of the great Chancellor, and who as regards these studies merely continued his master's teaching, recognizes his merit and priority."[2]

Although Grosseteste supported the theory of Divine Illumination, his interest in natural science led him to construct a theory of the universe in which light was the fundamental factor. The essence of the material universe is extension in three dimensions due to the form of corporeity which Grosseteste identifies with light. He describes light as a material element so rarefied in its nature as to be almost incorporeal. Thus it partakes of the nature

[1] GILSON, ETIENNE, *La Philosophie au Moyen Age* (Payot, Paris: 1930), p. 204.
[2] DE WULF, *op. cit.*, vol. ii, p. 89.

of both the material and the spiritual, a conception which is remarkably near to the modern idea of ether. He distinguishes light (*lux*) from *lumen*, which is the illumination produced by an incandescent body. Light behaves as though it were a power or energy which, starting from a point, diffuses itself in every direction until it generates an immense luminous sphere. The volume of this sphere expands until it either comes into contact with something which is contrary to light and puts an end to its expansion, or it reaches the extreme limit of its rarefaction when its diffusion naturally comes to an end. The diffusion of light is instantaneous, and it is the self-expanding energy of light which presents itself to the observer as matter and space. Thus light is not so much a motion through space as an instantaneous change which is perceived by us as space.

When the periphery of the sphere has expanded to its utmost limit it forms the firmament which in its turn reflects visible light (*lumen*) towards the centre of the earth. The activity of this reflected light produces in turn the nine heavenly spheres, the lowest of which is the moon, and through a process of condensation and rarefaction, the spheres of the four elements, fire, air, earth and water—*i.e.*, matter in its incandescent, gaseous, liquid and solid states. "It appears, then, that Grosseteste experienced the same difficulties as modern physicists. The functions he assigns to light, together with the preceding statements, show that he regards it as an energy; but his desire to speak of it as resembling body is strikingly like the present-day application of such terms as 'wavelengths' and 'rays' to the ether, which in itself is admitted to be imperceptible by the senses and is thought of only as the subject of activity or as that which is conserved throughout change. As a principle of unity in the universe, this light is comparable to the modern ether, which fills all space from the most distant stars to the interspace of the atom. Again, Grosseteste's theory is not unlike the modern hypothesis of the convertibility of matter and energy. Lastly, we find something resembling the modern etherial attributes of electricity, magnetism, and chemical activities in his view of *lux* as the source of all movement and life and as the basis of sound."[1]

Robert Grosseteste's conception of the origin of the material universe lent itself to the application of mathematics to the study of nature and the sciences. He found that the mathematical method

[1] SHARP, D. E., *Franciscan Philosophy at Oxford* (O.U.P.: 1930), p. 23.

was highly successful in dealing with the laws of the propagation reflection and refraction of light. Without geometry, which is concerned with lines, angles and figures, it is impossible to make an adequate study of natural science (*utilitas considerationis linearum, angulorum et figurarum est maxima, quoniam impossibile est scire naturalem philosphiam sine illis*). As Gilson remarks, "Truly, by the reduction of physics, of physiology and even of sensation to the rules of figure and movement, this philosopher of the 13th century is the real initiator of the Cartesian reform."[1]

Chronologically, Albert the Great (1206–80) does not belong to this chapter, but the nature of his teaching and the fact that, from one point of view, his labours were necessary for the finished synthesis accomplished by St. Thomas, may perhaps justify his inclusion at this point.[2] Albert came of a noble Swabian family which strongly supported the cause of the Emperor Frederick II. When his uncle left for Italy to take service with Frederick, young Albert accompanied him and started his university studies at Padua. It was here that he studied medicine and the arts and became acquainted with the Aristotelian *Physics* and *Ethics*. His biographers tell us that he spent nearly seven years journeying with his uncle to different parts of Italy. During this time, he no doubt amassed a great deal of information at first-hand but he showed special interest in astronomy, mineralogy, alchemy, zoology and botany. Albert was very anxious to investigate phenomena himself, and in his scientific writings he frequently informs us when his statements are the results of personal observation or if he is merely relying on second-hand information.

Albert's two treatises on animals (*De Animalibus*) and on plants (*De Vegetabilibus*) show that he was as eminent in science as in philosophy, and biologists of the present day treat his observations with great respect. "He was the first to mention spinach in western literature, the first to point out the difference between tree buds enveloped by scaly coverings and the buds of plants which are without them, the first to notice the influence of light and temperature on the growth of trees as affecting their height and spread, the first to establish that the sap in the root is tasteless, becoming more flavoured as it ascends—a phenomenon noted again by the English

[1] *op. cit.*, p. 208.
[2] Some accounts place the date of Albert's birth as early as 1193 and this is supported by one of his biographers who testified that he was well over eighty when he died.

E

naturalist Knight, at the beginning of the nineteenth century."[1] Similarly, in zoology, astronomy, anatomy, and climatology, Albert anticipated many of the modern theories.

Later, Albert philosophized on his scientific experiences and emphasized as strongly as Roger Bacon the importance of accurate observation and induction from experience. His maxim, *oportet experimentum non in uno modo, sed secundum omnes circumstantias probare*, has a very modern sound. It was only doing justice to his scientific work when, in 1941, Pope Pius XII proclaimed Albert the Patron of all Natural Science.

Whilst at Padua, Albert entered the Order of St. Dominic and became, in 1228, lecturer in theology at Cologne. He came to Paris in 1240 and received the doctorate in that subject in 1245. By this time he had achieved an international reputation, and at Paris was joined by the young Thomas Aquinas, who remained as his pupil in the university until 1248. In that year, Albert returned to Cologne to organize the *studium generale* in that city. Aquinas accompanied him, and on their return to Paris in 1252 Albert proposed him for the degree of bachelor. From 1254 to 1257 Albert was Provincial of his Order in Germany. These were very busy years for him, and he proved that in addition to being a scientist and philosopher he was an extremely able administrator. He then resumed his teaching at Cologne and from 1260 to 1262 occupied the see of Ratisbon. After the death of Aquinas, as soon as Albert heard that some of his pupil's doctrines had been included in the condemnation of 1277, he made a hurried journey to Paris and, although now an aged man, he vigorously defended the teaching of Aquinas.

Albert was a most prolific writer but the chronology of his works has not yet been definitely established. His most important scientific and philosophical treatises were begun in 1245 and he continued writing until after 1274. The second part of his *Summa* was written after the production of the *Summa Theologica* of St. Thomas, and is remarkable in containing no reference to nor showing any influence of the similar work of St. Thomas. Albert's works fall into four distinct groups; the *Summa de Creaturis* (1245–50); the *Commentary on the Sentences*, which appears to date from the same period; a number of original treatises written with special objects in view, such as the *Unity of the Intellect against the Averroists* and

[1] ALBERT, S. M., O.P., *Albert the Great* (Blackfriars, Oxford: 1948), p. 68.

the *Fifteen Problems*, produced between 1250 and 1270, and finally, his last work, the *Summa Theologica*. We are by no means sure that we possess all the works of Albert. Additional treatises may possibly be discovered, and some of those in the past attributed to him are now known to be of other authorship.

As has been said, one of the most important aspects of Albert's work was the popularizing of Aristotle in the West. He wrote commentaries on all the works of Aristotle which bear the titles and follow the sequence of the original treatises. Even in this task, Albert showed much originality. Gilson reminds us that the Middle Ages differentiated between the scribe (*scriptor*) who merely copied the original without introducing any variation, the compilator who made minor alterations, the commentator who contributed sufficient of his own as was necessary to explain the text, and the author (*auctor*) whose main object was to set forth his own ideas and only used the results of other thinkers as support for his own view. Albert was regarded as belonging to this last class by his contemporaries and his works were read and commented upon in the schools while he was yet alive. Gilson bids us notice the relation between author (*auctor*) and authority (*auctor-itas*).[1]

It is worthwhile emphasizing this since it is easy to underrate Albert's originality and to think of him as merely collecting material which the more orderly and critical mind of his famous pupil was able to utilize. Albert's claim to originality is also justified when one studies the doctrines developed in his philosophical treatises. Many views which have been attributed to St. Thomas may be found in his works. Albert was a wonderful scholar who had an intimate knowledge not only of Aristotle and his Greek commentators, but also of previous Christian thinkers and the doctrines of the Arabs. Unfortunately he was lacking in historical sense and made some most astonishing mistakes. Moreover, he incorporated in his works the views of other thinkers, so that it is often difficult to discover what he really thought. In his exposition he is guilty of many digressions and his Latin style is unpolished and sometimes his meaning is ambiguous, especially when contrasted with the concise, clear-cut expression of Aquinas. De Wulf sums up his philosophy in the words, "If one regards the philosophy of Albert from a constructive point of view, it lacks

---

[1] GILSON, E., *La Philosophie au Moyen Age*, 2nd edition (Payot, Paris: 1944), p. 505.

coherence and system. When he comments on Aristotle, he is an Aristotelian; when he comments on Neo-Platonic doctrines emanating from Arabian sources, he accommodates himself to them. Without taking into account that in certain respects he adheres to traditional teaching which does not fully agree with Aristotelianism, one can say of his philosophy in general terms what Schneider said of his psychology, that no opinion can be more false than that which looks upon it as a finished and unified system."[1]

Albert definitely broke new ground when he proclaimed that philosophy and theology belong to two distinct provinces of thought. Like Abelard, he had a tremendous faith in the power of human reason, and those modern writers who only see in Scholasticism a subservience to dogma are as much mistaken over Albert as they are about Aquinas. He never hesitated in applying reason to the elucidation of articles of faith. Aquinas followed him in this and completed Albert's work by developing a theory of the ultimate agreement that must exist between a true theology and reason rightly used.

Albert adopted the Aristotelian view of matter and form but he was unable to break away completely from the traditional teaching. For example, though he did not teach that matter has any part in the essence of the angels, he made a concession to the older view by insisting that the angelic form requires a fundamentum which, however, is not related to quantity. Again, he was not successful in wholly eliminating from his philosophy the belief in the plurality of forms and the existence of *rationes seminales* in matter. The same struggle between the old and the new is seen in his psychology. Thus, he is unable to decide whether the primacy in action should be assigned to the intellect or the will, and in considering the nature of the soul he agrees with Aristotle but tries to bring the latter's teaching into line with that of Plato. Thus, he regards the soul as an intellectual substance whose function it is to be the form of the body. Aquinas was able to produce a much neater solution of this particular problem.

On the other hand, the complete formulation of the solution of the Universals problem, so often attributed to St. Thomas, is really due to Albert. He taught that the universal can be considered in three stages, *ante rem*, *in re* and *post rem*. Before individual things came into existence, the universals were ideas or exemplars

---

[1] DE WULF, *op. cit.*, vol. ii, p. 136.

in the mind of God. In creating the world, God allotted appropriate forms to the matter of individual things. These forms are the likenesses of the Divine Ideas, and by their union with matter they not only produce concrete individual existences but also confer on the latter the property of being intelligible to human minds. In this sense, the universal may be said to be in the individual (*in re*). After the completed act of knowledge, the form or universal comes to dwell as an idea in the mind of the knowing subject, and once more comes to exist immaterially in a way analogous to that in which it originally existed in the Divine Mind. This solution was taken over by St. Thomas, who made it an integral part of his theory of knowledge.

SUGGESTIONS FOR FURTHER READING

A valuable though somewhat difficult account of the teaching of Robert Grosseteste is given in D. E. Sharp's *Franciscan Philosophy at Oxford* (O.U.P.: 1930).

Albert the Great, by S. M. Albert, O.P. (Blackfriars, Oxford: 1948), is a very readable account of the life and work of Albert. His achievements as a scientist are described with illustrative passages translated from his writings.

CHAPTER IX

ST. THOMAS AQUINAS

St. Thomas Aquinas, the youngest son of Landulf, Count of Aquino, was born about 1225 at Rocca Secca, near Naples. His two brothers were in the army of Frederick II, but young Thomas was not destined for a military career. When quite a small boy he was sent to study under his uncle Sinibald, Abbot of the Benedictine monastery of Monte Cassino which became well known from the events of the last World War. At the age of fourteen he was sent to complete his studies at Naples. In 1243 or 1244, he entered the Order of St. Dominic. Tradition states that this step was against the wishes of his family, who made every effort to dissuade him from following the religious life and even placed him in confinement for over a year. Their attempts were unsuccessful and St. Thomas is said to have escaped from the castle in which he was imprisoned by means of a rope let down from the castle tower. We do know, however, that he set out for Cologne to study under Albert the Great. His relations with his master have been described in the previous chapter. Tradition tells us that on account of his quiet and reserved manner he received from his fellow students the soubriquet of the Dumb Ox. Albert has been credited with prophetic foresight in exclaiming, "You may call him a dumb ox, but a time is coming when his bellowing will resound to the ends of the earth."

In 1252, his Order called him to teach at the University of Paris, and we have already seen that he took a prominent part in the disputes which divided the university. In 1260 or 1261 he was sent to Italy, where he formed a firm friendship with William of Moerbeke and Reginald, who became his biographer. About 1268, the doctrinal disputes in the university caused by the teaching of the Latin Averroists brought him back to Paris to occupy the Dominican chair for the second time. He left Paris in 1272 to organize, at the request of Charles of Anjou, a new *studium generale* at Naples. He

was not long in Italy before he was sent by Gregory X to take part
in the General Council of Lyons. His health had been undermined
by overwork and study and he was taken ill on the journey. He
lingered for about a month in the monastery of Fossa-Nuova and
passed away in 1274 at the early age of forty-eight or forty-nine.

St. Thomas has been described as "corpulent and tall—sufficiently tall to attract the notice of farm-labourers as he passed by.
He was brown, 'the colour of new wheat'; with an imposing head,
a trifle bald, with a powerful, peaceful face, well-formed lips,
penetrating eyes, and a quiet, frank expression."[1] "He slept little,
and often he would break his rest to consult some work, and
especially to dictate. He was painfully bored by meals, being
always absorbed and preoccupied in 'adapting his thought to the
world,' which he considered was a philosopher's purpose in life:
. . . He was kind and cordial to all, spoke little, and never without
good cause: he mixed as little as possible in crowds. By way of
recreation he would walk alone along the cloisters, at great speed,
head erect and uncovered. He went out rarely and only when it
was necessary. He made his work an excuse for refusing invitations
even to the court of St. Louis, and his only visit there was under
obedience. The story of how he behaved on that occasion is well
known. In the middle of dinner he suddenly struck the table and
exclaimed: 'Now that settles the Manicheans.' The Prior who was
present was afraid that the King would be offended, but, on the
contrary, a scribe was sent for to take down the Saint's new argument."[2] "The child-like simplicity of his private life, and the solid,
balanced, calm character of his public teaching are the salient
features of St. Thomas. Yet he seems to-day hardly a human being,
hardly real, so obscured is his private character by the impersonal
character of his thought."[3]

Like his master Albert, St. Thomas was in no way subservient
to the authority of Aristotle. He once wrote, "The object of
philosophical study is not to know men's opinions but the truth
of things." At the same time, he possessed a lively sense of the
value of studying the works of past thinkers. "Although a single
individual can contribute but little by his study and talent to the
knowledge of truth in comparison with what is known as true, yet

[1] SERTILLANGES, A. D., O.P., *St. Thomas Aquinas and his Work* (Burns, Oates and
Washbourne: 1932), p. 29.
[2] SERTILLANGES, *op. cit.*, p. 30.
[3] *ibid.*, pp. 33–4.

the results of inquiries when collected and analysed and systematic-
ally arranged, are great in magnitude, as is evident in the various
arts which have achieved a marvellous enrichment through the
studies and talents of different individuals." Again, he wrote,
"We must hear the views of the ancients whoever they may be.
This is doubly useful; first, that we may accept for our assistance
whatever they have said aright; secondly, that we may be prepared
against their errors." Aquinas certainly regarded Aristotle with
high respect and deep reverence, but he was no slave to that
authority. He could say with his master Albert, "The man who
holds Aristotle to have been a god, must believe him to be infallible,
but if he believes him human, then, certainly, he was liable to error
just like ourselves."

Aquinas was firmly convinced of the truth of revealed religion.
He was sincere in his belief that the teaching of the Church is in
accordance with reason, and although, at times, certain revealed
truths may be above reason, they are never contradictory to reason.
He accepts the authority of the Church and its teaching as reasonable and he has no doubts about the truth of any revealed doctrine.

It has been said that Aquinas was a Catholic from necessity and
an Aristotelian from choice. His synthesis is more than an exposition of Aristotle; it is a complete reconstruction. But, in making
use of Aristotelian principles, he neither tries to read Christian
theology into Aristotle nor alter his meaning to serve his own ends.
In his commentaries on Aristotle, he makes an honest attempt to
arrive at the philosopher's own thought. He develops and clarifies
Aristotle's meaning, and where there is a clash between Aristotle
and the doctrines of the Church, Aquinas shows that in certain
fundamentals he is more Platonic than Aristotelian.

From what source was this underlying current of Platonism
derived? Very little came from Plato direct. A Latin fragment of
the *Timaeus* was available but there is no evidence that Aquinas
had read it. A little may perhaps have come via Proclus; St.
Thomas' friend, William of Moerbeke, was an ardent student of
Neo-Platonism. The Platonic influence was mainly indirect,
through the Christian writers of Alexandria, St. Augustine, St.
John of Damascus, the Pseudo-Dionysius, and through Jewish
and Arabian thinkers, especially Avicenna and Maimonides.

His most important secondary authority was Dionysius. In his
works, Aquinas quotes 1702 times from the Areopagite. Although

446 different texts from Dionysius are quoted, some, such as "Bonum est sui diffusivum," are special favourites and occur frequently. Two translations of Dionysius were available to Aquinas, the earlier one of Erigena and the later and more accurate version of Sarracenus (about 1180). Aquinas makes use of both.

Did St. Thomas have access to original Greek texts? From internal evidence, it is quite clear that he had some knowledge of Greek but it was not sufficient for the purpose of translation. It was, however, enough to permit him to compare a Latin translation with the original. This is proved from a passage in the *De Unitate Intellectus*. In his attempt to prove the immortality of the individual human soul, he came to realize that Aristotle's teaching was vague and defective, but he still thought that the philosopher was a believer in personal immortality. He drew his arguments from such works of Aristotle as were available, and then suggested that further support might be found in the *Metaphysics*. "I have seen these books, fourteen in number, but they are not yet translated into our language." They were inaccessible to Aquinas owing to his insufficiency of Greek and he had to await the translations of William of Moerbeke. He was probably disappointed when he received them, for Aristotle did not even discuss the problem in the *Metaphysics*.

In the *Summa Theologica* St Thomas quite logically begins with God and the ways in which His existence may be proved, but the modern reader may probably appreciate St. Thomas' philosophy more easily if he commences with the doctrine of man. Questions lxxii to cii of the first part of the *Summa* deal with the human soul and its activities and might almost be considered independently under the title of the Psychology of St. Thomas. The author's experience in teaching Thomistic philosophy has convinced him that this is a sound arrangement to follow.

The previous part of the *Summa* had been concerned with purely spiritual substances, God and the angels, pure forms without matter. Man is a being who is not a pure spirit but consists of a soul or form which is united to a material body. Aquinas expresses his conception of this union by adopting Aristotle's definition of soul as the form or actuality of an organic body. In the 13th century such a position was a novelty. Earlier Christians had thought of the soul as a spiritual entity inhabiting a body. They were influenced by Plato and St. Augustine, and those who were biased towards asceticism had regarded the soul as the real man, the body being but a prison house of flesh. Aquinas had the task of developing Aristotle's doctrine and bringing it into agreement with the Christian conception of a self-subsistent spiritual substance which survives the death of the body.

He begins his argument by adopting a principle implicit in Aristotle but elaborated by Dionysius, namely, the conception of hierarchy in the universe. Aristotle's account in the *De Anima* suggests the general line of procedure but Aquinas emphasizes the idea of man as the mean between the pure intelligences and the animal creation; hence he is more explicit in his development.

The union of matter and form gives rise to concrete individual existences or substances. Matter and form should be understood as the result of purely metaphysical analysis which distinguishes in all material substances the two moments of an organizing principle, form, and that which is capable of being organized in a particular way, matter. In non-living substances the form is, so to speak, so completely embedded in the matter that, as a consequence, one can find no trace of those activities of assimilation of nourishment, or of growth and movement, that we associate with life. The universe presents us with a scale of existence, a chain of being, at the lower end of which are the inorganic substances, whilst at the summit is God, a purely spiritual Being. Even in non-living substances one can find a trace of hierarchical ordering. In the lodestone the form seems to display certain activities over and above its function of conferring being of a definite kind upon the matter which it informs.

When we ascend the scale, we reach a point at which form manifests powers and activities apart from the matter in which it is realized. Thus the essential characteristics of the living plant are its abilities to assimilate nourishment, to grow and to reproduce its kind. These are summed up by saying that the plant is alive, or that it possesses a nutritive soul. The animal has a sensitive soul and the form is able to organize the matter to a further degree of perfection. Thus the animal displays such powers as sense perception, appetition and locomotion. The plant has no differentiated organs, and so in the process of taking in nourishment from the soil it receives matter as well as form. In other words, its vital activities are exercised on the material level. The animal has sense organs enabling it to receive the form of an object without its matter. The higher animals are also capable of forming mental images and possess a superior power of appetition which corresponds to the modern conception of instinct.

Man is a creature who can transcend immediate perception by the use of reason. "We must observe that the nobler a form is, the more it rises above corporeal matter and the more it excels matter by its power and operation; hence we find that the form of a mixed body (what we should now call a chemical compound) has another operation not caused by its elemental qualities. And the higher we advance in the nobility of forms, the more we find that the power of form excels the elementary matter; as the vegetative soul excels the form of the metal and the sensitive soul is superior to the vegetative. Now the human soul is the highest and noblest of forms. Wherefore it excels corporeal matter in its power by the fact that it has an operation and a power in which corporeal matter has no share whatever. This power is called the intellect."[1]

The animate differs from the inanimate by living, whether that life manifests itself in the nutritive sphere alone, or in sense perception and reason. Soul is simply that by which we live. As soon as the first signs of life appear, soul is present. Hence the emphasis in Aristotle's definition on the "first actuality" to include the lowest manifestations of life.

A most important problem now arises. The animal soul possesses in addition to those belonging to the plant soul, the power of sense perception. Has the animal, therefore, two souls, a nutritive and a sensitive? Has man three souls, nutritive, sensitive and rational? Aquinas gives a definite answer. Unlike earlier thinkers, he teaches the principle known as the Unity of Forms. Only one substantial form can be realized in the matter of an object. As the human soul is the substantial form of the body, there cannot be three souls in man. "We must consider that the substantial form differs from the accidental in this, that the latter does not make a thing to be simply, but to be such; for example, heat does not confer being on an object but only makes it hot. . . . Now the substantial form confers being on an object; therefore by its advent a thing is said to be generated simply, and by its removal to be corrupted simply. . . . If besides the intellectual soul there existed beforehand in matter another substantial form by which the subject of the soul were made an actual being, it would follow that the soul does not give

[1] *S. Th.*, I.q. lxxvi. a. 1. c.

being simply, and, consequently, that it is not the substantial form. Thus, at the advent of soul there would not be simple generation, nor at its removal simple corruption, all of which is clearly false. Therefore we must conclude that there is no other substantial form in man besides the intellectual soul, and that this soul, as it implicitly contains the sensitive and nutritive souls, so does it virtually contain all inferior forms, and itself alone does whatever the imperfect forms do in other things."[1]

St. Thomas places the powers of the soul in ascending hierarchical order as vegetative, sensitive, appetitive, locomotive and intellectual. The same conception of hierarchical order applies to the functions of the vegetative soul, which are nutrition, growth and the reproduction of the species.

In his teaching on sense-perception, Aquinas follows Aristotle closely. Sense is the faculty whereby individual objects are perceived. The universal is, however, implicit in every act of sense perception for we perceive an object as belonging to a certain kind. Sense provides the data from which intellect through abstraction can obtain the universal. Sense is necessary to intellect. *Nihil est in intellectu quod non prius fuerit in sensu.* Sense, however, is not a material faculty; it receives the form of an external object without its matter. Aquinas is a definite opponent of materialism. On this view, perception takes place through physical emanations proceeding from the object. This was the error of the early Greek thinkers, who believed that like is known by like. They thought that the form of the object known must be in the knower in the same way as it existed in the object. Such an opinion is absurd, since nothing corporeal can affect that which is immaterial. *Nihil corporeum imprimere potest in rem incorporeum.*

Aquinas also steers clear of Subjective Idealism. He says, "Certain thinkers have asserted that the cognitive powers within us know nothing but their own affections—*i.e.*, sense perceives only the affections of the organs of sense. On this view, the intellect thinks nothing but its own affections—*i.e.*, the intelligible form received into itself—and hence this form is the very object of thought. This opinion is manifestly false, and for two reasons. First, it would follow that all the sciences would have as their objects, not the things existing outside the soul, but only the intelligible forms within the soul. Secondly, there would follow

[1] *S. Th.*, I.q. lxxvi. a. 4. c.

the error of the ancients who said that all appearance is true, and contradictions would likewise be true simultaneously. If taste perceived only its own affection, when anyone whose taste is sound judges honey to be sweet, he will judge truly; so likewise will he whose taste is defective judge truly when he judges honey to be bitter; for each will judge in accordance with the affection of his organ of taste; thus it follows that every opinion will be equally true."[1]

St. Thomas distinguishes between sense in potentiality and sense in actuality. In the former case, the actual object is external to the soul; in the latter, the sensible form in the object and the soul are one. The distinction between the knower and the object known has been partially transcended in the act of knowing. The same applies to thinking. "In one manner, the sensible form is in the object which is outside the soul, but in another it is in sense, which apprehends the forms of material and mobile objects without their matter, the colour of gold without the matter of gold. And, in the same way, intellect receives the forms of material and mobile objects immaterially and without their motion, according to its manner; for that which is received is in the recipient according to the manner of the recipient."[2]

In spite of this similarity between sense and intellect, there is also an important difference between the two. In sense-perception a sense organ and a medium are required—e.g., in hearing, the ear is the sense organ, and the air, in which certain vibrations are set up, is the medium. The intellect requires neither sense organ nor medium, nor is an external object necessary to stimulate the activity of thought. "It should be known that sense is a power residing in a corporeal organ. But the intellect is an immaterial power which is not the actuality of any corporeal organ."[3] Aristotle had taught this, but Aquinas goes a step further and uses the statement that intellect functions without a bodily organ to establish the self-subsistence of the human soul.

Aquinas recognizes five external senses arranged in hierarchical order. Vision is the highest because it is the least material. Hence, when we refer to the operations of the intelligence, we frequently describe them by metaphors borrowed from the sense of sight.

[1] *S. Th.*, I. q. lxxxv. a. 2. c.
[2] *S. Th.*, I. q. lxxxiv a. 1. c.
[3] *Com. de Anima*, lib. ii, lectio 12 b.

Touch is the lowest because the sense organ comes into physical contact with the objects it judges and is affected by them. Sense organs in the hand not only experience heat but become heated themselves. Why should God endow us with a sense so imperfect? Aquinas replies that it was due to the material He had to use, and explains what he means by the illustration of the carpenter and the saw. The carpenter desires a tool which will cut wood. The actual substance from which it is made is immaterial so long as it performs the function of cutting. The best substance for the purpose is steel but that has the disadvantage of being liable to rust and corrosion. The carpenter would prefer a metal which did not rust, but as he needs above all a keen cutting edge, he has to compromise.

The particular senses are not sufficient for the life of the perfect animal; there is need for a power which is able to discriminate between the reports of different senses and relate them to the object perceived. This function is carried out by the common sense. For a perfect life, the animal must also have the power of representing objects to itself when they are not present to the senses. Hence we find in the higher animals and man the power of forming *phantasmata*, or mental images. The latter are still individual images in which the universal is implicit. They do not remain passive in the imagination, but a certain amount of activity resulting in the formation of associations goes on. Aquinas considers the imagination a sense, for he attributes a bodily organ to it, namely, that part of the brain situated behind the frontal lobes. The importance of the mental image lies in the fact that it is the half-way house between sense and intellect—*cf.* Hobbes' description of the image as "decaying sense."

At the sense level there are two other powers to be considered, the *vis aestimativa* and the *vis cogitativa*. The former approximates to the modern instinct and is the power which leads an animal to recognize the utility or the harmful properties of an object. Thus, the sheep naturally experiences revulsion at the sight of the wolf, attraction to its own lamb and the ability to feel differently towards a lamb which is not its own. The bird sees straw and twigs and recognizes them as useful for a nest and so proceeds to collect them. The *vis aestimativa* implies a kind of judgment and choice, though the latter is not deliberate and does not involve the use of reason. Such instinctive action serves the animal as reason serves man.

In human beings, instinct directed by intelligence is the *vis cogitativa.* It is not reason because it is connected with the individual and the habitual. It is sometimes called Particular Reason and has an organ in the middle of the head. Thus, travelling upwards through the hierarchical arrangement of the powers of the soul, we are brought by stages to the very threshold of reason. The higher powers of sense in their operations foreshadow the activities of the intelligence. "The cogitative and memorative powers in man owe their excellence not to that which is proper to the sensitive part, but to a certain affinity and proximity to the universal reason, which, so to speak, overflows into them."[1]

So far the teaching of Aquinas has been largely an extension and reconstruction of the thought of Aristotle. In his synthesis Aquinas had to find room for the doctrines of the immortality of the soul and the resurrection of the body. Augustine had not encountered this difficulty since Platonists had always considered the soul as a self-subsistent spiritual entity, but Aquinas was forced to review the whole question in the light of his adoption of Aristotle's definition of soul.

In demonstrating the self-subsistence of the soul, Aquinas makes use of two principles. The first is Aristotelian, namely, that the intellect can function without using a bodily organ. The other is the hierarchical conception of Dionysius which emphasized that the highest activities of an intermediate order approximate to and foreshadow some of the perfections belonging to the rank next above it. By utilizing these principles, Aquinas is able to maintain the Aristotelian view of the soul as the form of the body but he also makes a concession to Neo-Platonism by insisting that, unlike other forms in nature, the human soul is a self-subsisting form. At the same time, he denied the Neo-Platonic doctrine that the human soul existed prior to the birth of the body, for in that case our life would commence by the degradation of the noblest element in human nature.

He begins his argument by demonstrating that all inorganic substances are composites of matter and form but the form is so embedded in matter that it has no activities apart from the matter on which it confers determinate being. Such simple bodies have no activities beyond those which are due to the active and passive qualities, or, in modern language, they exhibit only physical and chemical properties. Aquinas enumerates these qualities as heat

[1] *S. Th.,* I. q. lxxviii. a. 4. ad 5m.

and cold, wetness and dryness, denseness and rarity, heaviness and lightness. In every inorganic body these qualities are found in different proportions, and the nature of the substance is due to the various combinations of the active and passive qualities.[1]

The qualities were termed active and passive because it is their nature to act or to be acted upon by one another. Hot and wet are active, but cold, which is acted upon by heat, and dryness, which is affected by wetness, are passive. Yet even in the realm of inorganic nature certain mixed bodies, or, as we should now call them, chemical compounds, display an activity over and above that due to their chemical and physical properties. Magnetic iron ore, for instance, can attract iron from a distance, and in so doing it seems to foreshadow the attractive influences of the heavenly bodies—e.g., the attractive power of the sun and moon on the tides.

In organic nature, even in the lowliest forms of plant life, there exists the power of absorbing nourishment, of growth and of reproduction. Such activities are superior to those of inorganic substances where the form is so embedded in the matter that they exhibit none of those vital movements we find in plants and which are akin to the movements of the heavenly bodies. The animal soul, by virtue of its powers of sense-perception, is a cognitive soul. The vital powers of the animal show a likeness to the vital power that moves the heavens, but the animal soul is only able to exercise its functions of sense-perception through bodily organs.

In man, the soul has the power of thought which is not exercised through a bodily organ. It is true that its knowledge of immaterial things is dependent on the data given by sense-perception and stored up in memory, so that if, through illness or accident, the activity of any sense organ is impaired, the action of intellect in this

---

[1] The origin of the idea of the active and passive qualities is to be found in Empedocles, who regarded fire, air, water and earth as the four roots or elements of things. (See Burnet's *Early Greek Philosophy*, p. 263, and *Thales to Plato*, p. 72.) These elements became identified with the opposites, the hot and cold, and the dry and moist. This doctrine influenced Aristotle and the medical school, whose teaching is best known through Galen. For Aristotle, the most rudimentary form in which first matter actually exists is that of one of these elements. Fire is hot and dry, air hot and moist, water moist and cold, and earth cold and dry. It should be noted that these elements are arranged in order of increasing density and that each has one quality common with the next. Thus air is more dense than fire since flame rises, but fire is hot and dry and air hot and moist. Because air and fire possess the common quality of heat, fire can be transmuted to air and vice versa. Aristotle taught that this explained the changes in nature. The less dense becomes the more dense by condensation, and the more dense, through rarefaction, becomes the less dense.

particular aspect will be affected. In addition, the human soul is only potentially cognitive of immaterial things. The process we know as learning is necessary in order that the potentiality shall be transformed into actuality. Finally, the soul is united to the body since it confers being upon its body and therefore it must be the form of the body. Like the soul of the brute, the human soul is the form of the body, but, unlike the former, since it does not need a bodily organ, and what can function *per se* can exist *per se*, it is a self-subsisting spiritual substance.

Above the human soul are the angelic intelligences, pure forms knowing immaterial things intuitively and needing no process of learning to turn potential into actual knowledge. Man, in so far as his soul is his form, is a part of the physical world, but since it also has an existence as a spiritual being apart from the body, he shares the nature of the angelic spirits. The human soul occupies the intermediate position between the lower forms of the animals and the realm of pure spiritual existence. Such a view of the dignity of human nature and intelligence presents a marked contrast with the Greek. Aristotle regarded man as a little higher than the dogs and cattle. Aquinas lays emphasis on his kinship with the angels. The absolute value of every individual human soul is among the Christian thinker's strongest convictions.

One is immediately led to ask, "What is the origin of the independent existence of the soul? Did it exist prior to its union with the body? Is it produced by the act of propagation which brought the body into existence or is it created by God? If the latter, is it created at the same time as the body, or does it come into existence at a later period of the body's development? Since the soul is the form of the body, how is it that form whose essence is universal comes to be individualized? All these are questions which Aquinas has to answer. He rejects the doctrine that the soul as well as the body is produced by propagation, and also the Platonic view of the pre-existence of the soul. His answer is that soul and body were created simultaneously by God Who infused soul into body from without.

The view of St. Thomas is that in the generation of men and animals we are concerned with a very complex process which consists of a successive series of generations and corruptions, for one and the same substantial form cannot be developed into actuality by any gradual process. With the loss of form by the seed, a new

form is received which possesses vital powers of the kind belonging
to plants. As soon as the embryo begins to live a vegetative life, it is
disposed to receive an animal soul. When the time is ripe, the
vegetative soul disappears and its place is simultaneously taken by
an animal soul which exercises both vegetative and animal
functions. This is followed by another period of the disposing of
the matter to receive a new form. When the animal soul is lost,
it is immediately replaced by a rational soul created by God. This
rational soul exercises all the functions peculiar to the vegetable
and animal souls in addition to its own proper power of intelligence.

The difficult problem of the individuation of the human soul
remains to be considered. Perhaps the clearest method of approach
is to examine the way in which material substances are individualized. In the composite, neither matter nor form is individual.
First matter, having no qualities to differentiate it, is absolutely
indeterminate. Form is universal and is common to all members of
the species. In virtue of the form of man, Socrates, Plato, etc.,
are all men. Yet somehow an individual substance is constituted
by the union of matter and form. We may anticipate St. Thomas
by saying that in some sense he regards matter as the principle of
Individuation. This matter must be a matter which is already
endowed with some form. The latter cannot be a substantial form,
for in that case there would be two substantial forms in the same
individual which would contradict the principle of the Unity of
Form. The other alternative is that it must be an accidental form.
Can it be the form of quantity? It would seem that in virtue of
possessing the form of quantity matter can be distinguished in parts;
the matter belonging to this or that individual. "Remove quantity
and matter remains indivisible," says St. Thomas, quoting Aristotle.

Quantity is an accidental form, however, and if the principle
of individuation were an accident, then the individuality of
material substances and even human personality, the highest kind
of individuality we know, would depend on an accidental
modification.

In the solution of his problem, it is possible to see a gradual
development in the thought of St. Thomas. His earliest view was
given in the *Commentary on the Sentences*. In order to prove the
immateriality of the soul, he based his argument upon the fact
that the essence of a material body consists of extension in three
dimensions. Extension is due to the presence of the form of

corporeity. "The first form to be received into matter," he wrote, "is that of corporeity from which it is never separated."[1] Later, he said, "There can be no diversity prior to corporeity, for diversity presupposes the possession of parts and this cannot be unless divisibility is presupposed. Divisibility is the consequence of quantity, which cannot exist without corporeity. Therefore, all matter is clothed with the form of corporeity, so that if anything is incorporeal, it must be immaterial."[2]

In his *Commentary on the Trinity of Boethius*, St. Thomas develops another view which, like the former, was due to Averroes. This is the doctrine of indeterminate dimensions. There are two ways of regarding dimensions. A complete being, such as an oak tree, possesses determinate dimensions. It is so many feet in height and so many in thickness. Since, however, determinate dimensions change with the development of the individual, they cannot be the principle of Individuation. The oak grows in height and girth so that it would not remain numerically the same oak. Dimensions can be considered, however, without reference to definite measurement, though in point of fact they can no more exist apart from determination than a colour can exist without being some particular colour. Hence, indeterminate dimensions individuate form and make this stone distinct from that stone.

Later, St. Thomas feels that both corporeity and indeterminate dimensions are equally unsatisfactory as explanations. In his opusculum, *De Ente et Essentia*, Chapter I, he examines the definition of a species. The object of a definition is to state the essence of the thing which is defined; that which makes it what it is. Consider the definition of man as a rational animal. The conception of a rational animal includes the matter as well as the form. Will not the inclusion of matter in the essence render it particular and not universal? If so, definition would be impossible. One cannot define a particular, one can only point to it.

St. Thomas resolves the difficulty as follows. The inclusion of the matter as a part of the essence does not render the latter particular. In other words, matter itself does not constitute the principle of Individuation. "It should be understood that matter taken in its general meaning is not the principle of Individuation, but only *materia signata*—*i.e.*, matter in a determinate sense. I understand by the term *materia signata* a matter under determinate

---

[1] *In Sent.*, I.d. 8 q. v. a. 2.   [2] *In Sent.*, I. d. 3. q. i. a. 1.

dimensions." Hence, *materia signata* is not included in the definition of man. It would, however, be included in the definition of Socrates supposing such an individual could be defined. In the definition of man, this flesh and this bone is not part of the definition but only matter in a general sense—*i.e.*, *materia non signata.*

The term *materia signata* seems to have been borrowed from Avicenna, who also calls it *materia demonstrata.* Wicksteed refers to it as "earmarked matter."[1] The meaning of this shorthand term, for that is what it evidently was to Aquinas, can be made clear if one considers a simple example in which one substance is corrupted and another generated—*e.g.*, the burning of a log of wood. St. Thomas would describe this process as one in which the wood is transmuted to fire. Now the first thought that strikes one is that the destruction of the wood and the generation of fire must have a cause. The latter is the efficient agent who acts upon the wood, a composite of matter and form, by setting light to it, and his action ultimately affects the matter as well as the form. At the start, it is the accidents which are changed; the wood alters in colour, in shape and in bulk. While these accidental changes are taking place, the matter is being disposed for the reception of the substantial form of fire, but this does not occur until the appropriate moment has come. Then the wood ceases to be wood, and at the same moment the form of fire takes the place of the form of wood. A new substance has been generated, but is there anything belonging to the previous composite which is still present in the new? Obviously the matter has remained the same throughout the substantial change. The matter has been disposed by the activity of the efficient agent to receive the form of fire, and this matter is *signata*—*i.e.*, the efficient agent has set it aside or earmarked it for his operation and therefore his action has conferred on it determinate dimensions. We might say that he has selected a definite number of cubic inches of wood to burn. In using the term *materia signata*, the emphasis is not on the matter but on the selection of it by the efficient agent for his activity. There is no suggestion that the dimensions existed in the matter until the efficient agent stamped them upon it when he imposed form upon it.

Many texts of St. Thomas can be quoted to support this interpretation. Thus, "Dimensions should not be considered as

---

[1] WICKSTEED, P., *The Reactions between Dogma and Philosophy* (Constable: 1926), p. 368.

existing in matter in their full actuality before the advent of the natural forms, but in an incomplete actuality, and therefore they are prior in the order of generation, but form is prior in the order of perfection."[1] Again, "In the order of generation, dispositions to form are antecedent to form in matter, although in actual being they are later."[2] A more important quotation is from *Qq. disp. De Anima*, a. 9.

"From the fact that matter is determined as regards corporeal being through forms, it follows at once that there are dimensions in it by means of which matter is understood to be divisible into different parts and thus, according to different parts of itself, it is capable of receiving different forms. Furthermore, from the fact that matter is understood to be determined in a particular substantial being, it can be considered as capable of having accidental forms by which it is disposed to a further perfection, and through which the matter is rendered fit for the accomplishment of that further perfection. But *dispositions of this kind are forms presupposed and imposed by the agent upon matter.*"

The whole difficulty of the existence of the dispositions in matter rests upon the double meaning of the term "prior." The first is a temporal one. If dispositions existed in this sense, then forms would exist in matter prior in time to the advent of the substantial form, and the theory of *materia signata* would be open to the same criticism as the form of corporeity. The other meaning is that of prior in thought—*i.e.*, logically prior. It is in this sense that, in the composite, matter is prior to the substantial form. In a similar fashion, dispositions to determined quantity can be thought of as being imposed by the agent prior to the induction of the substantial form.

So far, however, only half the difficulty has been solved. We have seen that the distinction of corporeal things is due to *materia signata*, and the latter phrase has been given a meaning. This is quite sufficient to explain the individual distinctness of six pennies struck from the same die. When we deal with living things we find that a living being is not only distinct from others in the same

---

[1] *De Ver.*, q. v. a. 9. ad 6. Matter and form are beings existing in incomplete actuality (*actus incompletus*). The composite exists in *actu completo*. The dimensions are prior in order of generation, *i.e.*, the agent selects the matter of the wood on which to exercise his efficient causality, but the substance must exist, must receive the substantial form before it can have dimensions in *actu completo*.

[2] *Contra Gent.*, II. 71.

species, but it has a definite individuality of its own which at the human level becomes personality. Plato and Socrates are both men in virtue of possessing the form of humanity. Plato is distinguished from Socrates by his *materia signata*, but in disposition, temperament and character they are different personalities. What is the basis of this difference?

Dr. Wicksteed handles this problem[1] but he does not treat it in a manner which is wholly satisfactory. We have already seen how the four elementary forms of the hot, the dry, the cold and the moist give rise to the active and passive qualities of an elementary substance. What happens to the active and passive qualities in a mixed body—*i.e.*, a chemical compound? They neither retain their properties in actuality nor do they lose them entirely in the act of combining. As the animal soul virtually contains all the powers belonging to the plant soul, so the mixed body, which is a higher grade of being than the element, possesses potentially all the properties of the elementary substances that compose it.[2] Hence, the active and passive qualities are found in the mixed body combined and interacting in different ways and resulting in what St. Thomas terms a *complexio*. The balance or harmony of the active and passive qualities is called temperament.

Temperament does not represent a fixed numerical proportion. Like the mean of Aristotle's *Ethics*, it permits of a certain amount of variation. "Since to any kind there is given a certain *complexio*, this is not in accordance with some indivisible grade but is according to a certain latitude; so that there are limits beyond which the *complexio* of the kind is not kept intact. Within these limits, however, there is considerable difference, approaching to one extreme or the other. Thus the *complexio* of the human body is nicely balanced (*temperatissima*), but there are many kinds of temperament according to which some men are called melancholy, some choleric, and so on according to its nearness to the limits of the human *complexio*."[3]

[1] WICKSTEED, *op. cit.*, pp. 424-9. For passages in support of his view, see pp. 465-75.
[2] To illustrate by a modern example: The elementary substances, oxygen and hydrogen, combine to form the chemical compound known as water. The new substance has very different properties from the elements which constitute it, but these properties still belong potentially to water and may be actualized by electrolysis by which water is again separated into its elements.
[3] The upper and lower limits of variation in the *complexio* can be illustrated from the simple example of mixing cement and sand to make concrete. Suppose a

These differences, it is true, fall on the physical side but they ultimately affect the soul. "It is clear that the better the disposition of a body, the better the soul allotted to it; which clearly appears in things of different species; and the reason thereof is that act and form are received into matter according to the capacity of the matter; thus because some men have bodies of better dispositions, their souls have a greater power of understanding." Thus from the point of view of nature, Wicksteed's remark is just; "We have to realize the full implications of this doctrine by noting that not only the intellectual powers of the soul, but its moral predispositions, are conditioned, like its temperament, by the physical constitution of the body."[1] It is interesting to note that modern doctrines of temperament, like those of McDougall and Jung, would be subject to this criticism if this were all that could be said. But to leave the problem at this stage is to ignore the fact that Aquinas was a Christian. What the soul eventually becomes depends upon certain features of the individual's environment, his use or misuse of free will and his co-operation with the Creator through the Means of Grace.

All that Aquinas has done so far is to insist that, at the start, the individual is what he is because of physiological factors. The dispositions which give rise to temperament are certainly accidental. Plato and Socrates are both men because they both possess the same substantial form. They are distinct individuals since they are individuated by the *materia signata* which constitutes their bodies. Their personality, as far as we can estimate, depends in the first place upon accidental differences of temperament. Their fully developed personality, however, is largely due to the individuals themselves and the environmental influences brought to bear upon them. Their original disposition can be modified through experience, training and education, and as creatures possessing

---

concrete is obtained by a mixture of one measure of cement with three of sand. If the proportion is varied and one part of cement is mixed with five of sand, a concrete is still produced but of a more sandy character. A mixture of two measures of cement and three of sand would give a concrete which is more akin to cement, but there are certain limits to the proportions, beyond which concrete would not be obtained, and the result would be either sand or cement. In a similar way, the human *complexio* varies considerably with different individuals and thus the temperamental differences between them are produced. Beyond these limits the line between the normal and the abnormal is passed and the result is the pathological case.

[1] WICKSTEED, *op. cit.*, p. 473.

free will they can build up for themselves certain qualities of character which can be further refined and developed through the operation of Divine Grace.

St. Thomas now has to grapple with the problem how existences which are pure forms can be individuated. The case of God presents no difficulty. His nature is so unique that the co-existence of two beings of such a nature and attributes would be impossible —*impossibilia per se*—as Aquinas phrases it. The individuality and personality of God are individuality and personality at the highest possible level. The angels present a problem. They are separate substances which are not composites of matter and form. What is there, then, to distinguish one angel from another? Does the multitude of angelic beings form a single species comprising innumerable individuals? This is not possible unless it is granted that matter enters into the being of the angel.

Earlier thinkers had asserted that an angel possesses a spiritualized matter. They felt the difficulty acutely and wished to find some ground for maintaining the individuality of each angelic spirit. The view of St. Thomas is that each angel constitutes in himself a distinct species and is differentiated from others by his form alone. The different orders of angels are distinguished according to their varying capacities of knowing.

The personal individuality of each human soul is in one way dependent on the body. At the moment of creation, when the soul makes the first contact with its body, it is individuated, and, once individualized, it retains its individuality for ever. To say, however, that the soul's individuality is due to the quantified matter of the body is to ignore the efficient cause. It was shown earlier that, in the case of the lower forms, the efficient agent in imposing form on matter stamps the matter with determinate dimensions in the very act of conferring the form. In the case of the human soul, God is the agent who adapts each soul to a particular body, and it is because of His efficient causality that the soul becomes the soul of a particular body. Thus, after death, when the body has perished, the soul adapted to that body retains its individuality. "This soul differs numerically from that soul because of its relation (*habitudo*) to a numerically different body, and thus human souls are individuated according to their bodies, but not as though the individuation were caused by their bodies."[1]

[1] *Contra Gent.*, II. c. 75.

In the *De Ente et Essentia*, Aquinas is careful to say, "Though the soul's individuation depends upon the body as its occasion as regards its beginning, because individual being (*esse individuatum*) is only acquired by it in the body whose actuality it is, yet its individuality cannot be lost when the body is destroyed. For since it has absolute being (*esse absolutum*) from the time when it acquired individual being through becoming the form of this particular body, that being remains individual for ever; hence Avicenna's saying that the individuation and multiplication of souls depend on the body in respect of their beginning but not in respect to their end."

Aquinas draws the important corollary from the self-subsistent nature of the rational soul that it survives the death of the body and is immortal. "It is impossible that a substantial form should cease to be."[1] In the *Contra Gentiles*, II. c. 79, he develops a series of arguments designed to prove the personal immortality of the human soul. These depend upon the spiritual nature of the soul, but one of them is of a different character. Aquinas was convinced that God never implants a natural craving in a creature without at the same time supplying a means of satisfying it. Thus, earlier in the same treatise, he had shown that man has a natural craving for complete knowledge. The limitations of the human intellect prevent this desire from attaining its fruition on earth, but God provides for its satisfaction in two ways. On earth a partial satisfaction is possible. The knowledge that is unattainable in the present life, through the exercise of reason, has its deficiency supplied through the revelation of God in the Scriptures and in the teaching of the Catholic Church. Faith takes the place of reason in regard to the greater mysteries. Secondly, after death, the redeemed soul achieves the perfection of knowledge in the Beatific Vision of the Blessed Trinity.

The argument for the immortality of the soul is on similar lines. "Further, it is impossible for a natural craving to be frustrated. Man naturally craves after permanent existence, which is clear from the fact that, while existence is sought by all, man through his intellectual powers apprehends existence, not in the present only as animals do, but absolute existence. It follows, therefore, that man attains permanence on the part of his soul by which he apprehends being absolutely and for all time."

[1] *S. Th.*, I. q. lxxv. a. 6. c.

Not only the intellect but the whole soul, including its intellectual, sensible and vegetative faculties, is immortal. There is no contradiction in this statement. Though the rational soul alone is separable and immortal, yet the higher form contains in itself the powers of the lower. Hence the rational soul possesses virtually the lower functions of soul life which depend for their exercise, but not for their existence, on bodily organs. Soul is created *in ordine ad corpus*, and though it can exist independently of the body, it cannot enjoy the perfection of its nature apart from the body.

In strictness, the soul is not the form of the body but of the man. Man is a body-soul, and the soul cannot be considered by itself as constituting the man. After death, disembodied souls can only be termed men in a metaphorical sense. Aquinas discusses this in connection with the query whether Christ in the period between His death and resurrection was still true man. It is urged, "Aristotle says that each man is his intellect, Wherefore we invoke the soul of Peter departed this life, saying, 'Holy Peter, pray for us,' but after death, the Son of God was not separated from His intellectual soul. Therefore, in those days, the Son of God was true man."[1]

But since the intellectual soul is not the complete man, it would be more correct to say, "Holy Soul of Peter, pray for us." The appearance of Elijah and Moses at the Transfiguration raises a difficulty, but Aquinas shows that, though the former could truly be there, since he was assumed into heaven whilst still living, the latter could be present only through a special form provided for the occasion. "This does not mean that the soul of Moses had rejoined its body, but that his soul manifested itself by means of an assumed body in the same way that an angel manifests himself. Elijah, however, appeared in his own body, not indeed coming from the highest heaven, but from some other exalted sphere to which he was carried in the chariot of fire."[2]

Since soul without its body is not truly a human being, reason demands a final resurrection of the body so that the soul can enjoy once more that perfection of being for which it craves. After death, soul is a nude form crying for its matter and such a natural craving is bound in the end to be satisfied.

After discussing Scriptural arguments for the resurrection of the body, Aquinas adds, "It is clear from what has been said, that

[1] *S. Th.*, III. q. l. a. 4. ob. 2.   [2] *S. Th.*, III. q. xlv. a. 3. ad. 2m.

the soul is naturally united to the body, since through its essence it is the form of the body. It is, therefore, contrary to nature for the soul to be without the body, and nothing that is contrary to nature can be permanent. Therefore, the soul will not be for ever without the body. Since the soul itself is immortal, this demands that it will be united to the body again—*i.e.*, there will be a resurrection. The immortality of the soul seems to demand the future resurrection of the body."[1]

[1] *Contra Gent.*, IV. c. 79.

CHAPTER X

ST. THOMAS AQUINAS—*continued*

THE intermediate position of man as bridging the gulf between corporeal nature and the purely spiritual existences is, for St. Thomas, the key to the understanding of the activities of the intellect. "So therefore the human soul, although it is united to the body as its form, has a being elevated above the body and not depending on it. It is clear that it is constituted as a mean between bodily existences and the separate substances."[1]

Since soul is united to the body as its form, human knowledge in this present life is based on data received through sense perception and stored up by means of imagery. Like Kant, Aquinas emphasizes the sensible origin of intellectual knowledge, and like Kant, too, he is aware that intellectual activity is different from sense perception. In intellectual activity, the mind has the power of rising beyond the data of sense and arriving at a knowledge of the universal and immaterial. Abstraction is the outstanding feature of the operation of thought, and through abstraction the mind, setting aside all the individualizing conditions of objects, can rise to the consideration of the universal.

Universals, however, have no existence apart from the concrete things in which they are realized. Any being they have in the mind which has separated them out is a secondary being and must not be confused with real objective existence. Thus, Aquinas takes his stand as a Moderate Realist. Universals are obtained by abstraction from sense particulars; and because man is a body-soul, a process is necessary. Indeed, man is not, strictly speaking, an intelligence, but his soul is furnished with an intellectual principle which is in potentiality to all knowledge at the beginning. The process of learning is needed to make actually intelligible what was at first potentially intelligible. The following passages show quite clearly the teaching of Aquinas.

[1] *Qq. disp. de An.*, a. l. c.

(a) "The intellectual soul holds in the order of nature the lowest place among intellectual substances; inasmuch as it is not naturally gifted with the knowledge of truth, as the angels are, but has to gather knowledge from individual things by way of the senses."[1]

(b) "The angelic intellect is always in act as regards those things which it can understand, because of its proximity to the First Intellect, which is Pure Act. The human intellect, which is lowest in the order of intelligences and most remote from the perfection of the Divine Intellect, is in potentiality with regard to things intelligible, and is first like a clean tablet on which nothing is written."[2]

(c) "Angels, who according to their nature possess perfect knowledge of intelligible truth, have no need to advance from one thing to another, but apprehend the truth simply and without mental discussion. Man arrives at knowledge of the truth by advancing from one thing to another, and therefore he is called rational."[3]

(d) "The human intellect must needs understand through composition and division. . . . It does not gain perfect knowledge by its first act of apprehension, but it first grasps something about its object, such as its quiddity, and this is its first and proper object; and then it understands the properties and accidents and the various relations of the essence. Thus, it compares one thing with another by composition and division, and from one composition and division it proceeds to another, which is the process of reasoning. The angelic and the Divine Intellects, like all incorruptible things, have their perfection at once from the very beginning. Hence the angelic and Divine Intellects have the entire knowledge of a thing, at once and perfectly; hence also in knowing the quiddity of a thing they know at once whatever we can know by composition and reasoning."[4]

Aquinas unhesitatingly rejects any theory which suggests that universals may be innate and discovered by the mind within itself, or that they exist in a super-sensible world as the proper objects of human thought. Nor will he admit that they can be directly

[1] *S. Th.*, I. q. lxxvi. a. 5. c.   [3] *ibid.*, q. lxxix. a. 8. c.
[2] *ibid.*, q. lxxix. a. 2. c.   [4] *S. Th.*, I. q. lxxxv. a. 1. ad. 4m.

apprehended in the Divine Intelligence. Universals are derived
from sense images by the process of abstraction through the agency
of Active Intellect. There is no doubt whatever in the mind of St.
Thomas that Active Intellect is part of the individual human soul,
and he will not for one moment accept the hypothesis of the Arab
thinkers.

Active Intellect plays a twofold part in thought. In the first
place, it illumines mental imagery preparing it for the second
activity of abstraction. "Mental images are illumined by the Active
Intellect which then abstracts the intelligible species from them.
They are illumined so that the sensitive part of the soul may be
made more effective through union with the intellect, and so that
the images are rendered fit to have intelligible intentions abstracted
from them by the power of Active Intellect. Further, the Active
Intellect abstracts the intelligible species from sense imagery in so
far as through the power of Active Intellect we are enabled to
receive into our thought the nature of the species apart from their
individualizing conditions; after the likeness of which natures the
Possible Intellect is informed."[1]

The two functions of Active Intellect are again described in the
following passage: "On the one hand, the effect of the intellectual
light is to produce intelligibles in actuality, and on the other, it is
to perfect the Possible Intellect to knowing, which the species
illuminated by the light of Active Intellect effect in us."[2]

Aquinas is anxious, as was Aristotle, to do justice to the synthetic
activity of mind. He never entertains the idea of *a priori* forms of
the understanding in a Kantian sense. He insists that before the
beginning of the act of thought the Possible Intellect is devoid of
form. It is the work of Active Intellect, conceived under the analogy
of light, which provides for the synthetic activity of mind without,
at the same time, relinquishing the position that in knowing things
we know them as they are.

On the occasion of *phantasmata*, Active Intellect produces a
modification in the Possible Intellect. This is a new form abstracted
from sense imagery through the agency of Active Intellect. The
new form received by the Possible Intellect and actualized there is
the intelligible species (*species intelligibilis impressa*). It was implicit
in sense imagery and is called into existence in the Possible Intellect

[1] *S. Th.*, I. q. lxxxv., a. 1. ad 4m.
[2] *In Sent.*, III, l. 4. sol. 3.

as a purely universal form. It is not a transformation of *phantasmata* but an entirely distinct product. An individual may have many mental images of horses but only one intelligible species. We can refer to the intelligible species, for the present, as a rudimentary concept.

Before proceeding further with the psychology of St. Thomas, it will be necessary to consider his theory of knowledge, which throws considerable light on the former. He starts from two fundamental positions. The first is the intermediate place of man, and the second is that knowledge is none other than a mode of being. The latter requires elucidation. In the first place, we are told, "Knowing beings are distinguished from those that know not in this, that the latter have nothing save their own form, while that which knows has by nature also the form of another thing, since the form of the object known is in the knower. Whence it is manifest that the nature of a thing that knows not is more confined and limited, whereas the nature of a thing that knows has greater amplitude and enlargement."[1]

The nature of matter is to be receptive of form, and of form to communicate itself. Matter places restrictions upon the self-communication of form; hence the latter is received *ad modum recipientis*. Form communicates itself in two ways. In inanimate nature it confers being upon things. The form of stone, by communicating itself to the receptive matter of different stones, not only gives them being but produces a number of individuals of the same species. Form, however, can also communicate itself, *secundum modum recipientis* to knowing minds.

As knowledge consists in reception of form, it presents an analogy to the way in which form communicates itself to matter. Hence knowledge can be conceived on the analogy of becoming. Matter is only potentially the individual it becomes at the advent of form, and in a similar way the mind before it actually knows is only potentially the objects of its knowledge. Passing from ignorance to knowledge is really a transition from potentiality to actuality. In potential knowledge, a sharp distinction exists between the knower and the object known. I and the object I know are not one, but two. Aquinas rejects any theory of knowledge which would lead to Subjective Idealism.

[1] *S. Th.*, I. q. xiv. a. 1. c.

The form of stone by entering the mind of the knowing subject does so without prejudice to the being of the stone, for in the mind the object possesses a being different from its being as an object of nature. The latter is termed its natural being (*esse naturale*); the former its being as an object of thought (*esse intentionale, cf.* the *esse objectivum* of Descartes). The following passages make this distinction quite clear:

(a) "The form of the stone is truly in the mind but not according to the kind of being that it has in the stone."[1]

(b) "In this way, sense receives form without matter, since form has a mode of being in sense different from that in the sensible object. For in the sensible object it has *esse naturale* but in sense it has *esse intentionale et spirituale*."[2]

(c) "An external object which comes to be an object of our understanding does not exist in our intellect in its own proper nature, but the species of it must be in our intellect by means of which our understanding is actualized. The intellect actualized and informed by the species understands the thing itself."[3]

The *esse intentionale* is not an image of the object known but the thing itself, its being as seen or known. In knowledge we are naturally the subject and intentionally the object. The external reality enters the mind of the knower, and here lies the paradox, without going outside itself. In the living act of knowledge, the distinction between knower and known is partially transcended; the *esse naturale* and the *esse intentionale* coincide.

The same distinction can be applied to the knower himself. In his *esse naturale*, man is but a small fragment of the universe, but he possesses a spiritual nature. Thus, through knowledge, he transcends his finitude and can enlarge his being to include, as objects of thought, other finite fragments of the universe. This is what Aristotle meant by saying that in a sense the soul is all things.

The fact that man is a spiritual being with a material body restricts his thought in two ways. The human intellect is only potentially capable of knowing, and a process of learning is

[1] *De Verit.*, q. xxi. a. 3. c.   [2] *Com. in De Anima*, lib. ii, lectio 24 a.
[3] *Contra Gent.*, I.c. 53.

necessary by which potentiality is transformed into actuality. In addition, he is limited to what is abstracted from data accumulated by sense-perception. This second point is worthy of further consideration. Aristotle had taught this, and later Kant was to remind us that conception without perception is empty. The Active Intellect cannot function without a mental image which is the occasion rather than the cause on which the Possible Intellect is moved from potentiality to actuality. The necessity of mental imagery suggests that the human intellect is to a certain extent defective. It is true that the practised thinker can dispense with imagery, but it is always in the background ready to be called in when needed.

The dependence of intellect on material received through sense raises two important problems: (*a*) the nature of human knowledge after death, and (*b*) the knowledge of the angels and God. The first problem subdivides; how can soul separated from body grasp sensible realities; how is intellectual knowledge possible when no sense material is forthcoming? The former is answered by the principle that the higher faculty gathers up into itself the powers and functions of the lower, so that our intellect after death, and the angelic intellects, perceive sensible objects by means of the intellect alone.

Aquinas answers the latter by emphasizing that in the body the soul has one mode of being; freed from the body, it has another. When united to the body, according to that mode of existence, it naturally turns to imagery in order to understand. When disembodied, it turns to simple intelligible substances according to its new mode of existence, namely, that of a separate substance. Thus, in its intellectual activities, the disembodied soul apprehends in the same way as the angels. As spiritual beings without sense organs, they cannot think by means of intelligible species abstracted from sense imagery. Their intelligible species are part of their nature, implanted in them by God. Hence, with pure spirits there is no process of learning. Having innate ideas or Divinely infused species, their apprehension is immediate and intuitive.

In answer to the second problem, Aquinas is as emphatic as Kant in denying to man knowledge of the unconditioned. God and the angels possess such powers, but for man this is a privilege reserved for the redeemed in Paradise. Before, however, we discuss the problem of man's knowledge of God, we should

F

return to the psychology of Aquinas and study the manner in which concepts are formed.

The intelligible species has already been described as a rudimentary concept. In understanding the psychology of St. Thomas, it is important to grasp that the intelligible species is not the object known (*id quod intelligitur*), but the instrument by which we know the object (*id quo intelligitur*). He reminds us that the object of thought is the stone, not the species of the stone. Otherwise, the sciences would not be about things but about intelligible species. No question of representative concepts between knower and known arises. It is the thing, not the species, which is the object of thought.

It is possible, however, that, having thought the thing, the intellect may turn away from its primary object and reflect upon its thought of that object. This secondary object constitutes the second intention of the intellect. First intentions are the concrete objects of thought; second intentions, the manner in which those objects are thought as the result of reflection upon our own thinking. Natural science deals with first intentions but logic with second intentions.

The intelligible species, then, is the instrument through which we know the object, the guiding clue which moves the Possible Intellect to understand the universal. It is free from all materiality. Implicit in imagery, it becomes explicit in the Possible Intellect which receives it in its universality through the agency of the Active Intellect. It is not, however, the same as the concept. The latter is the completed thought of the object as actualized at the close of the intellectual process. The intelligible species is the intellectual starting point of the process and (though conceptual) is distinguished, as confused, from the finished concept, which is clear.

The union of the intelligible species with the Possible Intellect produces the concept. The word concept suggests the analogy of physical conception. The concept is the offspring in the mind of the union of the intelligible species and the Possible Intellect; a likeness of the intelligible object as the child is the likeness of the parent. It can also be thought of as the utterance of the thought of the object by the mind to itself, and as such is called the mental word (*verbum mentale*).

The whole process is explained in the following passage: "An external object which comes to be an object of our understanding does not thereby exist in our understanding in its own proper nature; but the species of it must be in our understanding, through which the latter becomes the understanding in act. The understanding, actualized and informed by the species, understands the thing in itself. The act of understanding is immanent in the mind and at the same time is in relation to the thing understood, inasmuch as the aforesaid impression, which is the starting point of the act of thought, is a likeness of the thing understood. Informed by the species of the thing, the understanding in act goes on to form in itself what we may call the concept of the thing. This concept is the idea of the thing and is denoted by the definition. . . . The understanding, however, has this advantage over the imagination, that it comprehends the thing apart from the individualizing conditions without which the thing does not exist in nature. This could not happen unless the understanding formed to itself the aforesaid concept.

"This concept in the understanding, being, we may say, the completed product of the intellectual activity, is different from the intelligible species which actualizes the understanding, and which must be considered the starting point of intellectual activity; yet, both the impression and the expression are likenesses of the thing in itself, which is the object of the understanding."[1]

Now that the psychology of the act of understanding has been explained, it is possible to return to the problem of man's knowledge of God. Aquinas denies that the human intellect in this present life can attain to a knowledge of the Divine Essence. We can know that God exists but not what He is. At the same time, St. Thomas is quite convinced that in addition to the assurance of revelation man can, by the exercise of reason, prove God's existence, and he severely criticizes those who think otherwise. The latter fall into two groups. In the first are those who accept the existence of God as an article of faith which is incapable of proof. Thus, Peter Damian and Manegold of Lauterbach in the 11th century, distrustful of human reason and the utility of philosophy, had insisted that the existence of God must be accepted as a matter of faith.

Aquinas allows a very generous field to the investigations of reason. Since reason and revelation have their ultimate source in

[1] *Contra Gent.*, I. c. 53.

God, it is unthinkable that the truths discovered by the former should contradict what is given by the latter. The highest truths of revelation, such as the doctrine of the Trinity, may be beyond the demonstration of reason, but the super-rational is not the irrational.[1]

In the view of St. Thomas, the 11th-century theologians made a very natural mistake. Whilst correctly affirming that God's Essence is identical with His existence, they erroneously concluded that because the former is beyond the reach of reason, the latter must also be incapable of proof. It is not necessary, however, in proving the existence of God to take His Essence as a premise. The only way open to man is to start from the effects of God's causality and argue to the existence of the cause.

The second group consists of those who believe that God's existence is so self-evident that it needs no formal proof. Aquinas, though he does not mention the name, is obviously thinking of Anselm's Ontological argument, and his criticism anticipates that of Kant, that it is not legitimate to argue from the idea of the Greatest Conceivable Being to His existence. He says, "Perchance, he who hears this name, God, does not understand it to mean something greater than which nothing can be conceived, for some thinkers have believed God to be a body. Granted, however, that anyone understands by the name God the meaning given above— *viz.*, something greater than which nothing can be conceived, it does not therefore follow that he understands what is signified by the name to exist *in rerum natura*, but in the apprehension of the intellect only. Neither can it be argued that it exists in fact, unless it be granted that there exists in fact a Being so great that we cannot conceive a greater, a position which those who deny the existence of God are unwilling to grant."[2]

Hence, Aquinas rejects the *a priori* form of proof in favour of the *a posteriori* and argues from the effects of God's causality to His existence. It might be objected that it is not a valid argument to pass from finite effects to a cause which is infinite and therefore disproportionate to them. Aquinas answers, "We cannot have perfect knowledge of the cause through effects which are not proportionate to it, yet from any effect it can be proved that a cause exists, and thus from the effects of God it can be proved that God

---

[1] See WICKSTEED, *op. cit.*, c. 4.
[2] *S. Th.*, I. q. ii. a. 1. ad. 2m.

exists, though we cannot through these effects know Him perfectly according to His Essence."[1]

The Thomistic proofs of God's existence are given in the *Summa Theologica* and the *Summa contra Gentiles*. Those in the former are arranged in a more concise and simplified form. The *Summa Theologica* was intended as a text-book for beginners, but the *Contra Gentiles*, written as a hand-book for the Christian missionary attempting the conversion of the Moslem, states and develops the proofs in greater detail and constantly appeals to the observations of sense.

The first proof (*S. Th.*, I. q. ii. a. 3) may be summarized thus. Sense experience shows us both that motion exists in the world and that every moving body is set in motion by another. Now, that which is moved is in potency with regard to that towards which it is moved, and the mover is only able to move in so far as it is in actuality. Thus fire, which is heat in act, makes wood, which is potentially hot, to become hot in actuality, and therefore moves or alters it.

It is impossible for a thing to be both in act and potency at the same time and in reference to the same thing—*e.g.*, if an object is actually hot, it cannot be actually, but only potentially cold. From this it follows that the same thing cannot be at the same time, and with reference to the same things, both mover and moved—*i.e.*, self-moved. Hence everything in motion must be moved by another. If the mover also is in motion, then it must have been set in motion by some other mover. We cannot, however, regress to infinity, for in that case there would be no first mover, nor, consequently, other movers, for the second mover imparts motion only because it has been set in motion by the first—*e.g.*, the stick moves only because the hand imparts motion to it. Therefore, we must grant a first mover which itself is unmoved, that is, not set in motion by any other mover. This First Mover is God.

To appreciate the force of this argument we must rid ourselves of the modern idea of motion being equivalent to locomotion. The latter is only a special case of motion. For St. Thomas, any actualization of a prior potentiality is a movement. Hence, movement is a generic term including not only motion in space, but alteration in quality and quantity and also generation

[1] *S. Th.*, I., q. ii. a. 2. c.

and destruction. In the *Contra Gentiles*, St. Thomas provides three arguments designed to prove that an infinite regress is impossible.

The second proof is based on the nature of efficient causality, and is again dependent on the belief in the impossibility of a regress to infinity. A similar proof had been advanced by Albert the Great and Avicenna, and St. Thomas follows the lines indicated by the latter. The argument begins with the premise that nothing in nature is self-caused, so that experience presents to us a causal series—*e.g.*, A is caused by B, B by C and so on. The series must either regress to infinity or a first cause must be granted. The former has been ruled out since, in a causal series, the first term is the cause of the middle term and the middle term the cause of the last. If the cause is removed, the effect disappears. Thus, if there is no first efficient cause, there can be no middle term nor a final effect, and this is obviously contrary to experience. Therefore we must assume God as the First Efficient Cause.

The third proof, which is absent from the *Contra Gentiles*, springs from the ideas of the possible and the necessary. Experience shows that the objects of nature have contingent being, for it is possible for them to be or not to be. If, however, all being were contingent, each one would be caused by another and we should have an infinite series of contingent beings. Such a regress is impossible, and therefore we must assume a Being existing necessarily, and this Being is God.

The fourth proof is based on the different grades of perfection existing in nature. Wherever a series manifesting varying grades of perfection exists there must be, as the upper limit, the completely perfect. We have such a series in nature so that the Most Perfect Being, God, must exist. In the *Contra Gentiles*, this argument is given as a third proof and varies in its form. St. Thomas remarks that Aristotle had shown in the *Metaphysics* that the objects which have the greatest degree of truth also possess the highest degree of being. He had declared also that there is a supreme degree of truth. Now, of two false statements, one always contains more of truth than the other. The terms, greater and lesser degree of truth, would have no meaning unless there exists a supreme and absolute truth against which they can be judged. Therefore, there exists something which is at once the supremely true and has the highest degree of being. This supreme Being is God.

The fifth proof of the *Summa Theologica* (the fourth of the *Contra Gentiles*) is based on the Divine Government of the world. In nature we see that all objects are ordered to some end (final causes), and therefore such a purpose running through the whole of nature demands a purposive intelligence directing all things to their appropriate ends. Such a Supreme Intelligence is God.

The Thomistic theory of knowledge showed quite clearly from the side of the knowing subject why it is impossible for man in this present life to attain to a knowledge of the Divine Essence. This is equally evident from the point of view of the object of knowledge. The Divine Nature is such that it is wholly beyond the grasp of any finite intelligence. Any positive predicate ascribed to God is entirely inadequate. He can only be described by the negative method (*via remotionis*). If we deny of God such qualities as materiality, finitude, evil and ignorance, we can arrive at a knowledge of what God is not. It is evident that such a method cannot supply a perfect knowledge of God. The Divine Nature is so immense, so unlike our experience, that we cannot ascribe to God the most fundamental notion we possess, that of being. God is indeed above and beyond all being.

The influence of Dionysius is apparent here and is acknowledged in the following passage. "Other terms (*nomina*) express determinate and particular being, as 'wise' expresses being of a certain sort. But this term 'Who is' expresses being absolute and undetermined by any addition. Thus St. John of Damascus says that it signifies not what God is, but an infinite ocean of substance being undetermined. Hence, when we advance to God by way of abstraction, we deny of Him, first, corporeal being, and after that intellectual things also in the manner in which they are found in creatures— *e.g.*, goodness and wisdom: so that there remains in our intellect only that He is, nothing more. Hence, He is as a kind of fusion. Finally, we remove from Him also this very being in the manner in which it is found among creatures, and then He remains in a certain darkness of our ignorance, through which ignorance we are, as pertains to our condition of life, most perfectly united with Him. As Dionysius says, this is a certain darkness in which God is said to dwell."[1]

Aquinas, however, guards himself against the dangers which threatened the teaching of Dionysius. The first chapter of this

[1] *In Sent.*, I. 8. sol. 1. a. 1 and 4.

book emphasized that the God of Dionysius in some ways approximated to the Absolute of modern thought, and tended to be an undetermined abstraction. The God of Aquinas is a personal God, an individual form. He appears to us as indeterminate because of the imperfections of our intellect which prevent us from seeing Him as He really is.

Dionysius had shown in the *Divine Names* that no title can be applied to God and a creature in the same sense—*i.e.*, univocally. Goodness in God is indeed different from goodness in creatures, but when we attribute goodness to God, there must surely be some meaning in the predication. As St. Thomas puts it: we are not making a statement that is a mere equivocation. His example of equivocation is the name *canis* applied both to a dog and a heavenly constellation (a modern example: the pen with which I write and the pen in which I keep my sheep). How far, then, are we justified in attributing to God qualities derived from our limited experience? This leads directly to the most difficult problem in Thomistic philosophy, the doctrine of Analogy.

St. Thomas believed that the attributes applied to the substance of God really indicate something which is true of the Divine Nature, though they describe it imperfectly. Such names express our intellectual grasp of God's nature. This is derived from creatures and, therefore, intelligence only knows God in so far as creatures mirror Him. No creature can mirror God as a Being of its own genus and species, but only as a superlative principle. The effect contains some likeness to its cause but it is always inferior to the cause.

Another difficulty arises: in trying to grasp God's nature, we are attempting to understand something which is absolutely simple and unique. We express our understanding of it by a number of judgments corresponding to the collection of ideas we have formed. This, however, does not indicate any diversity in the Divine Nature. The apparent distinctions are due to the imperfections of the human intellect.

Aquinas takes as his principle the teaching of Dionysius that inferior creatures imitate the activities and perfections of their superiors, as far as their nature will permit them. Thus, the created world endeavours, as far as is possible, to mirror the Creator. Since no single creature can express the likeness of God except in a most imperfect manner, what is impossible for the individual is approximated to by the multiplicity of things. The universe, through the multiplicity of parts, aims at representing the Divine Nature which is one and unique in its essence. In a similar way, the human intelligence gathers ideas from the effects of God's causality and tries to represent, by a collection of different statements, something that in its essence admits of no distinctions.

Although expressions which are used to denote the attributes of the Godhead are not true univocally of God and creatures, they are analogically true. The Thomistic doctrine of analogy is really an attempt to find a *via media* between agnosticism and pantheism. So far as we have described his theory of knowledge, St. Thomas appears to be heading for the former. He has denied to man direct knowledge of the being of God. The five proofs show only that God is, not what He is. The *via remotionis* does not take us much further. It allows us to see what God is not, but it is only by implication that it gives any positive assurance about the Divine Nature.

Analogy, however, does give us a positive knowledge about God. We argue from our experience of the world of finite existences to the knowledge of the infinite First Cause. As Fr. D'Arcy writes, "our knowledge provides us with a measuring rod even though some of the objects far surpass our range."[1]

What is the precise nature of the reasoning involved in this process? All Thomists are agreed that analogy leads us to a true though imperfect knowledge of God, but there are considerable differences about the form of the reasoning itself. The controversy is whether the analogy between God and creatures is one of proportion or attribution, or whether it is better stated as one of proportionality. Texts of St. Thomas can be quoted in support of either view. Cajetan and some modern Thomists accept proportionality while Suarez argues for proportion.

The statements of St. Thomas seem to conflict. Fr. D'Arcy suggests that Aquinas was feeling his way towards a final statement. On this theory, we should expect him to hold to the analogy of proportion in his earlier works and then, later, to adopt proportionality. This is precisely what St. Thomas does not do. He appeals in turn to proportion or proportionality, so that one can only admit that he has not given his attention to a definite theory of analogy but suits his terminology to the particular problem he

[1] D'ARCY, M. C., S. J., *Thomas Aquinas* (Ernest Benn: 1930 now published by O.U.P.), p. 131.

has in hand. The fullest analysis he gives is that in the *De Veritate*, where he chooses proportionality as the means of expressing the relation between God and creatures.

The terms "proportion" and "proportionality" themselves stand in need of explanation. The former is the continental way of expressing what in England we call a ratio. St. Thomas' proportionality is the same as our proportion—*e.g.*, 3 is to 6 as 5 is to 10, since 6 is twice 3 and 10 is twice 5. In the metaphysical sphere, an example of proportionality would be:

$$\frac{\text{created substance}}{\text{its being}} = \frac{\text{accident}}{\text{its being}}.$$

St. Thomas would seem to reject proportion for two reasons. In the first place, it implies that goodness in man is in a direct ratio to goodness in God—*i.e.*, that God's goodness is simply human goodness infinitely magnified. In general, it implies that any attribute applied to God and creatures is possessed by them to some degree in common. St. Thomas would vigorously deny this conclusion. You cannot have a relation which is a simple ratio when one term is finite and the other infinite. Secondly, if we predicate being of God and of man, and take the statement as expressing a ratio, we should mean that being primarily belongs to God (intrinsic) and is only accidental to men (extrinsic). This would at once open the door to pantheism which St. Thomas is as anxious to avoid as the opposite error of agnosticism.

To understand the points at issue, we must take the discussion further back. We predicate being both of God and man. By what right do we do this? What do we mean by being?

St. Thomas teaches that the idea of being is the first, the most fundamental and the most abstract notion that we possess. It results from the first contact of mind with reality. Such an idea is not clear and explicit. It is a confused idea which cannot be defined. A definition proceeds through genus and differences, but being is not a genus, not even the highest genus. Any differences to be found outside being are themselves being. It is an ultimate idea. Are we then to say that all being is one? In a sense, but in an analogous sense only. It is also a many. To assert that being is actually one, and that all differences of being are merely appearances, would lead to the position of Parmenides in ancient times or to pantheism in mediæval or modern times.

The Aristotelian categories should not be regarded as species of the genus being. They are the possible modes that being can take. In its ultimate meaning, being is an idea whose universality is absolutely unlimited and hence it cannot be a clear idea. In the categories, being has become contracted to narrower spheres, not by the addition of differences from without in the way that animality is contracted by rationality, but by a richer and fuller expression of the same idea.

Thus, we distinguish between Infinite Being, God, the finite being of created substance, and the being of an accident. It is true that being is not the same in substance and accident. Substance has being in itself, but accidental being is dependent on substantial being. The unity of being in substance and accident is expressed analogically as

$$\frac{\text{substance}}{\text{its being}} = \frac{\text{accident}}{\text{its being}}.$$

So far there is little difficulty because both substance and accident fall within the scope of human experience and are potentially, if not actually, determined in their limits. No further difficulty is caused by such an analogy as

$$\frac{\text{sensation}}{\text{sensible object}} = \frac{\text{thought}}{\text{intelligible object}}.$$

Neither analogate possesses determinate limits, but we have experience of both. In a similar way, the predication of being to God and man could be expressed as

$$\frac{\text{God}}{\text{His Being}} = \frac{\text{created object}}{\text{its being}}.$$

The objection might be raised that the left-hand side of this equation contains two unknowns, God and His Being, so that the analogy cannot lead to any knowledge of God.

The answer to the objection is that in reality there are not two unknowns in the equation. On the right-hand side, the terms are known directly through experience. On the left, God is known indirectly through the exercise of reason—*e.g.*, the five proofs. From these three terms, it is possible to infer the fourth.

Also, in created beings there is a composition of two moments, potentiality and actuality, in man, form and matter. In God there is no such composition; He is pure actuality. Now, in our experience, we conceive these perfections, being, knowledge, goodness etc., as realized to a higher degree, the more they are freed from potentiality. Hence, it is possible for us to have some meaning for such perfections as they exist in a Being Who is Pure Act. Thus in such equations as

$$\frac{\text{contingent being}}{\text{its being}} = \frac{\text{First Cause}}{\text{His Being}}$$

and

$$\frac{\text{material creature}}{\text{its intelligence}} = \frac{\text{First Immaterial Cause}}{\text{His Intelligence}}$$

the two terms representing finites are known directly through experience. The third term is known indirectly by way of causality, and from these we may infer the fourth term and come to know it also indirectly. Though we may not be able to understand it adequately, it still has a meaning for us.

By such analogical reasoning, we can infer the Divine Attributes and claim that every positive good in our experience belongs preeminently to God. Because each Divine Perfection is established by us through a separate act of inference, the Divine Attributes present themselves to us as distinct qualities. In God, however, they exist as one with each other and with His Being. No diversity exists in the Divine Nature, and God is none other than His goodness, wisdom, truth, justice and all His other attributes.

That knowledge which is denied to man on earth is the reward of the redeemed souls in heaven. The doctrine of St. Thomas on the Beatific Vision is bound up with his views concerning the supreme end of man. His conception of the latter is a combination of two points of view, the one Aristotelian, the other Christian and Platonic. In the *Nicomachean Ethics*, Aristotle had taught that happiness is the supreme good. All thinkers agree so far, but different people hold different opinions as to what constitutes happiness. Some believe it to be a life of sensual satisfaction; others the life of public activity the end of which is honour; while others, again, consider that happiness is to be found in the life of contemplation. Aristotle taught that the truly human life consists in the exercise of man's specifically human faculty, the life which is governed by reason. As the excellence of a harp player consists in playing the harp well, so the work of man will be an exercise of the soul in accord with excellence, or if excellence admits of degrees, in the way of the best and most perfect excellence in a complete life. He then showed that two kinds of excellence are required for the completely happy life. A man must be able to discover for himself the right rule of life, or at least recognize it when proposed by the teacher or lawgiver, and he must also be able to bring the lower appetites into subjection so that he obeys the rule. Hence the virtues may be divided into the intellectual and the moral virtues.

The highest kind of life of which man is capable is that which calls into play his highest faculties and is attended by the greatest and most perfect pleasures. This is the life of intellectual contemplation, and in the few brief moments of such experience as are possible to man he enters to some degree into that blessed life of self-contemplation which God ever enjoys.

When we compare this conception with that of the Christian Neo-Platonists, we become aware of a great difference. Dionysius, for example, constantly holds before us the possibility of an ecstatic experience transcending the life of reason and open to those who, by a holy and devout life, prayer, meditation, and contemplation, become assimilated to the Deity. To become Godlike is the highest end of the human spirit, and this goal is reached when the soul, leaving behind the things of sense and even of intellect, allows itself to be passively illuminated by the Divine Rays and become joined to its Creator in a glorious and ineffable union.

Aquinas takes both these conceptions and harmonizes them. Like Aristotle, he teaches that the life proper to man is a life in accordance with the exercise of his highest faculty, that of intelligence, and it is in the complete fruition of his intellectual desires that each individual will find his good. No created good can satisfy the soul of man, nor can he reach the state of perfect happiness through anything that this world can give. He writes, "It is impossible for the happiness of man to be in any created good. For happiness is perfect good, which entirely appeases desire: otherwise it would not be the last end, if still something remained to be desired. But the object of the will is universal good, as the object of the intellect is universal truth. Hence it is clear that nothing can set the will of man at rest but universal good, which is not found in anything created, but in God alone. Hence God alone can fill the heart of man."[1]

St. Thomas, unlike Duns Scotus, believes in the primacy of intellect over will, and therefore he teaches that happiness consists in an act of the understanding. The supreme end of man lies in the knowledge of God, the *Summum Bonum*. In the *Contra Gentiles*, chapters 37–40, he shows that happiness cannot consist in the knowledge of God gained through the effects of His causality, nor in that derived from demonstrations, nor even in that given to man through revelation and received by faith. The end of man is to know God in His Essence, and such is the completeness and perfection of this act of understanding and love that it merits the name of vision.

"The last and perfect happiness of man cannot be otherwise than in the vision of the Divine Essence. In evidence of this, two things must be considered. In the first place, man is not perfectly happy so long as there remains anything for him to desire and seek. Secondly, the perfection of every power is determined by the nature of its object. Now the object of the intellect is the essence of what is before it. Therefore, when a man knows an effect, and knows that it has a cause, there is in him an outstanding natural desire of knowing the essence of the cause. If, therefore, a human intellect knows the essence of a created effect without knowing anything of God, beyond the fact of His existence, the perfection of that intellect does not yet adequately reach the First Cause, but the intellect has an outstanding desire of searching into that Cause; hence it is not yet perfectly happy. For perfect happiness, therefore, it is necessary that the intellect shall reach as far as the very essence of the First Cause."[2]

The Thomistic theory of knowledge, however, excludes the possibility of such an intellectual vision for man in this present

[1] *S. Th.*, I. IIae. q. ii. a. 8. c.   [2] *ibid.*, q. iii. a. 8. c.

life. On this account, some have looked upon St. Thomas as a determined foe of mysticism. This is quite untrue. He holds most firmly that, as man is naturally constituted, he is unable by his own powers to see God, whether in this world or hereafter. What is, however, impossible for man by nature is possible by grace. How far, we may ask, is it possible for human beings aided by the grace of God to see the Divine Essence in this life? Aquinas considers it possible, but he is so jealous of the mystical treasure of the Church that he will only acknowledge two authenticated cases, those of Moses and St. Paul. He pays great attention to these instances, especially to the latter.

He states that it is impossible for anyone in this life while tied to sensible objects and perceptions to see the Divine Essence. It can only be realized through the miraculous state of rapture. The term "rapture" indicates, in its etymology, some kind of violent psychical upheaval by which the human soul is snatched from cognizance of sensible things and elevated to the supernatural through supernatural influence. It suggests a violent interference with the ordinary course of things. It is possible only when the soul is withdrawn from the body and from preoccupation with the sensible world and is open to impressions from the spiritual world.

Now there are three cases where the soul seems to be most removed from the body: in pathological cases, in demoniac possession, and lastly, when man comes under Divine Influence. The latter instance is rapture, and we say that a man is in this state when he is raised by the Divine Spirit to supernatural things and is alienated from all sensible impressions. It is important to grasp that the essence of rapture lies not so much in the exclusion of the sensible world which is its occasion, as in its being an experience which is not natural to man. There are degrees of rapture, the highest of which consists in the vision of the Divine Essence. "And such was the rapture of Paul and also of Moses, and this is meet, since Moses was the first teacher of the Jews and Paul of the Gentiles."[1]

The Scriptures tell us that St. Paul was caught up to the third heaven. Aquinas interprets this as meaning that the Divine Vision was vouchsafed to him in the same manner as the angels of the highest hierarchy see and enjoy God. During this state, he was

[1] *S. Th.*, I. IIae. q. clxxv. a. 3. c.

entirely alienated from sensible things, and such was the glory of the vision that the experience was beyond all thought and all expression in words.

St. Thomas, then, believed in the mystic's vision, but he held that we have only two instances in which we know for certain that it has occurred. All other mystic visions were on a lower plane. The prophets did not see God in His Essence but perceived some vision or appearance through which His will was manifested (*lumen propheticum*).

According to his biographers, St. Thomas was himself a mystic. "Hardly a day passed," we are told, "but that he was rapt out of his senses." Perhaps the most significant incident of his life, in this respect, is the well-known story related by his friend and companion, Brother Reginald. About two years before his death, while celebrating Mass in the Church of St. Nicholas at Naples, he fell into a trance, from which he was, some time later, awakened by Reginald. Then, turning to his friend, he said, "Reginald, my son, I am going to reveal to thee in secrecy what I prohibit thee to reveal to anyone during my life. An end has come to my writing, for such things have been shown unto me, that they make all that I have written and taught seem small. Now I await the closing of my life after that of my writing." He immediately put aside his writing materials, although the *Summa Theologica* was still unfinished, and wrote nothing more during the remaining months of his life. The truth is that St. Thomas, in spite of his intellectualism, was one of the greatest sources of inspiration for mediæval mysticism—*e.g.*, Dante and the German Dominicans.

The analogy of light in vision will help us to understand how the redeemed soul can see God. In seeing a material object, such as a tree, the medium which makes the tree visible (*medium sub quo*) is the light of the sun. The *medium quo*, the means by which we see the tree, is the sensible species of tree. Carrying over the analogy to intellectual knowledge, we find that the *medium quo*, by which thought is possible, is the mental image derived from sensible impressions. By its twofold operation of illumination and abstraction, the Active Intellect, the *medium sub quo*, renders conceptual thought possible. There is, however, a difference of object in the two kinds of knowledge. In visual perception, the object of sight is a material thing existing in nature. But in intellectual vision, the object of the intellect is a universal form grasped in abstraction from the particulars in which it is manifested. By its own natural powers, the human intellect can know God only through the effects of His causality, or, as Aquinas says, it can see God as though seeing an object reflected in a mirror. This incapacity of the human intellect is one of the results of the Fall, and man in his state of innocence, while he did not see God directly, had a more perfect knowledge of Him than is possible for us.

The redeemed souls are to see God face to face, but this is not possible in the feeble rays of Active Intellect. The light of the Divine Vision is so intense that the eyes of the soul would be blinded, just as the eyes of bats are unable to see in the full glare of the sun. Dionysius had taught that for union with God we must in some way become assimilated to Him. Aquinas teaches the same. To see God we must become like God, and this is brought about by the light of glory (*lumen gloriae*). "I answer that everything which is elevated to something which is above its nature needs to be disposed by some disposition which is above its nature. Thus, if air is to receive the form of fire, it must be disposed in some way to such a form. Whence, if any created intellect sees God through His Essence, that very Essence becomes the intelligible form of the intellect. Some supernatural disposition must therefore be added so as to raise it to so sublime a height. Since the natural powers of a created intellect do not suffice for seeing the Essence of God, as we have already shown, a power of understanding must be granted to it by Divine Grace, and this augmentation of the intellectual power we call the illumination of the intellect, and the intelligible itself is called light or brightness. And this is the light concerning which it is said in Revelations xxi. 23, 'for the glory of God did lighten it,' namely, the throng of the blessed who see God. And by this light they are made like to God (*deiformes*), as is said in 1 John iii. 2."[1]

The *lumen gloriae* is the light under which the blessed see God. But a further question arises. In the case of sensible vision, the tree was seen by reason of the presence of the visible species in the soul. Again, in intellectual knowledge, the intelligible species was necessary for understanding. Is there any equivalent species needed for the Vision of God? Do we see by means of the infused species by which angels and glorified souls intuit intelligibles?

[1] *S. Th.*, I. q. xii. a. 5. c.

Aquinas replies that no species can be adequate to the Vision of God. If we are to see Him, we must see Him directly without the intervention of any species. "In His light we shall see the light." Although the soul cannot directly approach God, yet God can enter the soul and inform it. Man is capable, when aided by Divine Grace, of the Vision of God. He is *capax Dei per gratiam.* Hence he says, "But since it is impossible for a natural desire to be frustrated, which would be the case if it were not possible to attain to a knowledge of the Divine Substance, since all minds naturally desire it, we must say that it is possible for the substance of God to be seen by the intellect and by the separate intellectual substances. . . . Yet we have shown that the Divine Substance cannot be seen by the intellect through any created species. Wherefore, if the Essence of God is to be seen, the intellect must see It through the Divine Essence Itself. So, in this vision, the Divine Essence is both that which is seen, and that by which It is seen."[1]

Again, "It is impossible for any created intellect through its own nature to see the Essence of God. Knowledge takes place according as the object known is in the knower according to the latter's mode of knowing. Whence the knowledge of any knowing subject is in proportion to the mode of his nature. If, therefore, the mode of being of any object known is more excellent than the mode of nature of the knower, the knowledge of that object must be above the nature of the knower. . . . It remains, accordingly, that knowledge of very Being Itself is connatural to the Divine Intellect alone and is above the natural power of any created intellect, since no creature is its own being but has participated being. A created intellect, then, cannot see God in His Essence except in so far as God through His Grace joins Himself to the created intellect, so that He is understood through Himself."[2]

Such is the supreme end of man: to know and see God in His Essence in his one true home (*in patria*), and, seeing Him, to see all things in Him as effects in their Cause. The doctrine of St. Thomas concerning the Beatific Vision cannot be more beautifully epitomized than in the sublime words of the great Italian poet and mystic:

"Oh grace abounding, wherein I presumed to fix my look on the eternal light so long that I consumed my sight thereon! Within its depths I saw ingathered, bound by love in one volume, the

[1] *Contra Gent.*, III. c. 51.   [2] *S. Th.* I. q. xii. a. 4. c.

scattered leaves of all the universe; substance and accidents and their relations, as though together fused, after such fashion that what I talk of is one simple flame. . . . Thus all suspended did my mind gaze fixed, immovable, intent, ever enkindled by its gazing.

"Such at that light, doth man become, that to turn to any other sight could not by possibility be ever yielded. For the good, which is the object of the will, is therein wholly gathered, and outside it that same thing is defective which therein is perfect."[1]

[1] DANTE, *Paradiso*, XXXIII. 85–105.

GOD	Pure Actuality without any mixture of Potentiality. Essence and Existence identical.	Knows all things in Himself and by His knowledge is the Cause of all being.
SEPARATE INTELLECTUAL SUBSTANCES (ANGELS)	**Pure Forms** without any mixture of matter. **Intuitive** grasp of universals. Finite beings in whom is distinction between Essence and Existence. ANGELIC HIERARCHIES 1st. Hier. **Seraphim** **Cherubim** **Thrones** 2nd Hier. **Dominions** **Virtues** **Powers** 3rd Hier. **Principalities** **Archangels** **Angels**	Know by means of infused intelligible species. FORM individuates; hence each angel a separate species.
HUMAN BEINGS	Capable of knowing universals abstracted from sense imagery by **Active Intellect.** Human soul is united to a material body as its form, but is a **Self Subsistent Spiritual Substance. Possible Intellect** in potentiality to intelligibles; hence, human reason is **Discursive.**	Intellect does not use a corporeal organ but depends upon data furnished by sense-experience. Powers of plant and animal souls implicit in rational soul.

ANIMALS	Sensitive soul having powers of sense-perception and, in higher animals, locomotion, appetition and memory. Functions arranged in Hierarchical Order.
	   Memory
	   Vis Æstimativa
	   Sense Imagery
	   Common Sense
	Special { **Vision, Hearing, Smell,**
	Senses { **Taste, Touch**
		Powers exercised through corporeal organs. Knowledge of individual sense objects. Sense receives form of objects without their matter.

PLANTS	Vegetative soul displaying powers of:
	   Generation
	   Growth
	   Nutrition
		Not capable of knowledge. Do not possess differentiated organs. Receive matter as well as form in nutrition.

OBJECTS OF INORGANIC NATURE	**Mixed Bodies** possess some activities over and above those due to active and passive qualities—*e.g.*, attractive force of magnet stone. **Elementary Bodies** display no activities beyond those due to active and passive qualities of matter.	Composites of matter and form. Individuated by *materia signata*.
FIRST MATTER	The potentiality of all things and the actuality of none. Can neither be known nor defined. First form received is that of quantity giving extension in three dimensions.	

CHAPTER XI

THE MORAL AND POLITICAL PHILOSOPHY
OF ST. THOMAS AQUINAS

THE framework of the moral theory of St. Thomas is Aristotelian, but this basis underwent a subtle transformation through two important influences that affected the ethical and political outlook of the Middle Ages. The first of these was Christianity, and its effect on mediæval moral and political philosophy has been amply acknowledged by most historians. The second influence sprang from the barbarian invaders of the Empire, especially the Teutonic races in the West, and strangely enough seems to have been overlooked in many accounts of the development of mediæval moral, legal and political thought. This influence was almost entirely one of custom, belief and tradition, but, nevertheless, it had important results and was responsible for the particular bias towards what we should now term democratic ideals, from John of Salisbury to the conclusion of the Middle Ages. It may be held that the views of Hobbes, Locke and other 17th-century thinkers are not altogether a product of their age but have a quite definite link with the Middle Ages. As Lord Acton once remarked, the first Whig was Aquinas.

Amongst the few who have emphasized the Teutonic influence was Professor W. G. de Burgh, who wrote, "The mediæval view of life, like the order of society from which it sprang, was the product of three factors, which came into fusion in Western Europe in the centuries following the break-up of the Roman Empire. There was the stream of Germanic and Scandinavian immigrants, who founded lordships and kingdoms in Britain, Gaul, Spain, and Italy between the fifth and eleventh centuries. Though these peoples brought with them no inheritance of learning or reflective thought, they had evolved a type of custom and belief, an unconscious 'way of life,' which left an enduring impress on the ideas of the Middle Ages. The convictions that monarchy was the rightful form of human government, and that law or right (*recht*) was not derived from, but superior to, the state, whose function was to realize and maintain law, were deeply rooted in the Germanic and Scandinavian mind; and found expression, at a later day, among the cardinal principles of political and legal theory. Above all, these races leavened mediæval thought with their strong sense of the worth of individual liberty. In this point their view of life harmonized with the teaching of Christianity, which had insisted on personal responsibility, and on the infinite value of the individual in the sight of God."[1]

One of the most important contributions to the study of ethics which was made by Aquinas was his careful and systematic analysis of the human act. From the preceding chapter, we saw that the object of the intellect is being and universal truth, but the nature of man as intermediate between the animal creation and the separate intelligences renders it impossible for his intellect to achieve its object, as does the angelic intellect, in one single act of intuition. The human intellect attains truth through the laborious path of learning and by many repeated acts of reasoning.

So, too, the human will stands in contrast to the angelic. The angels, from the moment of their creation, made an irrevocable choice between good and evil, and by a single act of free will either inclined towards God or turned away from Him for all eternity. With man, the situation is entirely different. "Our whole ethical outlook is to be determined by the fact . . . that man is intermediate between non-intelligent matter on the one hand, and the angels, who are pure incorporeal intelligences on the other. His perfection, therefore, must lie . . . in an operation akin to, yet wholly distinct from, the characteristic operations either of brutes or angels. He must not content himself with the life of a brute, but neither must he attempt to be an angel. In either case he will miss his own vocation, which is to be a man—a being composed of soul and body—neither more nor less."[2]

The nature of the human will inclines it to universal good, but in practice it is always concerned with particular goods. The latter are not able to satisfy the will and therefore do not determine

[1] DE BURGH, W. G., *The Legacy of the Ancient World* (Macdonald and Evans: 1924), pp. 364–5.
[2] KIRK, K., *The Vision of God* (Longmans, Green: new impression, 1946), p. 381.

it—*i.e.*, the will remains free to choose or reject them. "In the order of conduct, because man is neither mind nor body, but one being composed of both, he conceives the good in the vague and has to grow in knowledge of it and in virtue by the help of concrete choices in which the good is determined by specific ends and individual circumstances."[1] In contrast with the angel, the human will is not bound by a single choice of good or ill. Just as human knowledge is built up gradually from separate acts of thinking and judging, so morality is a growth and the virtues and vices are primarily habits formed through the constant repetition of single acts of a certain type.

Man differs also from the brutes, because, acting through reason and free will, he has lordship of his acts and chooses to do what he does. Every human act, properly so called, is a voluntary act. In so far as force, or fear, or ignorance enters into the act, it is made less voluntary. St. Thomas discusses at great length the degree to which fear or ignorance of various kinds reduce the voluntary nature of the action. Actions of a reflex or involuntary character are not human acts, though because they are carried out by the individual they may be called acts of the man. Moral action is concerned with the voluntary, but although the will may seem to be primarily involved, the intellect plays such a prominent part that St. Thomas, unlike Duns Scotus, assigns the primacy to the latter.

Aquinas distinguishes between the psychological, subjective aspect of an action, the order of intention as he calls it, and the practical and objective, the order of execution. Thus, although every voluntary action is performed in order to attain an end or a good, the latter is the last in the order of execution though the first in the agent's intention. Moral action is very complex and consists of a sequence of movements which concern both the intellect and the will. The first step is taken by the intellect, for although there can be no human act apart from the will, volition can be exercised only with regard to an end which has previously been presented to the intelligence. "If an object is proposed to us which is universally good in every point of view, our will necessarily tends to that, if we will at all, for we cannot will the opposite of it. Such a good is happiness. But if some special good

[1] D'ARCY, M. C., S.J., *Thomas Aquinas* (Ernest Benn: 1930; now published by O.U.P.), p. 231.

be presented to us which is good only from certain points of view, we do not necessarily will it. Being deficient, it may be regarded as not good, our attention being drawn to that deficiency. So the object may be rejected or approved by the will, since we may view the same thing in different lights."[1] In the former case, no further action follows, but if the end or good is approved by the will, desire is aroused, and the intellect may judge that the end is one worth seeking. As a consequence, if he judges the end is possible of attainment, the individual decides that he will pursue it. So far the sequence has been concerned with the end.

Once the individual has willed the attainment of the end, he makes use of his cognitive powers to find suitable means for carrying out his desire. Certain means may be rejected as not being practicable or not leading in the most direct way to the desired end. Those deemed to be effective are chosen, and the next step is for the will to assent to the employment of the means. There may be considerable delay before the final consent of the will is obtained, since the consideration of the means may be a very complicated process of deliberation involving much detailed planning—e.g., the case of a person deciding upon the career he wishes to follow. If the object is not eagerly desired, the process of deliberation may not issue in definite choice and the start of the action and may remain at the level of desire only. The whole of the sequence thus far belongs to the order of intention.

Now we come to the order of execution. As a result of deliberation, the agent makes up his mind to employ the means. He follows up his decision by putting into effect the action or series of actions he had chosen. If the action is successful and the end is achieved, the sequence is brought to a close and the individual experiences the feeling of joy and contentment at having satisfied his desire (*fruitio*). The stages in a complete act are shown in diagrammatic form on the opposite page.

This analysis leads to the problem of the goodness or badness which attaches to human actions. St. Thomas believes that the morality of an act is determined by the three factors of the end towards which the act is directed, the means adopted to attain that end, and the circumstances connected with the choice of the means. If end, means and circumstances are all good or all evil, the problem does not exist.

[1] *S. Th.*, I. IIae . q. x. a. 2. c.

ANALYSIS OF THE HUMAN ACT ACCORDING TO ST. THOMAS AQUINAS

COGNITIVE	VOLITIONAL

I. Order of Intention as related to the end.

1. Intellectual or sensual presentation of the end.	2. Natural inclination to the object presented.
3. Intellectual judgment that the end is worthwhile.	4. Desire to attain the object.

II. Order of Intention as related to the means.

5. Search for the means of attainment (*consilium*).	6. Approval of the means (*consensus*).
7. Choice of means best adapted to the end.	8. Actual choice of means (*electio*).

III. Order of Execution.

9. Act of will deciding to employ the means to the end.	10. The calling forth of the agent's powers for action.
11. Performance of the Act.	12. Content, pleasure, joy in successful accomplishment (*fruitio*).

Many actions, however, are more complex, so that St. Thomas remarks that "an action may have one element of goodness and be wanting in another. In this way an action that is good in its species, or in its circumstances, may be directed to an evil end, and vice versa. Still it is not simply a good action, unless it combines all the elements of good."[1]

To solve this problem, St. Thomas introduces the distinction between the formal and the material elements of an action. The latter refers to the overt action, the former to the end which the agent intends. The overt action may not be what the agent wills— *e.g.*, the man shooting at the target may be jogged by a comrade so that his aim goes wide and he kills another human being. Such an action would be involuntary and the person would not be judged guilty if he had taken all due precautions. Therefore, in judging an action, regard must first be given to the end the agent desires and wills. As Aristotle said, the person who steals to commit adultery is even more an adulterer than a thief. Abelard,

[1] *S. Th.*, I. IIae. q. xviii. a. 4. ad 3m.

as we previously saw, was inclined to judge the action solely by the intention of the agent. Not so St. Thomas, who saw the danger in the maxim that the end justifies the means. This would be true if only the end had to be taken into account, but the agent, when he wills the end, also chooses the means. In fact, as the means constitute the first step to be taken, they are willed more immediately than the end.

Moreover, the circumstances of the action have to be taken into consideration. "The fulness of the perfection of an action lies not wholly in its species, but some additional perfection is conferred in the way of accidents, or due circumstances. Hence, if anything be wanting that is requisite in point of due circumstances, the action will be evil."[1] St. Thomas foresaw the danger in selecting any one element of the action as a basis for our moral judgment. The latter is neither on the inward act of will, nor the exterior action, neither on intention, nor means nor circumstances. The moral judgment is concerned with the whole action; what is judged is the man doing the action. Hence, an act may be materially good but formally evil and vice versa. It is when the formal element, the intention of the agent, is wrong, that the act becomes a sin. "There may be a culpable perversion of the intellect, so that the man is the author of his own obliquity or defect of vision. When Saul persecuted the Christians, he probably sinned materially, not formally. When Caiaphas spoke the truth without knowing it, he said well materially, but ill formally."[2]

Earlier moral teaching had concentrated on the external action, and Abelard had shown the weakness of this practice by throwing into emphasis the intention of the agent. Like many reformers, he had exaggerated his point of view, but St. Thomas combines the old and the new by insisting upon the distinction between the intention, the internal act of will and the overt action.

In his account of moral virtue, St. Thomas follows Aristotle closely, but his Christian upbringing shows itself in one important deviation. To the Aristotelian classification of intellectual and moral virtues, he adds a third species: theological virtues. A virtue is a habit of doing the right thing, just as a vice consists in habitual wrongdoing. Since man is a body-soul, there will be habits of right

[1] *S. Th.*, I. IIae, q, xviii. a. 3. c.
[2] RICKABY, J., S.J., *Moral Philosophy* (Longmans, Green: 4th edition, 1923), p. 34.

action corresponding to each side of his composite nature. The error of Socrates was that he took cognizance only of the intellectual virtues and so concluded that virtue can be equated with knowledge and vice with ignorance. Something more than intellectual habits is required to produce a perfect character. "It is not enough for man merely to think, he must also live and act rightly; and to act rightly he needs to take count not only of what he has to do, but also of the manner of doing it. It is not enough just to take a decision; what matters is, to take a decision reasonably, not by blind impulse or passion. . . . It follows that an intellectual virtue must exist which enables reason to arrive at a suitable determination of means leading to the end in view; this virtue is prudence, *recta ratio agibilium*; and this is a virtue necessary for living rightly."[1]

Hence prudence, although a virtue of the rational side of man, is yet a moral virtue. "Prudence in its exercise is an intellectual virtue: but in its subject-matter it falls in with the moral virtues, being a right method of conduct; and in this respect it is counted among the moral virtues."[2] An indispensable factor in the moral life is the habit of bringing the appetites under the control of reason. Hence the necessity, as a prelude to the good life, of such moral virtues as temperance, courage, and justice.

The intellectual and moral virtues are sufficient for the natural principles of human action, but the Christian faith teaches that man's supreme end consists in something that is not proportionate to human nature, "a certain participation in the Deity." To achieve this, God adds to the natural virtues certain principles to enable man to attain his last end. These are the theological virtues of faith, hope, and charity, so called because God is their object and our knowledge of them comes from the Divine Revelation contained in the Scriptures.

It has frequently been asserted that Aristotle left no room in his ethical thought for the ideas of conscience and duty. The teaching of St. Thomas is not defective in these respects, and it is a natural corollary of his conception of law. The latter evolved from the fusion of four distinct streams, the philosophy of Aristotle, the traditional doctrines of the Church, the *Digest of Roman Law* made by Justinian, and the ideas handed on by the Teutonic invaders of the Empire. Aquinas defines law as a rule which either enjoins

[1] GILSON, ETIENNE, *The Philosophy of St. Thomas Aquinas* (Heffer: 1929), p. 322.
[2] *S. Th.*, I. IIae. q. lviii. a. 3. ad lm.

or forbids an action. The ultimate source of law is the *Lex Aeterna*, the law by which God wills the universe to be governed and which is none other than God Himself. "This Eternal Law is the timeless judgment of the Divine Reason, made binding by the Divine Will, known as it is by the blessed in paradise, and by us, through the reflections which flow from it."[1]

The reflections of the *Lex Aeterna* are the Divine Law (*lex divina*) made known to man through the Scriptures, and natural law (*lex naturalis*). The former is subdivided into the old law (*lex vetus*), and the new law (*lex nova*) according to whether its authority is derived from the Old or the New Testaments. The Eternal Law is binding upon all creatures and includes, besides the principles of morality, what we should now call laws of nature or scientific laws. Man is duty bound to know the Eternal Law and to obey it, but since he cannot know the commands of God by a direct vision of the Divine Nature, the Eternal Law is imprinted upon his soul, and is known as natural law, "the participation of the rational creature in the Eternal Law."

Human Law, in so far as it is just, is a derivation from natural law, which is above prince and state. The Greek moralists had conceived human law as being derived from the state, but Aquinas, influenced by the Teutonic tradition, emphatically declares that the state receives its authority from the law, and its duty is to secure the reign of law. In what way is natural law known to man?

To understand the answer to the above question, it is necessary to consider what St. Thomas means by the two terms "synderesis" and "conscience." In speaking of the intellectual powers of the human being, he informs us that just as reasoning has to make a start from certain axioms or self-evident principles, so too nature has bestowed upon us a number of practical principles which are also axiomatic. The following passages make his meaning clear:

"From the very nature of an intellectual soul it is proper to man that, as soon as he knows what a whole is and what a part is, he knows that every whole is greater than its part."[2]

In a similar way as regards practical reason, "The primary precepts of the law of nature stand to the practical reason as the first principles of scientific demonstrations do to the speculative reason: for both sets of principles are self-evident."[3]

[1] DE BURGH., *op. cit.*, p. 387.   [3] *ibid.*, q. xciv. a. 2. c.
[2] *S. Th.*, I. IIae. q. li. a. 1. c.

Synderesis is not a power but a habit of mind which is concerned with the primary moral principles of natural law. "Now it is clear that, as the speculative reason argues about speculative things, so the practical reason argues about practical things. Therefore we must have, bestowed upon us by nature, not only speculative principles; but also practical principles. Now the first practical principles bestowed on us by nature do not belong to a special power, but to a special habit . . . which we call synderesis."[1]

Synderesis must not be confused with conscience, which is the act whereby the principles of the natural law are applied by the individual to his own acts which he judges to be right or wrong. It is a practical judgment of the understanding which can be compared to the intellectual judgment that is the conclusion of a syllogism. Since conscience is a judgment, it is not infallible. Error may creep into it in various ways. The individual may be mistaken about the principles he applies; he may wrongly apply them to the particular circumstances, or he may misjudge his own motives and the circumstances in which the action is to be carried out. But conscience, however erroneous, is binding on a man. It is his only guide and he is obliged to follow it. Otherwise he would be acting immorally. Nevertheless, it may be his own fault that his conscience is erroneous. It may be blinded through wilful ignorance and carelessness or rendered less clear through constantly acting in an immoral fashion. Conscience, like every other activity, is capable of being educated, and the individual is at fault if he neglects its education.

The source of moral obligation or duty is to be found in the Eternal Law and its reflection in the minds of men, the natural law. The Eternal Law is not the arbitrary will of God, as Scotus was to suggest later. God is very reason, and He created man in His own image bestowing upon him a rational nature. He wills though He does not constrain that man should follow his rational nature. The moral law is part of this nature; it is therefore man's duty to obey it. If through the abuse of his free will the individual disobeys the command of the moral law, he is not only at fault intellectually, but he has, as it were, contracted out of God's intention for him; he has acted contrary to reason, and this is disobedience to the will of God and is called sin by the theologian.

The consideration of law leads naturally to St. Thomas' political

---

[1] *S. Th.*, IIae. q. lxxix., a. 12. c.

theory. There are three important sources for his views on the state. The first is his commentary on the *Politics* of Aristotle. Only half of this is the work of Aquinas; the latter part, according to Ptolemy of Lucca, was written by Peter of Spain. The continuity in style and method shows that the writer may possibly have had access to notes of St. Thomas or, at any rate, was one of his disciples.

Besides the commentary, St. Thomas was part author of a treatise called the *Rule of Princes* (*De regimine principum*), which had as its principal aim the instruction of a young prince in the theory of the state and the art of government. The particular prince for whom the book was intended is supposed to be Hugh III of Cyprus. The treatise consists of four books, and the work of St. Thomas breaks off suddenly in the middle of the second. The remainder of the treatise was written by Ptolemy of Lucca. The *Rule of Princes* was written about 1267. We know that Hugh died suddenly towards the end of that year, and this probably explains the cessation of St. Thomas' work.

The third authority is a section of the first division of the second part of the *Summa Theologica* (qq. xc to cviii), which deals with the theory of law. In addition to these sources, there are a few scattered references to the state, the powers of the ruler and the nature of law in other of his works.

For St. Thomas, the state takes its rise from human nature. It is not an artificial creation as was afterwards taught by Hobbes. Man is not intended to live alone. Aristotle had described him as "a social animal," but St. Thomas takes a further step and adds, "political animal." Man does not live with his fellows indiscriminately. He is a member of a number of social groups, family, clan, tribe or nation.

Society, like every natural organism, has its own proper end, and in order to attain it society must be organized and directed to that end. That which creates and maintains the organization and directs it towards its goal is termed by St. Thomas authority or power (*potestas*). Authority is vested in the government of the state. Government is necessary for co-ordinating particular interests for the good of the community. Hence, the principal concern of the governing body must be the common good. Each individual is responsible for his own behaviour and is free to live his own life according to his wishes, provided that his conduct is not contrary to the good of the community. The state, therefore, exists for the good of the people as a whole and on them rests the obligation of obedience.

St. Thomas teaches that the ultimate source of all authority is God, but in the sphere of government, as elsewhere, He works through secondary causes. He does not exercise His authority directly but through men. Although government in itself is divinely instituted, this does not apply to the rulers as individuals. St. Thomas never entertains the theory of the Divine Right of Kings as asserted by the Stuarts in the 17th century. Thus he tells us, "In its true sense, law has the public good as its primary and chief objective. But to legislate for the public good belongs by right to the people as a whole or to those who represent the people. Hence, to make a law is the right of the people as a whole or of the public personage into whose charge the welfare of the people is entrusted, since in all things to order means in relation to an end is the business of those whom the end concerns."[1]

Not only have the people the right of choosing their ruler, but he can be removed from office by the popular will if he abuses his power. St. Thomas teaches, "if it is the right of the people to choose the sovereign, they can without injustice remove the sovereign they have established or fix limitations to his power, if he abuses the royal power in a tyrannical manner. The people must not be considered as acting disloyally in so deposing a tyrant ... for he himself deserves this fate because he has not faithfully conducted the government of the nation according to his vocation as a ruler."[2]

We must not misunderstand St. Thomas here. He repudiates the view that individual patriots are justified in rebelling against or assassinating the tyrant. He declares, "It is more seemly to proceed to the overthrow of tyrants not according to personal presumption on the part of any one man, but on the public authority."[3]

Whence comes the right of the people to depose the tyrant? St. Thomas repeats that the object of government is to secure the good of the community. "The kingdom does not exist for the sovereign, but the sovereign for the sake of the kingdom." All government, in his view, rests implicitly upon a contract. In a state where the political sense of the people is sufficiently far advanced and the

---

[1] *S. Th.*, I. IIae. q. xc. a. 3.   [2] *De Reg. Princ.*, I. c. 6.   [3] *ibid.*

popular will educated, the circumstances of the pact may be more or less recognized. But in every state there is always the implicit understanding that the authority of the monarch depends upon a kind of contract. The sovereign, by the very fact that he assumes the government of the state, contracts to seek in all his acts the good of the community. If the sovereign breaks his part of the contract, the people remain free to break theirs.[1]

St. Thomas now proceeds to consider the different types of government with a view to discovering the kind of constitution best fitted for the state. He enters upon this task entirely free from bias or prejudice. He is firmly convinced that, wherever possible, the people should participate in the government of the state, but there are two dangers which his experience of actual 13th-century rule teaches him to avoid. He is determined at all costs to avoid a tyranny, or, what perhaps is worse, a state of anarchy. With these exceptions, he believes that different varieties of constitution are justifiable. The method of attaining the common good varies according to the circumstances. In some cases the political sense of the people may be sufficiently educated to enable them to see clearly what is necessary for the common good, and their experience in government may be such that they are able to devise means to secure it. In other cases, the people are unable to govern themselves but can approve measures taken by the government without themselves taking an active part in legislation. How far the people may be permitted to govern themselves depends upon their aptitude for the task. St. Thomas considers that it is extremely dangerous to assume that in every case a people is capable of

---

[1] The most explicit statement of the Social Contract theory in the Middle Ages was given by Manegold of Lautenbach. "King is not a name of nature but a title of office: nor does the people exalt him so high above itself in order to give him the free power of playing the tyrant against it, but to defend him from the tyranny of others. So soon as he begins to act the tyrant, is it not plain that he falls from the dignity granted to him and the people is free from his dominion? since it is evident that he has first broken that contract by virtue of which he was appointed. If one should engage a man for a fair wage to tend swine, and he find means not to tend but to steal or slay them, would not one remove him from his charge? . . . Since no one can create himself emperor or king, the people elevates a certain one person over itself to this end that he govern and rule it according to the principle of righteous government; but if in any wise he transgresses the contract by virtue of which he is chosen, he absolves the people from the obligation of submission, because he has first broken faith with it."—Quoted by R. L. Poole in *Illustrations of the History of Medieval Thought and Learning* (S.P.C.K.: 1920), p. 203.

Marsiglio of Padua (1270–1343) and John of Jandun, the joint authors of the *Defensor Pacis*, express the same type of theory, and in their desire to limit the power of the monarch they insisted that he should always be an elected ruler.

participation in the government or even of electing their ruler. The exercise of political power by a populace which is not ripe for it, in his opinion, exposes the state to perils as grave as those of government by an irresponsible monarch.

In theory, there is no doubt about the best form of government. The primary need of every state is unity, and this is best secured when the power is in the hands of one man. If a perfect monarch could be found, such a form of government would be ideal. But like Aristotle, he is impressed by the fact that the perfect man never turns up. The choice of such a ruler presupposes that he remains perfect and that the people who choose him possess infallible judgment. If that is so, why should they not take over control and realise a democratic republic rather than a monarchy? No, in practice an absolute monarch is always a potential danger. He can so easily become a despot. Hence the people must have safeguards against an undue extension of the monarch's power (*providendum de rege*). Although, in special cases, St. Thomas would choose an hereditary monarch, on the whole he prefers an elected one since every election gives the opportunity for the people to place new restrictions on his power, if these are deemed necessary. On the other hand, he shows that he realizes the advantages of an hereditary monarchy in the avoidance of the troubles attendant on a disputed succession. It is not the form of the constitution but rather its character that makes it a good or a bad one.

Following Aristotle, Aquinas distinguishes three forms of constitution according to whether the government is in the hands of one man, a few men or the many. These forms are monarchy, aristocracy, and democracy respectively. Another principle has also to be considered, whether the government is carried on in the interests of the people who are governed, or in the interest of the government itself. This gives rise to three perverted forms of constitution corresponding to the normal types previously mentioned: tyranny, oligarchy (the rule of a clique of rich and powerful men), and anarchy (mob rule).

St. Thomas feared tyranny and anarchy; hence he is suspicious of democracy. He describes a democratic constitution as one "in which all participate in political power and in judicial authority, all have the right to all offices and are called thereto in turn." He feared that democracy could easily get out of hand and lead to the abuse of liberty, mob tyranny and the oppression of the other classes in the state by the proletariat.

His own view of the best constitution is given in the *Summa Theologica*, I. IIae. q. xcv. a. 4. c. "Finally there is a form of government made up of all of these (*i.e.*, the normal types), and which is the best: and in this form we have law sanctioned by the lords and commons." Such a form of constitution is named a "mixed government" and approximates very closely to the English idea of a constitutional monarchy.

Such a constitution, St. Thomas thinks, was approved in the Old Testament. He informs us, "Two points should be noticed concerning the right ordering of rulers in a state or nation. One is that all should take some share in the government; for this form of constitution ensures peace among the people, commends itself to all and is most enduring. The other point to be considered in respect of the kinds of government is the different ways in which the constitutions are established. For whereas these differ in kind, nevertheless the first place is held by the kingdom, where the power of government is vested in one; and aristocracy, which signifies government by the best, where the power of government is vested in a few. Accordingly, the best form of government is in a state or kingdom wherein one is given the power to preside over all; while under him are others having governing powers; and yet a government of this kind is shared by all, both because all are eligible to govern, and because the rulers are chosen by all. For this is the best form of constitution, being partly kingdom, since there is one at the head of all; partly aristocracy, in so far as a number of persons are set in authority; partly democracy—*i.e.*, government by the people, in so far as the rulers can be chosen from the people and the people have the right to choose their rulers."[1]

It should be noted that the chief officers of state are to be chosen by the people. What does St. Thomas mean by the people? Has he some idea of universal suffrage? To answer this question it is necessary to remember that he is thinking of a Christian state, and any resident in the state who is not a Christian is *ipso facto* not a citizen. Those who are not Christians—*e.g.*, Jews—are to be tolerated by the state. In a letter to the Duchess of Brabant, Aquinas recommends that they should be treated kindly. They have civil rights according to the law of nature but they have no

[1] *S. Th.*, I. IIae. q. cv. a. 1. c.

political rights. They are not citizens and should have no part in the government of the state.

Another class is also excepted, the class termed *servi*. Considerable controversy has raged as to what particular group of people St. Thomas had in mind. Most authorities agree that they are not slaves and that St. Thomas did not countenance slavery as an institution. They were probably the serfs who were bound in certain respects to the lord of the manor. In England, they corresponded to the villeins in gross who were not only tied to the lord of the manor but could be sold at the will of their lord. There is no evidence to show that St. Thomas defended serfdom or suggested that the villeins constituted an integral part of society. He accepts the institution of serfdom as a social fact and believes that, as a body, they are unfitted to share in the government. In order to be fit to elect their rulers, they must be educated and acquire political sense and responsibility, and such can only take place by degrees. We know how in England the attempts of the servile classes to obtain education for their sons in the grammar schools met with violent opposition from the nobility. St. Thomas' attitude is another example of his belief that a people or a class in the community should enjoy only those political rights for which they become fitted. Thus he tells us, "if the people have a sense of moderation and responsibility and are most careful guardians of the common good it is right to enact a law allowing such a people to choose their own magistrates for the government of the commonwealth. But if, as time goes on, the same people become so corrupt as to sell their votes, and entrust the government to scoundrels and criminals, then the right of appointing their public officials is justly forfeit to such a people and the choice will fall upon a few good men."[1]

To sum up, St. Thomas believed that the real title to political power is merit and the people have only the right to rule themselves when they show by their conduct that they deserve it. If he had been living in our times, he would have probably said that the German people deserved the regime they obtained under the Nazis because they proved that they were unfit to rule themselves. He would also have questioned the British idea of hurriedly extending self-government to backward peoples. Before a race can be trusted to govern itself, it must be adequately educated and receive, by degrees, experience in managing its own affairs.

[1] *S. Th.*, I. IIae. q. xcvii. a. I. c.

The sources of St. Thomas' conception of the mixed form of government are threefold:

(*a*) Aristotle's *Politics*. Aristotle had decided in favour of a constitutional type of government, the polity, as being the best form in practice. Each class and interest in the community has its representation, and as all parts of the community have a stake in the government, it is to their interest to maintain stability. Thus the frequent revolutions to which the Greek state was subject could be avoided.

(*b*) Christianity. In the *Summa Theologica* St. Thomas analyses the political constitution of the Hebrews as it existed at the time of the Judges. He believed that it corresponded to the mixed type. Joshua and the Judges were princes under whom seventy-two elected magistrates governed the people. They were chosen by the people from the people. The choice of the prince, for a special reason, was in the hands of God. The history of Christianity added a further factor. In the classical ages, the priesthood was subordinate to the state. But Christ proclaimed the distinctness of the two orders when He said, "Render unto Cæsar the things which are Cæsar's and unto God the things which are God's." What is to distinguish between what belongs to God and what is Cæsar's? Christ made this pronouncement with regard to the payment of tribute money. Tribute is a symbol of submission to the state. Therefore, all that pertains to civil government is the affair of the state. God, however, is greater than Cæsar, and therefore God has the right to impose His laws, and the Catholic Church, in His name, can issue decrees which must be obeyed by the rulers of the state. The two spheres of civil and ecclesiastical authority are distinct and independent, but supposing a clash should arise, then God must be obeyed in preference to men. Thus, we may look upon the Church as providing an additional safeguard against the absolute power of the monarch.[1]

---

[1] It is interesting to compare the views of Aquinas with those expressed by Dante in the *De Monarchia*. Boccaccio affirmed that this treatise was written shortly after the expedition of the Emperor Henry VII to Italy (1310), and many authorities assign the date 1313 to its composition. There are, however, a number of scholars who advocate a date towards the end of Dante's life. On this point, see Wicksteed's appendix to the *De Monarchia* in *The Latin Works of Dante* (Temple Classics, Dent: 1904).

In the first book, Dante argues that a universal monarchy is necessary for the well-being of the world. "The conception that the goal of civilization is the realizing of all human potentialities is one of abiding significance. Divested of its mediæval garb, the Empire itself becomes a permanent court of international

(c) The actual practice of the 13th century was perhaps the most important source of St. Thomas' theory of government. That century saw the beginnings of the national monarchies in France, Spain and England. Already, in France, forces were at work which shortly after the death of Aquinas resulted in the calling of the States General. But it was in England that St. Thomas found his ideal of constitutional government an accomplished fact. Some writers have supposed that he visited London in 1263 to represent his order at a General Chapter of the Dominicans. There is no evidence to support this opinion, but it is unthinkable that as the personal friend of St. Louis of France, who was intimately concerned with English affairs, Aquinas was not well informed about the constitutional changes which were taking place in that country as the result of the parliamentary experiments of Simon de Montfort. In the Parliament of Simon de Montfort, for the first time, each of the three great classes of the realm was represented. Not only were the representatives of the clergy and the greater barons present, but also those from the knights of the shire and the citizens of the cities and boroughs.

One point in the political theory of St. Thomas remains to be discussed. Government has for its object the common good. In what does this consist? For St. Thomas, the state is the sum total of all the individuals who compose it. There is no suggestion, such as we find in modern authors, that the state is a personal entity, the most perfect expression of humanity, the supreme end of man. He would look upon the pretensions of both Fascist and Communist as

---

justice, a supreme and impartial tribunal of international arbitration. Within such a restored unity of civilization, nations and kingdoms and cities will develop freely and peacefully, in accordance with their own conditions and laws."—E. G. Gardner, *Dante* (Dent: 1923), p. 90. In other words, Dante's idea of the Empire is that of a United States of Europe.

The second book argues that the Empire belongs to the Roman people by right. It existed before the Papacy, and Christ acknowledged the jurisdiction of the Emperor when He consented to be born under the edict of Augustus. Further, since His death had to be the result of a sentence passed by the whole of mankind, only Pontius Pilate, as representing Cæsar, had the authority to do this. In the third book, Dante argues that the Empire is directly from God and not from the Pope. Man has two ends, blessedness in this life and Beatitude in the world to come. He has need, therefore, of two directives, that of the state and that of the Church. The state is supreme in all that concerns the present life. In this sphere the Emperor is absolutely independent of the Pope, but since "moral felicity is in a certain sense ordained with reference to immortal felicity, let Cæsar, therefore, observe that reverence to Peter which a first-born son should observe to a father, so that illuminated by the light of paternal grace he may with greater power irradiate the world, over which he is set by Him alone who is ruler of all things spiritual and temporal" (*De Mon.*, III. c. 16.).

nothing more or less than blasphemy. The principal business of the state is to promote the good of all the individuals who compose it, for without them the state would cease to exist.

On earth there is an immediate end for every individual man— a good life consisting in a harmonious use of his powers which tends to temporal happiness. But as we saw in the last chapter, man's ultimate end lies outside the sphere of the present life. It is the vision of the Essence of God in the world to come, and can be attained only through the gift of supernatural grace. The state cannot give this assistance, but there is a superior authority ordained by God which can supply it. The authority, St. Thomas tells us, "which will lead men to their supernatural end and which has not been entrusted to earthly rulers, is the Church." The state has reference to the immediate end of man on this earth and its aim is temporal good, but since the latter is related to the supreme good, the state can be regarded as co-operating with the Church.

The temporal good which is made possible for man through the government of the state is called by Aquinas the *bonum communne*, and can be achieved only through the good life. Hence, the state should be organized to establish the good life amongst its citizens, to maintain it and to develop it to a still higher level. The state achieves this by means of legislation, and this brings us once more to the conception of law, in this case, human or positive law. The function of the *lex humana* is to "force the wicked to abstain from evil so that others can live peacefully and so that they may gradually be brought through habit to do willingly what at first they did through coercion."[1]

Human law is of two kinds, the civil law and the *jus gentium*. It is called positive law because it is posited or enacted by human will. The twofold division of human law is dependent upon the way it is derived from the law of nature. The *jus gentium* consists of those principles which are necessary for the well-being of every organized community—*e.g.*, Thou shalt do no murder. It is, however, necessary to fix punishments for misdeeds, and this gives rise to civil law. Although the latter is derived from natural law it is subject to local and temporal determinations. Thus the punishment for a given crime will vary according to the different conditions of human society.

The views of St. Thomas on aesthetics have several points of

---

[1] *S. Th.* I. IIae. q. xcv. a. 1. c.

interest. In the first place, he steers a midway course between the extremes of subjectivism and objectivism. The former stresses that beauty is in the eye of the beholder; the latter, that it is a property of the object which is called beautiful. St. Thomas takes up a position which does justice to both ideas.

A beautiful object may be described in one of two ways. If we consider it from the point of view of its effects, it can be defined as that which gives pleasure on sight (*id quod visum placet*). If we seek its essence, then it is necessary to describe the particular features which make the object beautiful to our eyes.

In its essence, the beautiful is identical with the good. "The beautiful is the same as the good from which it is only mentally distinguished. For as the good is that which all things seek, its nature is to give rest to the appetite. But the specific nature of the beautiful is, that by its mere contemplation the appetite is set at rest; hence, those senses which belong most to the cognitive order especially perceive the beautiful—*viz.*, sight and hearing, which minister chiefly to the reason, for we speak of beautiful sights and beautiful sounds. We do not use the name beautiful in regard to the objects of the other senses, for we do not speak of beautiful tastes and smells. So it is clear that the beautiful adds to the notion of the good a special relation to the cognitive powers, and while the good is that which simply gratifies the appetite, the beautiful is said to be that which gratifies by its mere apprehension."[1] In this passage the emphasis on the disinterested nature of aesthetic appreciation should be noted.

If we ask what are the properties of the beautiful object which gratify the beholder, we are told, "for beauty, three things are necessary. In the first place, integrity or perfection, for whatsoever things are imperfect, by that very fact are ugly; and a right proportion or consonance; and again, splendour (*claritas*): hence brightly coloured objects are said to be beautiful."[2] The term *claritas* almost defies translation; splendour or glory are the nearest English equivalents.

Aquinas adds to this description in his commentary on the *Divine Names* of the Pseudo-Dionysius. He informs us that God as the supremely beautiful is the cause of beauty in all created things. "God imparts beauty in so far as He is the cause of proportion and splendour in things. Thus we say that a human being

---

[1] *S. Th.*, I. q. v. a. 4. ad 1m. [2] *ibid.*, q. xxxix. a. 8. c.

is beautiful because of the proper proportion of the parts of the body as regards size and position and because he has a clear and bright complexion. An object is called beautiful because it has the splendour of its kind, either spiritual or corporeal, and because it is constituted in the right proportion."[1]

Beauty is predicated of God per excessum; He is super-beautiful (*superpulcher*). "Splendour is also a quality of the beautiful as has been said. Every form, through which a thing has being, is a participation of the same divine splendour."[2]

"Form is a certain irradiation coming from the first splendour, for the latter belongs to the essence of the beautiful, as has been said."[3]

In truth, the Divine Beauty is the cause of the being of all that exists. "In the *Trinity* (of Boethius), St. Thomas goes on to say, the title Beauty is specially appropriated to the Son. As for integrity and perfection, He has truly and perfectly in Himself, without the least diminution, the nature of the Father. As for due proportion or consonance, He is the express image of the Father, a perfect likeness; and it is proportion which befits the picture as such. As for brilliance, He is the Word, the light and splendour of the mind."[4]

St. Thomas' view of aesthetic appreciation seems to be that it constitutes an intellectual intuition. In the beautiful object, the splendour of the form shines through the accompanying matter and is grasped by the mind, using the senses as its instruments, in all its purity, without the laborious process required in knowledge. Hence the delight which results on the contemplation of the beautiful. Kant was thinking along the same lines when he described the beautiful as that which gives pleasure universally without a concept.

SUGGESTIONS FOR FURTHER READING

There is no difficulty in obtaining English translations of the principal works of St. Thomas, and there are also numerous commentaries covering not only his philosophy as a whole, but special studies of important aspects of his thought.

(a) English Translations

The whole of the *Summa Theologica* is available in the English translation of the Dominican Order, published by Burns, Oates and Wash-

---

[1] *De Divin. Nomin.*, c. iv, lectio 5.
[2] *ibid.*   [3] *ibid.*, lectio 6.
[4] Maritain, J., *Art and Scholasticism* (Sheed and Ward: 1930), p. 32.

bourne. The *Summa contra Gentiles* is also issued by the same publishers. For the beginner, *Thomas Aquinas, Selected Writings*, by M. C. D'Arcy, S.J. (Dent, Everyman Library, No. 953), is specially recommended. For those who would like to make a start with the Latin text, *God and His Works and Studies in St. Thomas*, by A. G. Hebert (S.P.C.K.: 1936), is suitable. It contains selections from the *Summae* and has a useful article on mediæval Latin constructions.

(b) Studies of an Elementary Character

Probably the best general book on the philosophy of St. Thomas is *Thomas Aquinas*, by M. C. D'Arcy, S.J. (Ernest Benn: 1930; now published by O.U.P.). The essay on " St. Thomas Aquinas as a Philosopher," by A. E. Taylor, in his *Philosophical Studies* (Macmillan: 1934), is well worth reading.

Foundations of Thomistic Philosophy, by A. D. Sertillanges (Sands and Co.: 1931), provides a simple introduction.

(c) Special Studies for More Advanced Students

Dante and Aquinas (Dent: 1913) and *The Reactions between Dogma and Philosophy illustrated from the works of St. Thomas Aquinas* (Constable: 1926), both by P. H. Wicksteed, are studies by a scholar who, although he does not agree with the theology of Aquinas, yet shows a sympathetic and understanding attitude.

The Desire of God in the Philosophy of St. Thomas Aquinas, by J. E. O'Mahoney (Cork University Press: 1929), and *The Conception of God, in the Philosophy of St. Thomas Aquinas*, by R. L. Patterson (Allen and Unwin: 1933), are really able studies.

Professor Gilson's *Philosophy of St. Thomas Aquinas* (Heffer: 1929) is a detailed and valuable account which covers the whole ground of the thought of Aquinas.

Art and Scholasticism, by J. Maritain (Sheed and Ward: 1930), deals with the aesthetic theory of St. Thomas. Some of the views expressed are legitimate deductions from St. Thomas rather than views actually expressed by him.

St. Thomas and the Problem of the Soul, by A. C. Pegis (St. Michael's College, Toronto: 1934), is a valuable study by a Canadian writer of the psychology of St. Thomas. The *Introduction to the Theological Summa of St. Thomas*, by Grabmann-Zybura (Herder Book Co.: 1930), explains the scheme of the *Summa*, and contains a useful sketch of teaching in the mediæval university.

Modern Thomistic Philosophy, by R. P. Phillips (Burns, Oates and Washbourne: 2 vols., 1934), presents the teaching of St. Thomas in comparison with the views of modern philosophers.

CHAPTER XII

REPRESENTATIVE FRANCISCANS OF THE LATER
13TH CENTURY:
ST. BONAVENTURE AND ROGER BACON

ST. BONAVENTURE (John of Fidanza) was born in Tuscany in 1221. As Professor Gilson reminds us, no contemporary life of St. Bonaventure is extant, and therefore the account of his life has to be reconstructed, using evidence of varying degrees of reliability. As a baby, St. Bonaventure was stricken by a grave illness and his mother took him to St. Francis, who healed him. From that time he was dedicated to the service of the Franciscan Order, which he actually entered some time between 1238 and 1243. He studied under Alexander of Hales and his successor, John of La Rochelle, and by the time he obtained his bachelor's degree in 1245 he had definitely given his allegiance to the Augustinian tradition. He did this in full knowledge of the teaching of his Dominican colleagues, Albert the Great and St. Thomas Aquinas.

In 1248 St. Bonaventure received the licence to teach and was appointed to the Franciscan chair in the University of Paris. It was during this period of office that the disputes between the seculars and the mendicant Orders had reached their height, and Bonaventure took his place at the side of Albert and Aquinas in the defence of their Orders. On this account, he was temporarily excluded from the university in 1255, but he returned to his former office in the following year. In 1257 he was appointed Minister General of the Franciscan Order. This really marked the end of his university career, since for the rest of his life all his energies were given to the administration of the Order. He was created a cardinal in 1273, attended the Council of Lyons, where he preached on the subject of the reunion of the Eastern and Western Churches, and, after a brief illness, died in 1274.

St. Bonaventure's philosophical position may be described as conservative. There is no evidence to support the legend of his personal friendship with St. Thomas, and although he did not join in the attack upon him, there is no doubt of his disapproval of the latter's doctrine, which he regarded as an innovation. All through his life, St. Bonaventure was suspicious of the revived Aristotelianism, and the example of the Latin Averroists impressed him with the dangers that might follow from the acceptance of the new doctrines. He remained faithful to the Augustinian tradition he had received at the hands of Alexander of Hales, and later in life he recorded, "In the first book of the *Sentences* I adhered to the views of the masters, especially those of that master and father of happy memory, Alexander of Hales. . . . I do not intend to struggle to introduce new doctrines, but to defend and hold those commonly received and approved."

St. Bonaventure was a mystic and a theologian and in his eyes the initial mistake made by Aquinas was to separate philosophy from theology. "In principle he stands over against Aquinas; they represent two different and contrasted theories of the relation between faith and reason, between Christian theology and philosophy. His whole conception of knowledge differs essentially from the theory of Aristotle and the theory of St. Thomas Aquinas."[1]

Although Bonaventure rejected the Aristotelianism of Aquinas, at the same time he made use of the logical instrument which Aristotle had forged and retained those aspects of his teaching which could be reconciled with Christian Platonism. The key to the understanding of St. Bonaventure's theory of knowledge, as Professor Gilson has shown, lies in his interpretation of St. Augustine's doctrine of Divine Illumination.[2] Human knowledge, he believed, is due to the presence within us of the Divine Light. We see truth both in and by the eternal ideas. St. Bonaventure, however, was careful to point out that this does not involve the view that the eternal ideas are seen as they exist in God. They appear to us as faint reflections due to the sin of man. Before the Fall, the human race, in the state of innocency, enjoyed complete knowledge in the contemplation of God. Sin produced a defect in the human understanding, so that human knowledge will always be partial and incomplete.

[1] MELLONE, S. H., *Western Christian Thought in the Middle Ages* (William Blackwood: 1935), p. 152.
[2] GILSON, ETIENNE, *The Philosophy of St. Bonaventure* (Sheed and Ward: 1938), chapter xii.

St. Bonaventure's attitude towards Plato and Aristotle is interesting. He asserts that neither Plato nor Aristotle has expressed the whole truth about knowledge. Aristotle used the language of science and Plato that of wisdom, but St. Augustine, inspired by the Holy Spirit, speaks the language of both. Man can study truth in the objects of the physical world, or in himself, or in God. If he considers things by sense and the lower powers of the soul, he achieves only a relative certitude, but when he turns from nature to God he receives from Him an absolute certitude.

Corporeal things are perceived by sense, and the impressions gained through sense experience are stored in memory and form the data from which universal ideas are abstracted through the agency of Active Intellect. All the arts and sciences consist of universals abstracted from particulars, and Bonaventure is just as emphatic as Aquinas in declaring that without sense perception our knowledge of natural objects would be impossible.

It is when the soul turns from the external world to a knowledge of itself and God that an interior illumination is necessary. St. Bonaventure will not agree that all knowledge springs from sense experience. The knowledge that the soul gains of itself and God is not due to the agency of sense. To deny this is to ignore the operation of the interior light.

"The first principles of knowledge are known in virtue of no experience save the mind's experience of itself, of its nature and constitution, and of the things that are in it." Bonaventure accepts the Aristotelian distinction between the Possible and Active Intellects, but he introduces an important modification. He tells us that the Possible Intellect is not purely passive. It has the power of turning towards the intelligible, which is contained in the sensible species, abstracting it, and judging it through the assistance it receives from the Active Intellect. In a similar way, the Active Intellect is not completely in act. It cannot understand anything in virtue of its own powers and requires the help of the species which is held in the imagination.

This view is in complete opposition to the theory of St. Thomas. Professor Gilson summarizes it as follows: "St. Bonaventure's terminology then may remain Aristotelian; but it profoundly modifies the generally accepted conception of the Active Intellect, and it modifies still more profoundly the conception of the Possible Intellect and shows itself more and more irreconcilable with St.

Thomas as it advances further along its own lines. . . . The salient feature in this solution of the problem is that the inability of either of the two Intellects to exercise its activity without the effective co-operation of the other makes them in some way interdependent, the one participating in the passivity, the other in the activity of its partner, so that they are less like two faculties, less like complementary faculties even, than like two reciprocal movements in conjunction within a single operation."[1]

Knowledge of the soul and God present quite a different problem for St. Bonaventure. How, he asks, can one know a virtue of the soul such as charity? If the subject already possesses charity, he needs nothing besides to enable him to know it. But let us suppose that he does not possess charity. He cannot know it through a direct intuition of its essence, because charity is not present in the soul. Nor can he know it by means of an image derived from sense experience, for the virtues are not objects of sense perception. The only solution is to assume that our knowledge comes about through a species which is innate.

In the same way, the knowledge of God cannot be by means of sensible images nor through a direct intuition of the Divine Essence. We are forced to admit that the knowledge of God is implicit in the rational soul. "The human soul knows God simply by reflecting on itself, since it is made in the image of God; the knowledge by which it knows, the desire by which it loves, the memory by which it grasps and possesses itself, tend towards God, suppose and imply Him necessarily; the innateness of its knowledge of Him consists then in the power which it possesses of forming this knowledge without requiring fresh resources from the external world."[2]

Man, then, possesses a certain but an imperfect knowledge of the supreme object towards which he tends. The imperfection of human knowledge is due to the Fall whereby man's intelligence was blinded by sin. Therefore, at each step on the journey of the soul towards God, there is a need of Divine Illumination—*i.e.*, of the co-operation of God.

This idea is worked out in St. Bonaventure's *Itinerarium mentis in Deum* (*The Journey of the Mind towards God*). "Every object in the universe speaks to us of God, represents Him after its own manner, and invites us to turn to Him. The whole meaning of

[1] *op. cit.*, pp. 367–8.   [2] *ibid.*, p. 378.

life is to be a journey to God, and the world of our senses is the
pathway which leads us to Him. The things with which the path
is filled are all 'signs' or 'symbols' which at first appear utterly
mysterious to us. But when we study them attentively with our
reason illuminated by the light of faith, we read through the
multitudinous variety of characters the one Word—God. . . .
We thus are able, through created things, to rise to God."[1]

Man's journey commences, then, with the objects of the sense
world which are perceived through the eye of the flesh (*oculum
carnis*), and through the eye of reason (*oculum rationis*). To remain
at this stage, however, is to dwell in error. Man can also perceive
through the eye of contemplation (*oculum contemplationis*).

In his description of the ascent of the soul to God, St. Bonaventure differs considerably from the teaching of St. Thomas. The
latter regarded the objects of nature as the effects of God's causality,
so that we are enabled by analogy to gain some positive knowledge
of the Infinite First Cause. St. Bonaventure stresses the heart
rather than the head. Men must be recalled from preoccupation
with the visible world to the love of God Who is their Creator.

The first step to be taken is the contemplation of the shadows
of God as they are revealed in the sensible world (*vestigia*). Nature
is a book wherein the reader perceives the traces of the Creator
in the order, movement, beauty and disposition of things. The
next step is to contemplate God by the senses (*per vestigium*) and
through the imagination (*in vestigio*). These activities belong to
the realm of *Theologia Symbolica*. The next higher stage is that of
meditation, in which we learn to know and love God in His image
(*imago Dei*) in our own soul.

We see God through our soul (*per imaginem*), for, as St. Augustine
showed, the three faculties of memory, understanding and will,
mirror in us the Trinity and raise us to God. Memory preserves
for us the Divine Principles; the will is moved by the presentation
of the Supreme Good, and the understanding, illumined by the
Divine Rays, unites the soul to God. At the next stage, we need
the Divine Illumination to enable us to see God in our soul (*in
imagine*), and for this purpose we receive the Divine Grace,
bringing with it the virtues of faith, hope and charity.

Now we turn to God and contemplate Him, not as a cause, but
directly. From knowing God in His Being, we advance to Him in

[1] MELLONE, *op. cit.*, p. 155.

the knowledge of the boundless goodness of the Trinity. The last stage is the state of ecstasy in which we are united to the Infinite. This constitutes the *apex mentis* and is attended by raptures of delight and transports of love. Bonaventure is careful to avoid any tendency towards pantheism, and even at this supreme level the essential distinction between creature and Creator remains. The journey of the soul to God is shown diagrammatically below.

The "Itinerarium Mentis in Deum"

I. THEOLOGIA SYMBOLICA.

God as known in nature (*vestigia*)
by

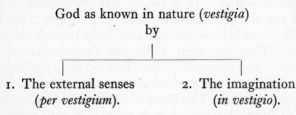

1. The external senses   2. The imagination
   (*per vestigium*).   (*in vestigio*).

II. MEDITATIO.

God as known in His Image in the soul.

3. Through the soul   4. In the soul
   (*per imaginem*).   (*in imagine*).
   (Faculties of memory, un-   (Divine Grace needed and
   derstanding and will.)   the virtues of faith, hope
                                   and charity.)

III. CONTEMPLATIO.

Direct knowledge of God.

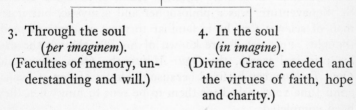

5. In His Being.   6. In the Blessed Trinity.   7. The *Apex Mentis*
                                                    (ecstasy).

Earlier in this chapter St. Bonaventure was described as a conservative thinker who preferred the traditional Augustinian teaching to the innovations of Albert and Aquinas. This is seen clearly in his account of matter and form, which follows largely the teaching he had received from Alexander of Hales. Thus, he affirmed that every created substance is a composite of matter (potentiality) and form (actuality), and extended this idea to include the angels. He taught that the possession of matter is the characteristic of the created being, and hence the human soul and the angel are both composites of matter and form. He says, "Taking matter in its widest sense as meaning that which exists in potentiality, one must say that the substance of the angel is composed of matter and form."

He also adopts the theory of the *rationes seminales*, so that in his eyes matter is not a pure potentiality but contains within itself a principle of activity. In a similar way, he upholds the older theory of the plurality of forms. The body, before it can receive a soul, must first become an organized body through the form of corporeity. This, the most noble and fundamental of forms, Bonaventure, like Grosseteste, describes by the term light (*lux*), and he asserts that it is the common nature belonging to all bodies, celestial or terrestrial. This form is not absorbed or replaced by subsequent forms, but serves, as it were, as a core round which the other forms are constituted and are rendered effective.

When we come to consider the teaching of Roger Bacon, we seem to enter an entirely different realm of thought. Bacon, like St. Bonaventure, was a philosopher and a mystic, but it is as a man of science that he is familiar to most students of mediæval thought. Few details are known of his life, though the dates of his principal works, the *Opus Maius*, the *Opus Minus* and the *Opus Tertium*, can be fixed because the letter of Pope Clement IV, 22nd June 1266, asked for them to be sent to him when they had been completed.

Bacon was probably born at Ilchester at some time between 1210 and 1215. When quite a young man, he studied at Oxford, having for his master Robert Grosseteste, for whom he showed a great regard during the whole of his later career. Bridges refers to the occurrence of Bacon's name in the chronicles of Matthew Paris. In 1233 Henry III assembled a council of barons at Oxford. They immediately protested against the favouritism that the king showed to foreigners, especially towards the arrogant Pierre des Roches, Bishop of Winchester. Matthew then relates that "a certain clerk who was present at the court, Roger Bacon by name, a man of mirthful speech, said with a pleasant yet pointed wit, 'My lord king, what is that which is most hurtful and fearful to those that sail across the sea?' 'Those know it,' the king replied, 'who have much experience of the waters.' 'My lord,' said the clerk, 'I will tell you; stones and rocks'; meaning thereby Pierre des Roches."[1]

In spite of his outspoken rejoinder, Bacon seems to have supported the king in the quarrels which arose between him and the barons. About 1245, Bacon left Oxford and is found teaching at Paris. It is not known for certain when he entered the Franciscan Order, but it was probably between 1251 and 1257. From his early youth he had been interested in languages and natural science, and on his return to Oxford we have his statement in the *Opus Tertium* that he continued those studies and spent more than two thousand pounds in buying books and instruments.

It was at Paris that he met Peter of Maricourt, whom he eulogized as a master of experimental science. All that is known of Peter is what Bacon has to say about him in the *Opus Tertium* and *Opus Maius*. Bacon tells us also that he heard William of Auvergne lecturing at Paris on the Active Intellect. As William died in 1249, this gives an indication of the date at which Bacon was teaching at Paris.

On his return to Oxford, Bacon seems to have incurred the hostility of the members of his order and he was forbidden to publish his work. A change came when his friend Clement IV became Pope. The new Pope requested him in 1266 to send for his perusal the works that were intended for publication. Thus, the *Opus Maius* and *Opus Minus* and, later, the *Opus Tertium* were sent to Clement. On the Pope's death, Bacon's enemies united against him, partly for doctrinal and partly for political reasons. In 1278 Jerome d'Ascoli, who had succeeded St. Bonaventure as General of the Franciscan Order, condemned the teaching of Bacon and the latter was committed to imprisonment. Tradition states that he was held in what was probably honourable confinement until 1292, and his death took place a short time after his release.

Bacon's teaching presents what at first sight appears to be a curious mixture of opposing tendencies. As a Franciscan, he upheld many of the traditional doctrines of the school, such as the

[1] BRIDGES, J. H., *The Life and Work of Roger Bacon* (Williams and Norgate: 1914), p. 15.

presence of *rationes seminales* in first matter, the ascription of matter to the angelic spirits, and the plurality of substantial forms.

His devotion to experimental science was, however, not inconsistent with his seemingly conservative attitude. He believed that knowledge can be obtained through three distinct means: from authority, from reason, and through experience. Authority must be supported by reason and the latter, again, by experimental investigation.

Hence, there are two aspects of Bacon's thought. On the one hand, he was a natural scientist and a mathematician. He wrote on optics, astronomy, geography, alchemy and languages. There is good reason to believe that even if he did not actually possess them he was well on the way to the construction of a telescope and a microscope. His discovery of gunpowder is well authenticated, and his recipe for making the explosive is extant. He did not, however, conceive the idea of using the explosive force of gunpowder for the propulsion of a projectile. He dabbled in chemistry and prepared a scheme for the reform of the calendar which anticipated that of Pope Gregory. His speculations as regards geography, given in the *Opus Maius* and later copied by Pierre d'Ailly in his *Imago Mundi*, played an important rôle in persuading Columbus to undertake his voyage of discovery. Many of Bacon's contributions to science were written in cipher and it is still possible that others may come to light. Bacon did not despise Aristotle, as some authors have assumed. On the contrary, he admired him greatly, but he reproached his contemporaries for making use of inaccurate Latin translations. He was intensely interested in the development of thought, and the *Opus Maius* contains a miniature history of philosophy.

On the other hand, Bacon as a traditionalist taught that the essential aim of philosophy is to explain the Scriptures. He regarded philosophy as the instrument of theology. "Either there is one science the mistress of the others, namely theology (to which the rest are entirely necessary; and without the others it cannot attain to its effect; their excellence it claims as its right; the rest of the sciences obey its nod and authority), or better, there is only one perfect wisdom which is contained wholly in the Sacred Scriptures, to be explained by canon law and philosophy."[1]

[1] McKEON, R., *Selections from Medieval Philosophers* (Charles Scribner's Sons: 1931), vol. ii, pp. 17–18.

On the subject of universals, Bacon insisted that the individual alone exists. "An individual possesses more reality," he wrote, "than all the universals taken together." He accepted the division of created beings into the two moments of matter and form; and while insisting on the individual distinctness of creatures, he regarded the whole of being as united in one vast causal series. Every being acts upon and is acted upon by others. Superior grades of being act on inferior, spirits upon bodies and the heavenly upon earthly bodies. Every action of one being upon another is termed by Bacon a species. Each act of knowledge is a species, for it is due to the direct union of the knower and the object known. Such an intuitive theory of knowledge had no use for the operation of the individual Active Intellect in the manner which St. Thomas taught. Thus, we find that Bacon, whilst acknowledging that the Possible Intellect or understanding is a part of the individual human soul, teaches that the Active Intellect is outside the soul. He wrote, "And thus the Active Intellect, according to the ancient philosophers, is not part of the soul, but is an intellectual substance other than and separated in essence from the Possible Intellect."[1] He considered that this was the view of Aristotle, and recorded, "For I twice saw and heard, at convocations of the University of Paris, the venerable priest, Master William, Bishop of Paris, of blessed memory, declare in the presence of all that the Active Intellect can not be part of the soul; and Master Robert, Bishop of Lincoln, and brother Adam of the Marsh and elders of this sort supported the same opinion."[2]

Was Roger Bacon, then, an Averroist? Renan took these words at their face value and jumped to the conclusion that he was. If he had read a few more pages of the *Opus Maius*, his error would have been corrected. Bacon was simply affirming the traditional Augustinian doctrine of Divine Illumination. At the end of the same chapter Bacon summed up his position. After quoting St. Augustine in support of his view, he wrote, "All these things are evidence that the Active Principle illuminating and influencing the Possible Intellect is a separated substance, that is, God Himself."[3]

All knowledge ultimately leads to God, Who taught men to be philosophers by revealing the truth to them, but the wickedness of human beings provoked God's anger, and, withholding His

[1] McKeon, *op. cit.*, p. 28.   [2] *ibid.*, p. 31.   [3] *ibid.*, pp. 33-4.

revelation, He permitted error to be mixed with it. Progress in philosophy is really a rediscovery of this primitive revelation. Hence the value of studying the ancient philosophers. We must study them and the Scriptures to find the truth, but such a study makes great demands upon the seeker after wisdom. He needs to possess a knowledge of languages and also of mathematics, since the latter study is necessary for progress in understanding natural science and grasping the truth of the Scriptures.

In the *Opus Maius*, in a manner reminiscent of his better-known namesake, Francis Bacon, he enumerates the causes of human ignorance. It is due to dependence upon "frail and unsuited authority," long duration of custom, giving heed to the opinion of the unlearned crowd, and concealment of one's own ignorance in the display of apparent wisdom. "Every one in all the acts of life and study and every occupation uses three of the worst arguments to the same conclusion: namely, (1) this has been exemplified by our ancestors, (2) this is the custom, (3) this is the common belief: therefore, it must be held."[1]

In the search for knowledge, experience is the sole source of certainty. Bacon expounds his view in the following passages: (*a*) "I wish now to take up the roots of experimental science, because without experience nothing can be known sufficiently. There are, in fact, two ways of knowing, namely, by argumentation and experience. Argumentation concludes and makes us grant the conclusion, but does not make certain nor remove doubt that the mind may be quiet in the contemplation of truth, unless it finds truth by way of experience. . . . If a man who has never seen fire should prove by sufficient argument that fire burns and that it injures things and destroys them, the mind of one hearing it would never be satisfied by that nor would a hearer avoid fire until he had put a hand or a combustible object into the fire that he might prove by experience what argument had taught. But once he had had experience of combustion, his mind is made sure and rests in the brightness of truth. Therefore, argumentation does not suffice, but experience does."[2]

(*b*) "But experience is double: one is by means of the exterior senses, and such are those experiences which show things that are in the heavens through instruments made for these experiments and those things that we find below by visual ascertainments.

[1] McKeon, *op. cit.*, p. 9.   [2] *ibid.*, p. 73.

We know things which are not present in the places in which we are, through other wise men who have experienced them. . . . This experience is human and philosophical, as much as man can do in accordance with the grace given him; but this experience does not suffice man, in that it does not certify fully concerning corporeal things because of its difficulty, and it touches on nothing at all of spiritual things."[1]

Therefore such knowledge is supplemented by interior illuminations, which enabled the patriarchs and prophets of earlier times to give science to the world. Bacon speaks of seven grades of interior knowledge ; purely scientific illuminations, virtues, the seven gifts of the Spirit, the beatitudes, the spiritual senses, the sixth "is in fruits among which is the peace of the Lord which exceeds all understanding", and the last is rapture. The latter three refer to supernatural states experienced by the mystics.

Bacon was interested in what we now call scientific method, and in the *Opus Maius* there occurs a passage in which he develops his ideas about the lines which should be followed by the experimental scientist. He chooses the example of the investigation of the phenomena connected with the rainbow. The first task of the experimenter is to ascertain the different instances in which these phenomena are present. If the hexagonal stones of Ireland and India are held in the rays of the sun as they shine through a window, the observer will find in the shadow which is cast all the colours of the rainbow and in the same order. He may be tempted to conclude that this is due to the hexagonal shape, but this may be ruled out because other crystalline stones of a different regular shape will yield the same result. Has the fact that all these stones are white anything to do with the cause of the phenomena? This can be tested by using black crystalline stones. "He will find it, too, in another figure than the hexagonal, provided the surfaces are corrugated like the Irish stone and neither altogether polished nor more rough than they are, and provided they are such property of surface as nature produces in the Irish, for the diversity of wrinkles produces a diversity of colours." The reader will probably have noticed that the method described by Bacon has more than a superficial similarity to J. S. Mill's *Method of Agreement*, and he will find it interesting to compare the last example with the experiments of Sir David Brewster, which were

[1] MCKEON, *op. cit.*, p. 75.

designed to show that the colours seen upon mother-of-pearl are due to the texture of the surface.[1]

Bacon then lists a number of other instances where the colours of the rainbow occur. Bridges sums up the investigation as follows: "He begins with a collection of phenomena, colours in crystals or half-polished surfaces, in spray from a mill-wheel, or from an oar when lit by the sun, and the like, which, as Whewell says, 'are almost all examples of the same kind as the phenomena under consideration.' He combines astronomical theory with astronomical observation in explaining the connexion between the altitude of the bow and that of the sun. In his proof that the centre of the bow, of the eye, and of the sun are always in one straight line, the union of theory with observation is equally marked. The conclusion that each observer sees a distinct rainbow is clearly drawn. Not less striking is his discussion of the form of the rainbow, which was pushed as far towards the truth as was possible at a time when the law of variation in the angles of refraction was still undiscovered."

"With regard to the colour of the rainbow, and indeed with regard to colour in general, he shared the ignorance, not of his own time only, but of the three centuries and a half that followed, till Descartes initiated the analysis of white light into the spectrum."

There are two other points of interest in Bacon's teaching. The first concerns his views on mathematics. In Part IV of the *Opus Maius* he shows at considerable length that every science requires mathematics. Speaking of the sciences of his day, he says, "The door and key of these sciences is mathematics . . . since he who ignores it can not know the other sciences nor the things of this world." His discussion of the uses of mathematics shows that he was well acquainted with Euclid, whose works had reached Europe more than a century before Bacon's time. He also knew the work of many of the Arabian scientists and mathematicians such as Al Kindi and Alhazen. The latter is frequently quoted by Bacon in the fifth part of the *Opus Maius*, which deals with optics.

In the unfinished *Scriptum Principale*, Bacon deals with the principles of mathematics, but he shows that his interest is more in the practical applications than in developing mathematical

---

[1] See JEVONS, W. S., *Elementary Lessons in Logic* (Macmillan: 1895), p. 214.
[2] BRIDGES, *op. cit.*, pp. 158–9.

theory. He mentions the use of the ball frame or abacus in com-
putation and the study of algebra. But as Bridges remarks, "Bacon
had made himself acquainted with the highest mathematics of his
time; though no evidence is forthcoming to show that he contributed personally to the advance of the science. . . . Whether
the study of equations as carried on by the Italians algebraists of
the fourteenth and fifteenth centuries would have interested him
is doubtful. But he would have eagerly welcomed the invention
of logarithms, as facilitating the construction of astronomical
tables."[1]

The other point of interest in Bacon's work is the attention he
gave to languages. Once again he was motivated by a practical
interest. He was anxious for the publication of an accurate text of
the Bible, but, above all, he wished to see a faithful translation
of Aristotle. Nor was he unmindful of the practical advantages
of a knowledge of languages to those who were engaged in foreign
trade. He believed that the universities should undertake the
comparative study of language, and he suggested that Hebrew,
Arabic and Greek with their dialects should form the basis of such
a study. How far Bacon knew Hebrew and Arabic is a matter
for conjecture. The *Opus Tertium* reveals that he knew the Hebrew
alphabet, but his knowledge of Greek is shown by part of a Greek
grammar that he wrote and which is still extant.[2] In the third
part of the *Opus Maius* Bacon enumerates eight reasons why the
study of Latin, and the languages from which Latin is derived,
is of great importance. Bacon criticized many of the current
translations of Aristotle, not only those made from Arabian versions, but also William of Moerbeke's translation from the original
Greek. He considered the weak point of the latter was William's
ignorance of natural science which was responsible for a number
of errors.

Because Bacon was a man with such many-sided interests, it is
difficult to assess his stature as a thinker. It has been said of
Francis Bacon that it is easy both to exaggerate and to minimize
his achievements. The same is true of Roger Bacon. It is beyond
doubt that he owed much to Grosseteste, to the Arabians and to
contemporary thinkers, but he was no mere copyist. His writings

---

[1] BRIDGES, *op. cit.*, pp. 82–3.
[2] Bacon's grammar was published by C.U.P. in 1902 under the title of *The Greek
Grammar of Roger Bacon and a Fragment of his Hebrew Grammar*, ed. E. Nolan
and S. A. Hirsch.

give evidence of a keen and inquiring mind, and even when he borrowed most he transmuted what he had acquired in the light of his own interests and purposes. In the opinion of many historians, he compares very favourably with his namesake of the early 17th century. Mellone hardly does him justice when he speaks of the "self-centred claims which Roger Bacon makes for his own achievement, his critical attitude to his contemporaries, his monotonous dispraise of what he calls 'authority' and his exaltation of experimental science,"[1] although he admits later that he was "a man moved by a passionate conviction that the natural sciences are of vast importance to humanity and to the Church, and that no further advance is possible but by an intellectual return to nature."[2]

Suggestions for Further Reading

The most complete study of St. Bonaventure is that of Professor Gilson—*The Philosophy of St. Bonaventure* (Sheed and Ward: 1938). McKeon gives translations of selected passages from St. Bonaventure and Roger Bacon. A very readable account of the achievements of Bacon is contained in the work of J. H. Bridges, *The Life and Work of Roger Bacon* (Williams and Norgate: 1914).

[1] MELLONE, *op. cit.*, p. 227.   [2] *ibid.*, p. 233.

CHAPTER XIII

DUNS SCOTUS

As St. Thomas Aquinas represented the culmination of philosophical speculation amongst the Dominicans of the 13th century, so we may regard Duns Scotus as the outstanding thinker among the Franciscans. Unfortunately very few details are known about his career. Even the date and place of his birth have been a matter for controversy. He is supposed to have been born in 1266 at Maxton in the county of Roxburgh. Some authorities place the date of his birth as late as 1274, but what evidence we possess seems to favour the earlier date. He has been claimed also as an Englishman born in Northumbria, but even the evidence of his nationality is inconclusive. Where authentic records are wanting, tradition has attempted to supply the defect. He is said to have been educated at a school at Haddington, and then to have been sent to the Franciscan convent at Dumfries. The famous Scottish scholar, John Major (1470–1550), claimed Scotus as a Scot and asserted that Duns was a place name. He also tells us that Scotus entered the Franciscan Order in 1281 and went to Oxford some time before 1290. There is also a record to the effect that he was ordained a priest at Northampton on 17th March, 1291. He seems to have lectured on the *Sentences* at Oxford about 1300 after a visit to Paris. In 1302 he returned to Paris, where he taught as a master and, according to the legend, defended the doctrine of the Immaculate Conception. He also seems to have opposed the anti-Papal policy of Philip the Fair and was banished for a short time. He went back once more to Paris in 1304 and obtained his doctorate in the following year. He was sent to Cologne in 1307 and died towards the end of the next year.

The uncertainty which surrounds the events of his life is apparent also when an attempt is made to compile a list of his works. Modern criticism has shown that many of the treatises attributed to him were certainly not his. For example, the complete edition of his works was published by L. Wadding in 1639 and reprinted in 1891–5. This is the only collected edition of his works we have at present, and it contains a number which are undoubtedly spurious and others about which a good deal of controversy still rages. The works of which the authenticity has been established fall into two groups, those written at Oxford and those at Paris. The former are in many ways superior to the latter. His two most important treaties were the commentaries on the *Sentences*, known as the Oxford and Paris works, respectively. Besides these, certain treatises on logic, the *Questions on the Metaphysics*, the *Quodlibeta* and the *De primo principio*, are considered genuine. These alone represent a formidable accomplishment when we realize that he died at the early age of forty-two.

The *Theoremata* are generally agreed to have been written some years after his death, since they contain opinions similar to those held by Ockham. The main controversy has been in connection with the *De Rerum Principio*. B. Landry, in his much-criticized work on Scotus, accepted the *De Rerum Principio* as genuine. Its authenticity has been rejected by Dr. P. Minges and Fr. Longpré, but Dr. C. R. S. Harris considers that it is an early work of Scotus, written at Oxford when he was strongly influenced by Augustinianism and the teaching of John Peckham.[1] D. E. Sharpe supports the view of Longpré and points out that the Augustinian influence at Oxford has been overrated, and that other works of Scotus, presumably of this period, are markedly Aristotelian and show little trace of the influence of St. Augustine.

The question of the authenticity of the *De Rerum Principio* is an important one. If the work is not the production of Scotus, then the traditional account of his teaching was greatly in error. It is difficult to believe that the treatise represents an earlier period of the thought of Scotus, since what then have to be regarded as later developments seem to have no relation to the earlier work, but are in flat contradiction to it. There is only one manuscript of the work and this cannot be put earlier than the end of the 14th century. John of Reading, the friend of Scotus who compiled a list of his works, does not mention it, and Ockham, who makes many references to the writings of Scotus, is quite silent

---

[1] Dr. Harris gives the evidence for his view in *Duns Scotus* (Clarendon Press: 1927), appendix iii (b) to vol. i.

on the *De Rerum Principio.* The best policy, under the circumstances, is to regard its authenticity as so highly doubtful that it should be ignored in attempting to summarize the opinions of Scotus.

Duns Scotus, perhaps more than any scholastic philosopher, has suffered from the gibes of after generations. This is probably due to his outspoken advocacy of the Papacy, and the Reformation leaders so completely identified him with the old order that Thomas Cromwell specially selected him as an object for attack. The very name Duns was corrupted into our modern Dunce. In the 19th century Scotus was held to have spent serious consideration on the problem of how many angels can dance on the point of a needle, and this was quoted as an example of the trivial questions with which the Schoolmen concerned themselves. The real problem which he was discussing was how far a spiritual substance is subject to the same spatial and temporal limitations that apply to a material body.

Scotus was recognized by his contemporaries as a thinker of great critical power and they rewarded him by the title of the Subtle Doctor. It is only of late years that his genius has been accorded full recognition. When, towards the close of the 19th century, interest in Scholasticism revived, it was the work of St. Thomas Aquinas that first attracted attention and Scotus tended to be overshadowed by the Angelic Doctor. The issue of a critical edition of his works would do much to restore him to the place which he deserves in the history of thought.

Those who accept the *De Rerum Principio* assert that in his earlier period Scotus taught a theory of matter which he afterwards repudiated. In his commentaries on the *Sentences* Scotus only admits one form of matter which is not regarded as a pure potentiality. It must have some degree of actuality if it exists, but he emphasizes that matter possesses the very minimum of actuality. This is just sufficient to make it capable of becoming a subject for the reception of forms. Since it possesses a degree of actuality, matter imitates the Divine Nature so that God has a distinct idea of it. A further consequence is that matter is accessible to intelligence and does not, therefore, present a barrier to knowledge of the individual.

It would be quite possible for God to create matter without form though such an existence would be a mere travesty. In human experience, matter is always united to form but the union is to a certain extent accidental. From the point of view of first matter, there is no reason why matter should be united to this form rather than to that. Any tendency towards a particular form would favour the doctrine of *rationes seminales* which Scotus unhesitatingly rejects.

In a similar way, although form is identified with actuality, it is not a pure actuality, but a degree of potentiality is present. Thus in the case of a substance which becomes hot, the matter has a potentiality to receive the form of heat, but the form has also a potentiality to supervene upon the body which is not yet hot. Scotus distinguishes between the double meaning of potentiality by saying that matter has a *potentia subiectiva* whilst that of form is a *potentia obiectiva*. All corporeal substances are composites of matter and form. Like matter, there is nothing in the nature of form to prevent it from existing apart from matter, but God did not choose to have it so. Hence, in nature, forms are not found existing apart from matter. As regards the existence of matter in the heavenly bodies and in the angelic nature, Scotus is uncertain. In some passages he seems to grant the existence of a spiritual matter in such cases, and in at least two places he speaks as though he believed in the hylomorphic composition of the angels. He certainly marks the distinction between essence and existence, but on the question of the existence of matter in the angel he is not decided.

The author of the *De Rerum Principio* insists upon the unity of matter in all created beings. In fact, the unity of being is due to the same first matter as the basis of all things. Hence he makes use of the well-known analogy of the world as a magnificent tree. "It is clear that the world may be likened to a most beautiful tree, whose root and seed vessel is first matter and whose falling leaves are accidents; the leaves and branches are created contingent beings; the flower, the rational soul and the fruit is the angelic spirit. . . . The root issues forth immediately in two branches, one of which consists of spiritual, the other of material, substances. The spiritual branch is divided into three hierarchies, each of which is subdivided into three orders each consisting of millions of angels. . . . The material branch divides into two more branches, the corruptible and the incorruptible, each of which is split into a multitude of twigs."[1]

---

[1] Translated from R. P. Deodati Marie's *Capitalia Opera B. Joan. D. Scoti*, vol. i: *Praeparatio philosophica*, 19th edition (La Bonne Parole, Le Havre), p. 297.

In the genuine works, Scotus teaches that matter is only one from an abstract point of view. The same applies to being. The unity of being is true only if one takes its meaning in the widest and most abstract way possible.

Scotus arranges forms in a hierarchy which starts with the least perfect, the forms of the elementary substances. These are the least in perfection since they are more closely allied to corporeal matter than are the other members of the hierarchy. Above them are the forms of mixed bodies (compounds) which manifest certain activities independent of the matter. Thus certain herbs have the power of stopping the flow of blood from a wound. Above these, again, come the plant and animal forms. The highest of the corporeal forms is the human soul. In man the form attains its full independence and is so far removed from matter that it constitutes a spiritual substance. Thus the human soul can survive the death of the body and is capable of still further development before it rejoins its glorified body. Moreover, this hierarchy constitutes a continuous series; nature does not proceed by jumps. "The time for the discovery of phylogenetic evolution was not yet come. How nearly Scotus passed it by, however, is shown in his recognition of the fundamental similarity of all living phenomena, and his conception of the rudimentary form of liberty in plant life."[1]

Scotus teaches that in the mixed body, the forms of the elements do not continue to exist in addition to the higher form of the compound. It would seem, then, that at first sight he taught the doctrine of the unity of the substantial form. He, however, makes certain exceptions which are of fundamental importance. In the first place, it would seem that there are two forms in the animal. Its body is the result of the form of corporeity which acts directly upon the matter. The body is now ready to receive another form which confers life upon it. This second form gives to the creature its determinate character.

The human composite is much more complex. The body, considered apart from the soul, is a mixture of elements. These are ordered in particular ways to form organs. Each bodily organ possesses its proper substantial form, otherwise a limb when torn from the body would not continue to exist. When the embryo is formed, the organs are constituted into an organism by the form

[1] HARRIS, C. R. S., *Duns Scotus* (Clarendon Press: 1927), vol. ii, p. 113.

of corporeity. It is due to this latter form that a corpse retains its identity for a time. The rational soul appears as soon as the organs have been organized. Hence, Scotus is able to teach that the soul is to the body as form to matter. How then does he maintain the unity of the individual? His answer is that the body by itself is incomplete and it receives its perfection through the final form, the intellectual soul, which makes the composite to be what it is. It is in this way that Scotus considers that the plurality of forms in organic nature does not interfere with the unity of the creature.

Scotus had an extremely high appreciation of individuality and personality. He rejected the view of St. Thomas that *materia signata* is the principle of individuation. He had not realized the full meaning of the latter's doctrine, and therefore he asked how matter, which, according to the Thomist view, is a pure potentiality, can be responsible for those positive determinations which constitute the individual. If the emphasis is laid on dimensions, does that not make the individual depend upon an accident?

The solution offered by Scotus is characteristic of the change in the outlook of 14th-century thought. In every individual he distinguished two realities, one universal, the other individual. The universal is common to all individuals of the species, but the individual element is a positive reality which is quite distinct from the essence. The principle of Individuation is not an accident but is grounded in the essence itself. It may be described as a mode of real substance. Thus, Socrates is constituted by the meeting of two different lines of reality. As a member of the human race, he shares in its common humanity. But he is also Socrates and not Plato, and as such possesses a number of characteristics that are peculiar to him and different from those belonging to Plato. The reality which makes Socrates just the individual that he is, is called by Scotus, Thisness (*haecceitas*). It brings to the nature of Socrates the property of being incommunicable.

Strictly speaking, *haecceitas* is not a form, since it does not modify the specific nature. It confers on the individual a positive determination which is not a property of the species. From this point of view, the individual has more perfection than the species. On the other hand, *haecceitas* may be thought of as approximating to matter in so far as it restricts the form and makes it of a particular kind. From the standpoint of its restrictive operation, it would follow that the individual has less perfection than the species.

Scotus teaches that there are six entities in the individual composite. The following diagram shows clearly how these entities are united in the individual.

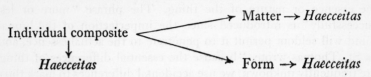

It might be objected that Scotus breaks up the unity of the individual by creating these distinctions. The answer is contained in his conception of the Formal distinction (*distinctio formalis a parte rei*), and so frequently does he use this idea that the term "Formalism" has been applied to his philosophy. The *distinctio realis* is a real distinction between two things which are in fact quite different. Thus the distinction between the oak and the ash is a real one because it distinguishes between what are in reality two different things (*res*). We do, however, in thought, draw a distinction between the different elements which logically constitute one individual. Thus, in considering the species, we make a distinction between what is common to the genus and the differences which mark off the species from others in the same genus.

Scotus terms such distinctions Formal distinctions, and since the things differentiated have no separate existence in reality, he coins the word "formalities" (*formalitates*) to indicate them. Such distinctions are more than mere mental differentiations (*distinctiones rationis*), because they are based upon a reality which enters into the existence of the object. This is expressed by calling them *distinctiones formalis a parte rei* to show that they are not merely subjective but have also an objective reference. "For example, in Socrates the intellectual and sensitive soul may be conceptually distinguished, though they are not two things, for Socrates has only one soul. And yet the distinction is not a mere fiction of the mind, for Socrates' sensational and intellectual processes are objectively different."[1]

Another example of the use of the Formal distinction is in regard to the problem of essence and existence. We saw that in created substances St. Thomas held that there is a real distinction between the two. The visible world is composed of a number of

[1] HARRIS, *op. cit.*, vol. ii, p. 115.

individual substances, men, horses, trees or stones. If we ask what any one of these substances is, the answer will take the form of a definition, which attempts to give, more or less successfully, the essence or nature of the thing. The phrase "more or less successfully" is introduced since the imperfection of the human mind will seldom permit it to penetrate to the actual essence, and, as St. Thomas wrote, "because the essential differences of things are frequently unknown, we use accidental differences to mark those which are essential."[1] The definition of a triangle as a three-sided rectilineal figure, or of a human being as a rational animal, expresses the essences of a triangle or a man, respectively.

St. Thomas argued, however, that to know the essence is no guarantee that an object possessing that nature exists. It may be possible to express the essence of a fabulous creature such as a unicorn, but we know that no such animal exists. A naturalist can describe the characteristics of the great auk although such a bird has been extinct for well over a century. Hence, St. Thomas believed that in an actually existent creature there is a real distinction between its essence and its existence, the former being related to the latter as potentiality to actuality. We saw that this distinction held good for the angelic nature. Only with regard to the Supreme Being, God, can it be said that His Essence is identical with His Existence.

Scotus is not so radical as St. Thomas. "It is quite false to say that being is distinct from essence," he wrote. At the same time, he realized, with St. Thomas, that identity of essence and existence in a finite being would destroy the distinction between God and creatures. He felt that the truth that the creature does not derive its existence from itself, but from God, had to be emphasized. Therefore, whilst denying the real distinction between essence and existence, Scotus taught that there is a *distinctio formalis a parte rei*.

His psychology and theory of knowledge also are quite distinct from those of the Thomist. St. Thomas had upheld a real distinction between the soul and its faculties. From the modern point of view, this doctrine readily lends itself to the faculty psychology which was popular in some quarters in the 19th century. For Scotus, the soul is a unity and its faculties are only names to describe the activities of the one substance. The distinction between such powers as those of the will and the

[1] *In Lib. de An.*, lect. 1.

intelligence is a *distinctio formalis a parte rei*. In the same way, the faculties are formally distinct from the essence of the soul.

Scotus emphatically declares that the intelligence can know the individual. He argues that if the theological definition of sin as an inordinate affection for a particular object is accepted, our will cannot love that particular unless it can first be known through the intellect. Hence, he criticizes the Thomistic theory of knowledge as resting upon the false assumption that the universal alone is knowable. In truth, the individual is highest in the rank of being and, far from being unintelligible, it forms the very basis of our knowledge. The intellect has a direct intuition of the individual. All our judgments are in the form of universals, but none of these universals, not even the whole collection of them, can constitute the individual for us. The universal is obtained through a process of abstraction from the singular, so that before we can know it, the mind must first gain a knowledge of the individual.

The intuition of the individual is, however, vague and confused as compared with the clear and distinct knowledge which flows from the grasp of the universal. Scotus believed that this was due to the defect of our intellect because of the conditions of its earthly existence, and not to any perfection in the object of knowledge. Thus, perfect knowledge, as it exists in God, is intuitive and presents a contrast to the human mind which only grasps intuitively certain general aspects of the individual such as its numerical unity, its independent existence and its characteristic of being incommunicable.

Scotus criticized the Arabians for their view of the passivity of the intellect. They compared the intellect to matter as being a capacity for receiving intelligibles. In essence, the intellect is an activity, and this characteristic is manifest in its interpretation of sense experience. Although there is a superficial resemblance in the terms used by Scotus and St. Thomas, the actual meaning given to the Active and Passive Intellects by Scotus is quite different. The Active Intellect is the intellect in as far as it is active. It perceives the sensible image and from it produces, in the Passive Intellect, a species which is the representation of the universal. The elaboration of this species through the activity of the intellect results in the completed concept. Like St. Bonaventure, Scotus believed that the Possible Intellect is not purely passive. All through the process, Scotus emphasizes the activity rather than the

H

passivity of intellect. His objection to the Thomist theory was that it leant too much to the Arabians by making the rôle of intellect one of the passive reception of truth.

The species makes no positive contribution to the act of thought. It is a co-agent rather than a principal cause, and acts rather as a restriction to thought. In its true nature, the intellect is able to know all being, the super-sensible as well as the sensible. In knowing a particular thing, its power is limited and restricted.

Aquinas has often been described as an intellectualist and Scotus as a voluntarist. The latter taught that the intellect and the will together form the rational nature of man, but the will is the superior. The intellect is always determined by its object, but the will is free and is never restricted by the intellectual presentation of the good. "The intellect itself as active and passive and the intelligible object are the sufficient cause of the act of cognition. The will itself contributes nothing to the understanding—it is not even a concurrent cause; it lies wholly outside the sphere of the knowing process."[1]

It is quite true, Scotus affirms, that knowledge of the good must precede action, but the sequence of knowledge and action is a succession without a necessary connection. The will is a *potentia libera*; it is free to turn away from the good presented by the intellect. Hence, although the intellect may guide the will, it cannot determine it. The will is determined by nothing other than itself. It is in fact the power of self-determination. Even in the presence of the Supreme Good, the will preserves its freedom and can turn away from the intellectual presentation. In this way, the primacy belongs to the will and not to the intellect. Both the will and the intellect are in the end directed to one object, God, but it is through an exercise of the will that man gains possession of his last end.

Scotus was not at all satisfied with the Thomistic proofs of the existence of God. He agreed with St. Thomas on one point, namely, that as we do not in this life have an intuitive knowledge of God, it is necessary to prove His existence, and that our argument must be *a posteriori*, from the effects to their cause. We have no innate idea of God's existence, nor is it possible to deduce this truth from the bare notion of a being than whom no greater can be conceived. The latter was the mistake of St. Anselm, and

[1] HARRIS, *op. cit.*, vol. ii., p. 286.

like Aquinas, Scotus rejects the Ontological argument. God is the Infinite, and the idea of Him is a very complex one which is a product of our own experience. It is not, however, to be rejected. Although it is not adequate to express the nature of God, it does represent truthfully certain aspects of His nature. Thus the reason, without the help of Divine Revelation, can form some notion of God as the Infinite.

In opposition to St. Thomas, Scotus puts forward the theory that we have of God and creatures a concept that is univocal; namely, the concept of being. It is easy to misread him on this point. St. Thomas had taught that terms drawn from our finite experience, and applied to God, describe Him in an analogical sense. Scotus thinks this goes too far in the direction of agnosticism. But does not his own teaching lead towards pantheism? He is careful not to compromise himself, and he avoids doing so by drawing a distinction between the logical and the metaphysical genus. God has no place in the ten categories into which being in the logical sense can be classified. They deal with creatures which have being, but God is Being. But God and creatures can be included in the same metaphysical genus. The distinction between them is that of being *per se* and being *per participationem*. The being of God and of creatures are, therefore, not the same, but Scotus wishes to express the idea that the same term, being, when applied to God, has the same meaning as in its application to creatures, though in the former case, it means so much more. In the creature, being is limited by the fact that a creature is finite; it is this, not that. God, on the other hand, is unlimited and infinite. Finitude is the intrinsic mode of being applicable to the creature, whilst infinity belongs to God alone.

Scotus does not employ the argument from motion. He challenges the fundamental assumption that everything in motion is moved by something other than itself, and he no doubt looked upon the proof as a special case of the more general argument from efficient causality. He may also have thought it dangerous for a Christian to use a proof which was pagan in its origin.

Scotus offers three main arguments for the existence of God. The first is based on the idea of contingency. Experience shows us that the beings of the visible universe are liable to change. Therefore, it is necessary to assign to them a cause which is outside them, for we cannot assume that they came into being from nothing. This involves a hierarchy of causes, and since there cannot be a regress to infinity, it is necessary to postulate a Being which contains within itself the reason for its existence. Such a Being is necessary and eternal; otherwise the unity of the universe would be destroyed.

He also argues from the existence of degrees of perfection in the world which demand a Supreme Perfection which is God. Lastly, our inner conscience forces us to admit that only an infinite Good is able to satisfy the will. Our conscience is the source of all certitude; therefore, God, the Infinite Good, exists.

Dr. D. J. B. Hawkins sums up the position of Scotus in the words: "Such is the third of the great thirteenth-century metaphysical systems. St. Bonaventure, although deeply affected by the rediscovery of Aristotle, had deliberately kept as close as he could to the tradition of St. Augustine. St. Thomas Aquinas, basing himself wholeheartedly on Aristotelian principles, showed that the new philosophy was capable of reconquering the religious conclusions of the old. Duns Scotus occupies something of an intermediate position, liking to follow Bonaventure but taking a considerably more Aristotelian line."[1]

Suggestions for Further Reading

McKeon (vol. ii) gives a translation of selections from Duns Scotus.

C. R. S. Harris's *Duns Scotus*, 2 vols. (Clarendon Press: 1927), is a very complete account of the philosophy of Scotus, but it suffers from the defect that he makes considerable use of the *De Rerum Principio*, which is of doubtful authenticity.

D. E. Sharp's *Franciscan Philosophy at Oxford* (O.U.P.: 1930) contains a valuable account of Scotus. Dr. Sharp does not accept the *De Rerum Principio* as genuine.

[1] HAWKINS, D. J. B., *A Sketch of Medieval Philosophy* (Sheed & Ward: 1946), p. 112.

CHAPTER XIV

WILLIAM OF OCKHAM AND HIS FOLLOWERS

It has been customary to date the decline of Scholasticism from the 14th century, and many writers have asserted that William of Ockham represents the beginning of the deterioration. Such a belief does less than justice to the thinkers of the 14th century and completely overlooks the part played by this period in the development of mediæval philosophy. As was previously said, the 13th century was an age of construction, and its achievements were followed by a period of criticism. The transition from synthesis and construction to criticism showed its first signs in the thought of Roger Bacon and Duns Scotus, who began to question many of the conclusions arrived at by previous thinkers. It was overshadowed by their own constructive achievements, but it became more marked in the early 14th century and reached its zenith in the school of William of Ockham.

Before dealing with Ockham's teaching, it is important to say something of two of his predecessors, who, working independently, arrived at a number of significant conclusions. The first was the Dominican, Durandus of Saint-Pourçain. He was a pupil of Jacques of Metz, a faithful follower of St. Thomas. Durandus was born at some time between 1270 and 1275 and was teaching as a Master of Theology at Paris in 1312. His chief work was the *Commentary on the Sentences*. J. Koch has shown that an earlier and a later edition of the work exist. In its earlier form, the commentary earned the censure of the Dominican Order which had proclaimed St. Thomas as its official teacher and doctor. The objection of his superiors caused Durandus to modify some of his statements in the revised treatise. Nevertheless, certain of his doctrines were condemned by the Order in 1314.

At this time, Durandus was residing at the Papal court at Avignon, and he saw fit to withdraw most of the statements which had caused such stringent criticism. His philosophical teaching, however, did not seem to hinder his ecclesiastical preferment, since he became Bishop of Limoux in 1317 and died as Bishop of Meaux in 1334. Evidently, as Bishop of Meaux, Durandus felt himself more independent, for he issued a third version of his *Commentary* in which he returned to the views he had held in his earlier days.

Durandus rejected the Thomistic theory of knowledge on the ground that it involved the doctrine of Representative Perception. In his view, both the sensible and intelligible species and the Active Intellect which abstracts the species are redundant. Every real existence is an individual, so that universal concepts have no existence outside the mind, but they are definitely related to the objects which they represent. In other words, thought can give a true picture of external reality. Durandus has been labelled sometimes as a Nominalist, sometimes as a Conceptualist, but, as De Wulf remarks, "Durandus, then, remains faithful to the Realism of Abelard, St. Thomas and Scotus. The destructive influence of Conceptualism does not begin with him as was for a long time believed."[1]

Durandus believed that there was no need to concern ourselves with the problem of individuation. Since experience gives us the individual, it is the universal which stands in need of explanation. The same reality when grasped in a determinate fashion is singular, and it is universal when conceived indeterminately.

Another thinker of the same period was Peter Aureolus. He is supposed to have been a pupil of Scotus at Paris in 1304. He became a master at Paris in 1318, Bishop of Aix in 1321, and died in 1322. His principal work was the *Commentary on the Sentences*, which exists in two versions. This work is a critique of the value and function of the universal in knowledge. Like Durandus, he dispenses with the Thomist mechanism of knowledge. All that is necessary to explain knowledge, he declares, is the existence of individual things which are to be known and the intellect which knows them. Conception is the activity through which the intellect apprehends its object, and the thing, in as far as it is known, is a concept. The latter is a representation of the object known and, as such, exists only in the intellect. Nevertheless, although the concept does not belong to the real order of existence, it does bring the mind into direct contact with reality.

[1] DE WULF, *op. cit.*, vol. iii., p. 21.

Peter tells us that "it is more noble to know an individual and particular thing than to know it in an abstract and universal manner." Knowledge by means of universals is confused and indistinct, whilst the knowledge of the individual is the exemplar and the sign of our grasp of the universal, since it explains and illustrates the latter and is more clear and certain. The true object of knowledge is the external individual thing, whilst the universal is due to the activity of the mind. In knowledge, the mind comes into direct contact with the object it knows, and, therefore, the Active Intellect and the species are not required. Peter, using a principle often attributed to Ockham, gives as his reason for the rejection of the species and Active Intellect, "It is useless to explain through many causes what can be explained by fewer (*Frustra fit per plura quod fieri potest per pauciora*)."[1]

Peter Aureolus, like Durandus, has been termed a Nominalist, but the outline of his teaching given above seems to show that he still remained a Realist, but in his dissatisfaction with the Thomist and Scotist theories of knowledge, he was feeling his way towards the Conceptualist position. In some ways, too, his statements suggest that he was harking back to the older Augustinian theory of sense-perception which he extended to cover the operations of the intellect. The Conceptualist view was expressed unequivocally by William of Ockham, who was a determined critic of Realism, whether in the more extreme form which is found in St. Anselm or in the more moderate standpoint of St. Thomas.

William was born about 1290 at Ockham in Surrey. Few details are known about his early life. He studied at Oxford, probably between 1310 and 1318, and received his bachelor's degree in 1324. Modern criticism has dealt severely with the traditions which have grown up in regard to William's career. There is no evidence to show that he studied under Duns Scotus, or taught at Paris, or obtained his master's degree. His *Commentary on the Sentences* was written at Oxford about 1318–19.

William's teaching provoked a good deal of opposition, and in 1324 he was summoned to Avignon to give an account of his views. It was evidently not considered satisfactory, for he was placed in confinement for three years. The date of his entry into

---

[1] The so-called " Ockham's Razor " runs *Entia non sunt multiplicanda praeter necessitatum*—*i.e.*, we are not entitled to assume the existence of anything more than is necessary to account for our experience.

the Franciscan Order is not known, but it is believed to have been when he was quite a young man.

William took a leading part in contemporary politics. Since 1305, the Papal court had resided in Avignon and was subjected to French influence. The crisis came in 1316, when John XXII was chosen as Pope, after the Church had been without a chief Bishop for two years and four months. John's chief characteristic was his greed for money. In order to defray the expenses of his establishment, he seized every opportunity of extorting money from the different European countries, and his exactions in England aroused extreme discontent. John sold benefices in the open market, and his subjection to the French king and his antagonism towards the Emperor did not make for popularity in either England or Germany.

About this time a dispute arose with regard to the Imperial crown. The claimants were the Archduke Frederic of Austria and Lewis of Bavaria, and John endeavoured to secure the rôle of arbitrator for himself. After seven years of civil war, Lewis became Emperor under the title of Lewis IV. He immediately formed an alliance directed against the Pope. John replied by excommunicating him and placed his lands under an interdict. Lewis demanded the assembly of a General Council of the Church. Many writers supported him, none more enthusiastically than William of Ockham, who appeared in the guise of a champion of the secular power against the Papacy. His arguments were similar to those employed two centuries later by Luther, who acknowledged his debt to William. Tradition states that his writings were condemned and that he was seized and imprisoned by John at Avignon. He managed to escape and sought refuge with Lewis, and historians have credited William with the saying, *Tu me defendas gladio, ego te defendam calamo* ("If you will protect me by your sword, I will defend you with my pen"). Lewis wanted his son's adulterous marriage, which was in open defiance of the laws of the Church, declared valid. William was prepared to undertake this defence and declared that the state is supreme in all political matters. After the death of Lewis, William became reconciled with the Church and died in 1349 or 1350.

William's chief philosophical works are his *Commentary on the Sentences*, the *Quodlibeta* and the *Commentaries on Aristotle*. His logical teaching is contained in the *Expositio Aurea* ("a Golden and Extremely useful Exposition of the Ancient Art") and the *Summa Totius Logica* (Sum of all Logic). In addition, he wrote a number of political treatises.

As Ockham taught at Oxford, he was naturally influenced by the interest in experimental and natural science which, as we have seen, was so attractive to Roger Bacon. In fact, the term empiricist can be applied to him so long as we do not understand it in the sense it acquired in the 17th and 18th centuries.

Direct evidence, he believed, is the only proof of any assertion. This, of course, does not rule out the truth of a proposition which is deduced from a previous one that has been established by immediate evidence. Our assertions may be classified as either abstract or intuitive. In the former case, the assertion has relevance only in regard to the relations which exist between our ideas. Even when logic has established the validity of these relations, there is no guarantee that the order and relation of our ideas correspond to anything real in the external world. Thus the old problem of the correspondence of thought and reality recurs.

William solves it in a very drastic fashion. He states that the assertion based on direct intuition alone guarantees both its truth and the existence of the reality it affirms. The actual state of affairs in the external world is known only through intuition. It is only by the seeing something white that enables one to affirm with confidence that this object is white. Direct experience as given in intuition provides for certainty in our knowledge. It should, however, be noted that sensible intuition is not the only kind; the mind can have a direct intuition of its states and activities, for it experiences them in its thinking, feeling and willing. Intuition, then, is the starting point of knowledge, and by generalizing our knowledge of individuals, we arrive at the universal propositions which are the basic principles of all science.

Ockham applies this principle to the study of the Aristotelian categories. He warns us that although he accepts them in their logical signification, he does not imply that the distinctions between the ten categories are distinctions that can be observed in the real world. Thus, the categories of quantity and quality refer to the same thing as the category of substance, and time and space are only adverbial determinations which add no further reality to the things concerned. He is especially interested in the category of relation. One of the essential relations in knowledge is that of cause and effect. He asserts that a relation contains no other reality except that of the two objects related. Let us suppose the contrary. It follows that when I raise my finger, thus changing all the relations of position between my finger and every other object in the world, I am creating an infinite number of new beings. Relation is therefore a mental, not a real fact. Apply this to the conception of cause and effect. The maxim of economy (the so-called razor) forbids us to assume the existence of anything that is not guaranteed by experience. Hence, to obtain definite knowledge of the cause of any phenomenon, it is necessary to have recourse to experience. A is the cause of the effect B, if experience shows that when A is present, whatever other factors are absent, the phenomenon occurs; and conversely, that if A is absent and all other circumstances are present, the effect is not produced.

With these ideas in his mind, William rejects as redundant the intelligible species of the Thomists. He declares most emphatically that in the real world, only individuals exist. The universal has no existence outside the mind of the knowing subject.

"There is no universal really existing outside the mind . . . its extra-mental existence is as impossible as it is impossible for a man to exist as an ass." Again, "Every real thing outside the mind is in its nature an individual (*Omnis res positiva extra animam eo ipso est singularis*)." The process of learning starts with the particular and concrete or, as Ockham phrases it, "according to the primacy of generation, the understanding knows the individual first."

The Thomists, who teach that the universal is realized in the multitude of particulars in the sense world, come up against a paradox which defies reconciliation. If the universal is one, how can it be multiplied and shared by a number of individuals? If it is so multiplied, it is impossible to see how it can be one.

But what kind of being does the universal possess in the mind? The answer to this question involves an inquiry into the nature of knowledge. Consider what happens when I hear such a statement as, Man is mortal. The speaker's vocal organs have produced a number of vibrations in the air which reach my ears so that I hear a number of words or sounds. Such statements as, Man is a rational animal, are accepted as true although in their essential nature they are reduced to nothing more than a collection of words. Even scientific knowledge, which consists of universal propositions, is ultimately a sequence of words. What guarantees the validity of these propositions?

If we examine different assertions, we shall find that they fall into two distinct classes. In some propositions, the words stand for real objects existing outside the mind. In others, they merely represent ideas in the mind. The former give us the real sciences which are concerned with the objects of the physical world; the others furnish us with such rational sciences as logic. But the important point is that all universal propositions, whether they contain the real or the rational, are composed of words and can be ultimately reduced to nothing more than utterances of the voice. One can see why many of his contemporaries called Ockham a Nominalist. But his particular brand of Nominalism is quite different from the so-called Nominalism of Roscelin or that of thinkers like Hobbes or the Mills.

The latter will be evident if we carry our analysis of William's teaching a stage further. The words of a proposition can stand for either other words, or ideas, or objects. The first is of mere grammatical interest; the two latter are more important. Granted the first assumption that only the individual exists, it seems reasonable to conclude that words which represent concepts really stand for a collection of individuals. The problem, however, is more difficult than this. When an object is presented to the mind it can be perceived either distinctly or in a confused manner so that it is not possible to single out the object in its distinction from others which resemble it. A distinct conception enables us to differentiate the object from others. Since only individuals have a real existence, it follows that they are the cause of both clear and confused knowledge. If my impression of Socrates is a confused one, when he approaches me in the street, I recognize him as a man but not as Socrates, and the term "man" stands for a confused conception because I cannot distinguish him from Plato. If, however, I have a distinct impression of Socrates, I can single him out from other men and pointing to him say, "There is Socrates." In the latter case, my statement refers to an individual person, an object and not a concept. But both terms, man and Socrates, refer to the same object; the one confusedly, the other distinctly. The sole difference lies in the way in which I consider the object. "The term man is a universal because it can be true indifferently of this or that individual. It is universal

by its signification, or in so far as it is a sign; but it is not a conventional or arbitrary sign. It is a natural sign independent of the
word which expresses it. Ockham therefore reaches the positive
conclusion that the universal is not an object but a function. It is
this function that he calls a sign or symbol."[1]

In order to simplify the relation between the mind and the
individuals which are the objects of its knowledge, it is necessary
to dispense with everything that is irrelevant. Two things and two
things only are needed to explain knowledge; the knowing subject
and the object which he knows. When the knower comes face
to face with the object, we have all that is necessary to explain
knowledge, and the intelligible species is redundant. In any case,
nobody can see a species or have a direct intuition of it. Ockham,
therefore, shows himself a staunch antagonist of any view which
suggests the possibility of representative perception, and he
occupies a position similar to that of Reid and the Common Sense
school of the 18th century.[2]

Dr. Mellone sums up the psychology of the formation of
universals as follows: "We have then innumerable acts of sense-
perception directly related to external objects. Every such act
leaves behind it a mental trace or mental disposition (*habitus*)
resembling itself; and when several such acts, or their mental
traces, occur together, their common elements (*consimilia*) are
assimilated. . . . The intellect is nothing but a derivative con-
tinuation of this primary sense-elaboration of given material.
That it should be so is a fundamental law of the mind which we
have simply to accept. The procedure of the intellect is always the
same. Abstracting from the variable particulars of sense experience,
it retains the common or permanent elements; and with the
indispensable help of language forms what logic calls 'class
concepts.' The only existence which the concepts have consists
in these ever-recurring acts of mental abstraction, which, again
with the indispensable help of language, are combined into
propositions and arguments."[3]

Ockham now turns to deal with the nature of scientific knowledge.

[1] BREHIER, EMILE, *La Philosophie du Moyen Age* (Albin Michel, Paris: 1937),
p. 400.

[2] Sir William Hamilton in his edition of the works of Thomas Reid (Longmans:
1863), pp. 970–1, states that Reid obtained his doctrine of perception from Ockham
through the medium of Gassendi.

[3] MELLONE, *op. cit.*, pp. 252–3.

How far, for example, is such knowledge valid? His answer is contained in the theory of Signification. We have already seen that the universal has no existence apart from the particular object or groups of objects which it represents or for which it stands (*supponere*). It is a sign (*signum*) of something that exists outside the mind. A class name such as "man" or "tree" stands for the multitude of different individuals considered from the standpoint of certain common elements. When Ockham terms the universals "fabrications" (*ficta*), he does not mean that they give us an untrue picture of reality. He is emphasizing that they are mental constructions which have no real counterpart in the external world. Thus he defines the universal as "a mental conception signifying univocally several individuals."

Ockham distinguished two kinds of signs—natural and conventional. The former stand for objects existing outside the mind. Conventional signs, however, signify concepts. Thus, the spoken or written word is a conventional sign because it has been selected to represent what the corresponding concept signifies naturally. Men of his own age called Ockham a Nominalist, but such a term does not truly represent his position. He agrees that universals have a real existence in the mind, where they perform functions which are essential to thinking; he draws a distinction between sense perception and conceptual thinking, and he admits that such concepts are valid in interpreting the world of experience. "The universal is no mere figment to which there is no correspondence of anything like it in objective being, as that is figured in the thinker." Many mediæval writers referred to his system as Terminism, but from the modern point of view he would be called a Conceptualist.

Ockham's Terminism is apparent in his treatment of logic. He considers logic as a science of the second intention. Real sciences have, for their objects, terms of the first intention—*i.e.*, existing things in nature. They investigate natural objects and their properties, but they study them apart from such accidental determinations as particular time or place. In the business of investigating nature, the sciences employ terms which stand for concepts which, in their turn, signify individual things. Logic is a rational science because it studies the intentions or fabrications of the mind. Hence it is no concern to the logician whether the propositions with which he deals do or do not accord with fact. His function is to consider the form of the proposition and the relations that should exist between its terms. The logician does not bother his head about the objects which the terms signify. His interest in them is from the point of view of the different forms of signification. Hence, logic can be justly called a formal science.

William applied his theory of knowledge to natural theology. He attacked the validity of the Aristotelian and Thomistic argument for the existence of God, an argument based on the idea of a First Unmoved Cause of motion. He challenged the statement that a thing cannot be self-moved—e.g., an angel or the soul is self-moved —and denied that a regress to infinity is impossible. The fact that it cannot be thought is no proof of its non-existence. "There are even cases where it is necessary to assume an infinite regression. If I strike the end of a stick so that the vibration is carried step by step in the direction of the opposite end, then it must be granted that an infinite number of moving causes are brought into play, since there will be an infinite number of parts to a given length. It is, then, not impossible but, on the contrary, it is necessary to affirm the existence of an infinite chain of causes."[1]

Ockham did not believe that any rational argument can prove the existence of God. All that the so-called proofs are able to do is to affirm that God's existence is probable. Nor is intuitive knowledge of God possible to man in this present life (as a wayfarer); that is the prerogative of the blessed in heaven. The idea of God cannot be demonstrated. It is a complex idea and its elements consist of abstractions from finite experience which have been magnified indefinitely. Nor can the Attributes of God be demonstrated. Knowledge of God and His Attributes depends entirely on revelation; it is the concern not of philosophy but of faith. "With Occam, Scripture, revelation, is absolutely infallible, neither requiring nor admitting the proofs of reason. To be sure he coordinates with it the law of nature, which God has implanted in our minds. But otherwise theology, faith, stands alone, very isolated, although on the alleged most certain of foundations. The provinces of science and faith are different. . . . So the breach in the old scholastic, Thomist, unity was made utter and irreparable. Theology stands on the surest of bases, but isolated, unsupported; philosophy, all human knowledge, extends around and below it, and is discredited because irrelevant to highest truth."[2]

---

[1] GILSON, ETIENNE, *La Philosophie au Moyen Age* (Payot, Paris: 1947), p. 649.
[2] TAYLOR, H. O., *The Mediaeval Mind* (Macmillan: 1919), p. 549.

In his moral teaching, William pushes to the extreme the primacy of the will as taught by Duns Scotus. The sole difference between good and evil is that God has willed certain actions to be meritorious and others to be sinful. He acts in a purely arbitrary fashion. If He wished, God could make theft and adultery moral acts, but, in fact, He has not done so. The only basis of morality lies in the Divine Will. In a similar way, God could cause a person to have an intuition of an object which does not exist. There are no limits to His arbitrary power. Ockham is trying to say that what we call rational is so because God willed it. God could have willed an entirely topsy-turvy world, and then we should call good those things which we now call evil.

The teaching of William of Ockham spread rapidly during the 14th and 15th centuries, especially at Paris. The new ideas were so enthusiastically received that the followers of St. Thomas and Duns Scotus were called *antiqui* in distinction from the *moderni* who embraced the teaching of Ockham. Terminism even invaded the Dominican Order, which could be regarded as definitely conservative in its outlook.

The ecclesiastical authorities were actively suspicious of the new tendencies. In 1339, the teaching of Terminism was condemned, and the faculty of arts at Paris deprived of their chairs certain professors who held these views. In 1346, Clement VI wrote to masters and students of the university warning them of the dangerous tendencies of Ockhamism. Even as late as 1425, the Prince Elector demanded that the masters at Cologne should justify their preference for Ockham rather than for St. Thomas. But as Gilson remarks, the opposition to the introduction of Aristotle's works in the 13th century did not prevent them from being read, and, in a similar way, ecclesiastical censure could not hinder the spread of Ockham's teaching.

At Oxford, Terminism was defended by the Franciscan, Adam Woodham (d. 1358), and at Cambridge by Robert Holkot, the Dominican (d. 1349). The latter pushed the voluntaryism of Ockham to its furthest extreme. He maintained that God could be the immediate cause of sin. Since by His absolute power (*potentia absoluta*), God could command a man to hate him, "sequitur necessario quod Deus sit immediata causa peccati." One of the best-known members of Ockham's school was Nicholas of Autrecourt, who taught at Paris and was summoned by Benedict

XII to Rome in 1340 to answer a charge of heresy. After the condemnation of his doctrines, he retracted and died some time after 1350. Nicholas was called by Rashdall "the Hume of the Middle Ages."

Following the teaching of Ockham, Nicholas believed that experience is the only guide as to whether an Object exists or does not exist. Therefore, it is not legitimate to argue that because one thing exists that fact must lead us to assume the existence of another. He applies this principle to the idea of substance. Experience reveals the existence of certain qualities or accidents, but this does not justify the view that a substance in which these qualities inhere must also exist. In the same way, there is no necessary connection between our experience of the activity of willing and the existence of a faculty of will. All that experience entitles us to do in such cases is to suggest that the existence of the corresponding substance or faculty is a possibility. Necessity is replaced by possibility.

Nicholas considered the relation between cause and effect on similar lines. Experience shows me that, in the past, A has always been followed by B. Therefore, given the same conditions, I can expect A to be followed by B in the future. "Because it was evident to me in the past that my hand became warm when I brought it close to the fire, I conclude that at the present moment it will probably become warm if I place it near the fire (*Quia mihi fuit evidens aliquando, quod quando ponebam manum ad ignem eram calidus, ideo probabile est mihi, quod si nunc ponerem quod essem calidus*)." Holding this conception of causality, Nicholas will not surprise us when he refuses to accept any proof of the existence of God which is dependent on the notion of cause and effect.

He also rejects the Scholastic view of the relation of soul to body as that of form to matter, and he substitutes a materialistic explanation. He adopts the atomism of Epicurus, and instead of atrributing generation and corruption to the coming into being or the passing away of a form, he speaks of the coming together or the disintegration of atoms. "When we speak of the corruption of a thing, this is none other than the dispersal and division of the particles which compose it." When, at death, the atoms which form the body disintegrate, the intellect and sense, being spiritual realities, continue to exist.

Nicholas is not only a materialist, but is also a phenomenalist.

We judge truly only when we judge on the basis of appearance. Thus Protagoras was right when he asserted that honey is sweet to a person whose taste is sound but bitter to him whose taste is impaired and that both judge truly, so that two contradictories can be true at the same time. The same applies to dreams; as appearances they are true. If one dreams of fighting the Saracens or that he is a cardinal, the images of the dream are true. "If anyone dreams he is a cardinal, he really is a cardinal (*Si quis somniat se esse cardinalem, sic erit*)."

At the same time, Nicholas thought it prudent to convince the world of his orthodoxy. He wrote in the prologue to his treatise, "I wish to protest that neither in this treatise nor in any others do I desire to assert anything that is contrary to the articles of the faith or the decisions of the Church, or against the articles, the opposites of which were condemned at Paris." The last phrase refers to the condemnation of 1277 and is reminiscent of the Latin Averroists and their doctrine of the two truths.

Ockham's teaching was responsible for quite a different line of development. Just as some of his followers threw overboard the metaphysics of their predecessors, so others applied his teaching to natural science, and Gilson suggests that the foundations of modern astronomy and physics were laid in the 14th century. Ockham himself initiated this, for he had inherited the Oxford interest in the study of natural science. He was profoundly dissatisfied with the accepted explanation of motion, which was based on Aristotle. According to this view, the form is the cause of movement in living creatures. This explanation was extended to the case of the stone which is dropped and the feather which is released by the hand. The stone is naturally heavy and therefore it seeks its natural place on the ground whilst the feather has the quality of lightness and tends to rise. But how are we to explain a violent movement such as that of a stone cast by the hand or an arrow shot by the archer? The difficulty lies in the fact that the stone continues to move after the impelling force, the hand, has been withdrawn. Moreover, it moves upwards, a direction contrary to its natural place. Aristotle had explained this by supposing that the air surrounding the stone is set in motion. We can picture the disturbance of the air on the analogy of the ripples produced on the surface of a pond into which a pebble has been cast. The ripples spread outwards in wider and wider circles. So the movement induced in the air spreads and carries the moving body forwards in its movement. When this movement is spent, the stone ceases to move and returns to its natural place on the ground.

Ockham considered that this solution of the problem was very unsatisfactory. Suppose two archers shoot towards one another and the arrows meet midway. On Aristotle's hypothesis one would have to say that the air at the meeting point moved in two opposite directions. Nor does the hand in throwing a stone transmit motion to it. Ockham argued that experience shows that when the hand is brought slowly and gently into contact with a body, the latter does not move. In modern terms, the force applied must be sufficiently great to overcome the inertia of a body at rest before motion is initiated. Using his principle of economy, he suggested that no other assumption is necessary to explain movement other than the moving body itself. Once a body has begun to move in one direction, it will continue in the same until it meets with interference. This speculation presents an interesting parallel to Newton's First Law of Motion. Ockham was also opposed to the view that the mover must be in contact with the moving body, either directly or through a medium. In contradiction, he cited two instances given by experience in which a force is able to act over a distance: the sun's rays passing to the earth, and the magnet attracting iron.

The study of motion was continued by John Buridan, who was born at Béthune shortly after the commencement of the century. He was rector of the University of Paris in 1328 and again in 1340, and died shortly after 1358. Buridan carried his speculations further than Ockham. He explained the continuance of motion in a moving body by supposing that when the mover sets it in motion he imparts an impetus to it. This impetus is proportional to the speed with which the mover moves that which is in motion and to the amount of matter contained in the moving body. When the resistance of the air and the weight of the body are able to overcome the original impetus, the body falls to the ground. This hypothesis explained also why a heavy body can be thrown a greater distance than a lighter one. It shows also why a stone dropped from a height continually accelerates in its journey to the ground. It begins its movement because of its weight, but at the same time the weight adds a certain impetus to it. This results in an increase of the speed with which it falls. The more the body is accelerated in its motion, the greater becomes the impetus, and so the acceleration increases. The movements of the heavenly bodies can be explained in a similar way. Ockham had shown already that the belief that they are composed of a matter different from that of terrestrial bodies is untenable. Buridan suggests that the same laws of motion apply to both. When God created the heavenly bodies, He imparted an impetus to them which keeps them continually in motion.

Buridan is well known for his doctrine of psychological determinism. He taught that the will chooses the good in general terms, but if faced by two concrete goods, it must of necessity choose the one which appears to be the better. The will is, however, free to the extent that it can refrain from action so that the reason can make a fresh investigation of the alternatives. Ultimately, its choice will be the good that is judged to be the superior. Buridan's contemporaries ridiculed his view by the story of the ass which is placed midway between two bundles of hay equal in size and quality. The poor beast is attracted equally by each bundle and, unable to come to a decision, dies of hunger within reach of food.

Buridan's pupil was Albert of Saxe, sometimes called Albert the Little to distinguish him from Albert the Great. He was born about 1316 and studied at the newly formed University of Prague. Later he taught at Paris, became rector in 1337, and in 1365 was chosen as the first rector of the new University of Vienna. He was created Bishop of Helmstedt, which office he held until his death in 1390.

Albert developed Buridan's theory of falling bodies and, not content with the statement that a heavy body naturally falls to the earth, he asked the question, "To what part of the earth? Is it to the surface or towards the centre?" He distinguished two centres in a heavy body, what we should now call the centre of volume and the centre of gravity. These centres coincide only in a homogeneous body of regular shape. He investigated also the problem of the acceleration of falling bodies, but was unable to come to any definite conclusions. The heavy body, he concluded, falls to the earth as its natural place because its centre of gravity tends to union with the centre of the earth. Albert also considered the hypothesis of the rotation of the earth about its axis, but, coming to the conclusion that the evidence was insufficient to support the theory, he rejected it.

Nicholas of Oresme was one of the most interesting members of the school of Ockham. He was studying at Paris in 1348, became head of the college at Navarre in 1356, and finished his days as Bishop of Lisieux in 1382. He earns the distinction of being the first philosopher to write an important work in the vernacular. He translated the *Ethics* and *Politics* of Aristotle into French. Nicholas also wrote a treatise on the coinage and others on mathematics and physics. In the latter, he anticipated modern thought in a remarkable way. To him, rather than to Descartes, belongs the credit of founding analytical geometry. He also anticipated Galileo in his formulation of the laws governing the acceleration of falling bodies due to gravity. The latter arrived at the same conclusions experimentally. Finally, Nicholas developed a theory similar to that of Copernicus, that it is the earth and not the heavens which moves. Earlier thinkers had agreed that the earth is stationary with the heavens moving round it.

SUGGESTIONS FOR FURTHER READING

A translation of passages from Ockham is given in vol. ii. of McKeon's *Selections*. E. A. Moody's *The Logic of William of Ockham* (Sheed & Ward: 1935) is a difficult book but well repays reading. Moody contends that far from despising Aristotle, Ockham was concerned to clear his logical doctrines from the accretions which had accumulated during the centuries. L. J. Walker, S.J., contributes an interesting essay, " Nicholas of Autrecourt's Refutation of Aristotelianism," to the *Downside Review*, Jan., 1949.

CHAPTER XV

NICHOLAS OF CUSA

NICHOLAS OF CUSA took his name from the village of Cues on the left bank of the Moselle, where he was born in 1401. When quite a small child, he showed an interest in reading, but his father, who was a boat owner, had no sympathy with his studious habits, and on one occasion, it is said, he knocked his son overboard with an oar. When quite a youth, Nicholas sought refuge with Count Theodoric of Manderschied, who sent him to the school of the Brothers of the Common Life, where both Thomas à Kempis and Erasmus were educated. In 1416 he matriculated at Heidelburg, and in the following year he entered the faculty of law at the University of Padua.

Here Nicholas became friendly with a number of famous scholars including his own master, Giuliano Cesarini, a well-known lawyer and theologian, and Toscanelli, the celebrated physician. In 1425, we find Nicholas at Cologne, where he became secretary to Cardinal Giordano Orsini, the Papal legate. This office involved frequent journeys to Italy, where the Renaissance was in full swing, and thus he was able to make contact with the most important of the Italian humanists of the time.

The early life of Nicholas was passed in what is often known as the conciliar period; the Council of Constance met in 1414. He was also a contemporary of the Hussite movement in Bohemia. Nicholas already held several ecclesiastical benefices, but the Council of Basle, which opened in 1431, offered him an opportunity of entering public life. He took a prominent part in the business of the Council, and at this time he commenced his first important work, the *De Concordantia Catholica*. During this period he was enthusiastic about the conciliar idea, and in his treatise he showed himself definitely anti-Papal. The *De Concordantia* discussed the rights and powers of a general council and defended the claim of the council to overthrow the Pope.

Four years later, Nicholas completely changed his views and for the rest of his life remained a faithful defender of the Papacy. Probably the anarchy into which the Council was falling was the main cause of his defection. In spite of his change of front, Nicholas maintained his interest in the new ideas which were soon to alter the whole outlook of Western Europe. He was essentially a man of the Renaissance in many ways, and this explains why he has sometimes been classified amongst modern thinkers. On the other hand, much of his thought was influenced by earlier philosophers, especially the Christian Neo-Platonists such as the Pseudo-Dionysius and Erigena.

One of the great hopes of the age, in which Nicholas shared, was the healing of the breach between the Eastern and the Western Churches. Negotiations were opened for reunion, and the diplomacy displayed by Nicholas was one of the main causes which led to the temporary union of the Greek and Latin Churches in 1438. For this service, amongst other rewards, Nicholas was given the cardinal's hat. He was nominated in 1446, but was actually elevated to that position in 1450, when he became Bishop of Brixen and Papal legate to Germany. He found a low standard of life combined with moral laxity amongst the German clergy, and he at once set about introducing reforms. The German clergy did not wish to be reformed, and very soon Nicholas encountered considerable opposition which led to open hostility between him and Duke Sigismund. Eventually, the latter declared war on the cardinal and marched against him with an army. Nicholas retired to his castle, but he had not reckoned on the increased power that the use of gunpowder had conferred on a besieging force. He found that it was hopeless to defend the castle, and he had to make an ignominious surrender to Sigismund in 1459. The Pope supported Nicholas and laid the lands of Sigismund under an interdict. The Emperor also was induced to support the Pope, and in the fighting which followed, Sigismund was defeated, but the war still dragged on until a compromise peace was arranged in 1464. Nicholas did not live to see the peace, for he fell ill and died about three weeks before it was concluded.

The most important works of Nicholas were the *De Docta Ignorantia*, written in 1440, the *De Conjecturis*, in 1449, and the *De Possest*, in 1460. In addition, he wrote his *Apologia* in 1449 as a reply to a charge of heresy, and also a number of smaller treatises on mathematical and scientific subjects. Of his works, the *De Docta Ignorantia* and the *De Possest* are the most important from the philosophical point of view.

Bett speaks of Nicholas as an apostle of reconciliation and unity whose hope was to discover one unifying formula which would unite all the religions and philosophies of the world.[1] No doubt the age in which he lived did much to encourage this attitude. His experience of the Council of Basle, the healing of the Great Schism, and the union of the Latin and Greek Churches were responsible for his outlook. The same spirit pervaded his philosophy, and he was attracted by that aspect of Neo-Platonic thought which sought to bridge the gulf between the One and the multiplicity of the visible world. Such attempts are apparent in the thought of Plotinus and Proclus and their Christian successors, the Pseudo-Dionysius and Erigena.

The root principle of the thought of Nicholas was nothing more or less than the identification of the opposites. The very title of his earlier work—*De Docta Ignorantia*—suggests the line he adopts, and the name of the later treatise—*De Possest*—is equally significant. The most outstanding antithesis in Scholastic philosophy was that between matter and form, potentiality and actuality. "The aim of the *Docta Ignorantia*, as of all the works which followed it, is to show the identity of two opposite terms. The *Possest* from this point of view is a commentary on the *Docta Ignorantia*. It is the synthesis of potentiality (*posse*) and of actuality, which is being in its fulness (*est*)."[2] "What is the world," wrote Nicholas, "but the visible appearance of the invisible God? What is God, but the invisible aspect of visible things?" Such phrases recall the expressions of Scotus Erigena from whom they were derived. It must be confessed that many of the statements of Nicholas have a pantheistic flavour, and it is small wonder that later he had to clear himself of the charge of heresy.

God and the world are equally necessary to each other. Nicholas, because of his interest in natural science, appeals to motion and rest to illustrate his doctrine. Motion and rest cannot be conceived except in terms of each other. One is the opposite of the other, and the existence of motion implies the possibility of rest and vice versa.

[1] BETT, H., *Nicholas of Cusa* (Methuen: 1932), pp. 101-2.
[2] Translation from *De la Docte Ignorance*, by L. Moulinier (Félix Alcan, Paris: 1930), p. 18.

Motion starts from and ends in rest. Although rest is prior to motion, it contains motion within itself. The relation of God to the world is parallel to that of motion and rest. All begins and ends in God (as in Erigena). God is all of all that is, and at the same time, nothing of all that is. All being is implicit in God but explicit in the universe, the latter being the development of a limited potentiality into a limited actuality. Since multiplicity is the characteristic of the finite; the universe is the multiple, but it develops from unity.

Nicholas illustrates the idea of the One giving rise to the many by referring to the process of knowledge. The mind is able to grasp the idea of a multiplicity of individuals within one species, but this ability is dependent upon its power of understanding the nature of the species. The many have become one in God, and by a reverse process, the multiplicity of the visible world has its origin in the Divine Unity. In a similar fashion, unity is the principle of number. It is the minimum, but the end of number is the maximum. Nicholas means that number starts from unity, and by adding one at a time all numbers are formed. The process of adding ones can continue to infinity.

The Divine Nature is a pure Unity without any differentiation. God's attributes are identical with His Essence and with each other. They appear different to us only because of the finitude of our intelligence. God's Nature is too immense for us to grasp in its entirety, and therefore we have to conceive Him first from this aspect and then from that. All opposites meet in God. He is the Same, for everything that can be conceived coincides in Him. He is the *Non Aliud* because nothing exists to which He is other, because He is the Absolute and the Unconditioned. He is the *Possest* because in Him potentiality and actuality coincide.

If the language used by Nicholas to describe creation is taken in a literal sense, it would seem to fall into line with the views of Dionysius and Erigena and to have strong leanings towards pantheism. The world would appear to be the result of an emanation from the Deity. "With God, to see is to create, and He sees nothing but Himself: how then can He create what is not Himself?" It is quite certain that Nicholas regards the creation of the world as a necessary consequence of God's Nature. Like Dionysius, he asserts that God creates of necessity since it is of the nature of the Good to communicate Itself. At the same time, however, he is equally insistent that creation is a free act of the Divine Will, for God's

Will is identical with His Nature, which is free in the sense that it is subject to no external restraint.

Nicholas also guards himself against the accusation of pantheism by his care in the use of terms. He leaves no doubt in the mind of his reader that God and creatures are distinct. God is the Infinite, but the creature is contingent, having its being not from itself but from God. The perfect Unity and Infinity of God is the origin of the finitude, contingency, and multiplicity of creatures. To explain how this is possible, Nicholas employs the terms *complicatio* (aggregate) and *explicatio* (development). He writes, "God is the aggregate of all in the sense that all is in Him; He is also the development of all, in the meaning that He is present in all things."

Thus, finite things are the development or evolution of God; that which is in God the infinite, the perfect, and the absolute unity, becomes in the world the finite, the imperfect and the multiple, and, since the *explicatio* necessitates a falling off from the perfect, the imperfect. Nicholas uses the analogy of the original and the multiple images in the mirror to illustrate the relation between God and creatures.

Nicholas also employs a third term, *contractio*, to explain the nature of the finite world. Like St. Thomas, he believed that all created things mirror the Creator. The universe, which sprang from the Supreme Unity of the Divine Nature, has its own unity, the unity of creation. From this springs a third unity, that of the genus, and a fourth, that of the species. Looking at the same process from the point of view of an ascending scale, individuals through their common nature are united in the species, and in the same way, species in genera, and the latter in the wider unity of the created universe. In this way, the Divine Unity is manifest throughout nature.

God is also a Trinity, and in a similar fashion the triune nature of God is reflected in creation. Nicholas regards every concrete existence as a composite of that which is contracted (*contrahabile*) and that which contracts (*contrahens*), and the two are bound together by the *nexus* or bond. He identifies the *contrahabile* with potentiality and the *contrahens* with actuality, the two being associated together to produce the actual existent.

We have seen the importance to Nicholas of the conception of the coincidence of the opposites in God. He makes frequent appeal to mathematics to illustrate this central idea of his system of thought.

These illustrations are interesting in that they show an outlook upon geometry which is modern rather than mediæval. Thus, in the *Docta Ignorantia*, Nicholas tells us that the coincidence of the maximum and minimum in God is well illustrated through geometrical figures, which are more abstract in their nature than material objects and therefore more clearly reflect the Divine Nature.

"I assert that if you have an infinite line, it will be at the same time a straight line, a triangle, a circle, and a sphere. Similarly, if you have an infinite sphere, it will also be a triangle, a circle, and a line; and the same must be said of the infinite triangle and the infinite circle. . . . There will remain no doubt of this if one sees

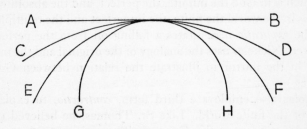

in the accompanying figure how the arc CD, the arc of a larger circle, is less curved than the arc EF, the arc of a smaller circle. It therefore follows that the straight line AB will be the arc of the maximum (infinite) circle. Thus, it is seen that the maximum and infinite line is necessarily the straightest and that the nature of the curve is not opposed, or rather, that the curvity of the maximum line is the same as straightness."[1] Nicholas repeats a similar argument for the triangle.

In the next figure, suppose the point A is fixed and the line AB revolves until B reaches the point C. The result of the rotation is the triangle ABC. If AB continues to rotate until B reaches the position D, opposite its original position, it has described a semi-circle. If, again, the diameter BD is fixed and a semi-circle is described about it, a sphere will be produced. From this, Nicholas argues that the infinite in actuality is what the finite is in potentiality.

[1] *De Docta Ignorantia*, I. c. 13.

Nicholas of Cusa offers a theory of knowledge which has a remarkably modern appearance. He begins with the affirmation that, through a Divine Grace, all things spontaneously desire a higher mode of existence than their own nature will permit. Hence, the intelligence naturally desires the attainment of truth, but this attainment of truth is relative. There is no end to knowledge. When we have reached one stage in the attainment of truth we can always look forward to a further stage. "Thus the intelligence, which is not the truth, never lays hold of the truth with such precision that it cannot be grasped in a more precise way by the infinite. The intelligence is to the truth what the polygon is to the circle; the greater the number of angles possessed by the inscribed polygon, the more like to a circle it is, but even when the number of angles is multiplied to infinity, it is not absolutely identical with the circle. Therefore, it is clear that all we know of the truth is that we know that it is impossible to reach it absolutely; for the truth, which is an absolute necessity and which can be nothing more or less than it is, presents itself to our intelligence as a possibility. Therefore, the essential nature of things, which is the truth of beings, cannot be reached in its purity."[1]

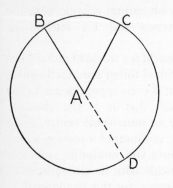

Human knowledge, therefore, can never be more than an approximation to the truth. The truth is absolute and indivisible, not admitting degrees, but our knowledge of it is relative and can be more or less, *cf.* Kant's view that *noumena* are not accessible to thought. To represent the idea of approximation, Nicholas uses the term *coniectura*. True wisdom recognizes this and is a learned ignorance (*docta ignorantia*) which strives incessantly to attain the truth. In his view, knowledge is valid but it is limited and relative. His use of the term *coniectura* emphasizes that our conclusions are true only to a limited degree.

Mention has already been made of the preference shown by Nicholas for mathematical illustrations of his metaphysical

[1] *De Docta Ignorantia,* I. c. 3.

principles. His interest in mathematics was a direct consequence of his study of the Pythagoreans and Platonists, the Neo-Pythagoreans and Neo-Platonists. The illustrations given above indicate that he had advanced beyond the closed and static geometrical system of Euclid and regarded the world from a dynamic point of view. He looked upon mathematics, and dynamics, the study of movement and rest, as providing a key to the understanding of the physical world. Hence, his views on natural science were the outcome of his philosophical doctrines and his interest in mathematics.

Nicholas emphasizes that the sense world is a world of individuals which are so graded that no two individual things are exactly alike. Nothing in the universe is so large that it even approximates to the absolute maximum; nothing so small that it is the absolute minimum. The universe cannot have an immovable centre, since that would be the point of the absolute minimum for motion which is rest. Further, because the maximum and minimum coincide, the centre of the universe would coincide with its circumference. Nor can the universe have a circumference, for this would enclose it by limits outside of which would be absolute and unlimited space. The conclusion is that God is both the centre and the circumference of the universe.

Nicholas argues against the mediæval conception of the earth as static, with the sun and the heavenly bodies moving round it. The earth has a twofold motion. Like the spinning top, it not only revolves but it has a lateral movement. It appears motionless to us who live on it because we become aware of movement only in relation to something which does not move. Thus (and here Nicholas recalls the memory of early days spent on his father's craft), a man in a boat floating downstream can tell that he is moving by comparison with the banks which he regards as stationary. We see here a faint anticipation of the modern view of the relativity of movement.

Nicholas now anticipates the conclusions of Copernicus and Kepler and even of Newton. Indeed, Kepler acknowledged his debt to Nicholas. The earth cannot be the centre of the universe, for the latter has no centre save God. It is neither the centre of the eighth nor of any other sphere. The earth approximates to a sphere, but it is not a perfect sphere. The mediævals had considered the sphere to be the perfect figure and the motion in a circle to be the exemplar of all motion. Therefore, the earth does not move, according to Nicholas, in a perfect circle. The same applies to the other heavenly bodies. The planets, although they may appear to us to move in circles, have each their own orbit which is only approximately circular. All is in motion, and when we measure the rate of movement of anything, we base our calculations upon the assumption that some other point is fixed. As there is no such fixed point, not even the so-called sphere of the fixed stars, all measurement of motion must be relative to a point which is regarded for our purpose as being motionless.

The earth is a star, a "noble star," and in this respect it is similar to the other stars, from which it receives light and heat. The sun and the other stars are much larger than the earth, but this does not warrant the conclusion that the earth is inferior to them. On the other hand, the earth is larger than the moon and perhaps larger than Mercury and some other stars. The relative sizes of the sun, earth and moon can be deduced from the shadows cast during an eclipse. In other words, the earth as regards its matter and its movement is just like any other star, and the older view that the heavenly bodies are composed of a superior kind of matter is a false one.

Nicholas speaks of the possibility that the other heavenly bodies are inhabited, but just as we cannot know whether their region is more or less perfection than the region of the earth, so it is impossible for us to say whether their plants and animals and inhabitants, if they have any, are nobler or less noble than their terrestrial counterparts.

We may sum up the teaching of Nicholas by saying that he belongs equally to the mediæval and modern worlds. His metaphysics hark back to the Christian Neo-Platonists of an earlier age, but even then they are not a mere repetition but a reconstruction containing many points of novelty. His speculations about mathematics and science make him a forerunner of the new outlook which we usually associate with the name of Descartes.

SUGGESTION FOR FURTHER READING

The only account of Nicholas of Cusa in English is that contained in H. Bett's study, *Nicholas of Cusa* (Methuen: 1932).

CHAPTER XVI

MEDIÆVAL MYSTICISM

No outline of the history of mediæval philosophy would be complete without some reference to the great mystical theologians of the period, but space forbids all but the briefest summary of their teaching. The reader will have already noticed that many of the leading thinkers were at the same time mystics. This is especially true of the Pseudo-Dionysius, Scotus, Erigena and St. Bonaventure, but it applies also to St. Thomas Aquinas, though in his case his intellectual achievements tend to overshadow all other aspects of his personality.

The mystic is not a phenomenon peculiar to the mediæval period. He has appeared at all ages and in all lands. Although individual mystics have differed greatly in their character and belief, they all possess one thing in common. Their master aim in life is the search for and the attainment of Absolute Truth. The 19th century was very sceptical on the subject of mysticism and tended to regard the mystic as a dreamer who lived in an unreal world of his own imagination which appeared to him as more real than the objects of his every-day life. He claimed to have experienced something that was both stupendous and unique, but he was not able to substantiate his claims to the satisfaction of the scientific inquirer. In short, the mystic's vision was entirely subjective, and his claim that it yielded a knowledge far more certain, and indeed more intimate, than that given by philosophy and science, was something that could not be taken seriously in an enlightened and scientific age.

Lest we fall into the same error as the scientific materialists of the 19th century, it is worth while asking what it is that the mystic aims at achieving, and how he plans to reach his goal. The answer is that the mystic's quest is for ultimate reality. So far, his aim seems akin to that of the believer in magic, but there is an essential difference. The latter seeks in order to obtain power that he may use for his own selfish ends. The former surrenders his self that he may attain to union with the object of his love. Magic seeks to get; the mystic wants to give.

For the Christian mystic, the end of his quest is God, and he is sustained in his search by an intense conviction that he will succeed where the scientist and philosopher have failed. They make use of the senses and the intellect for the business of acquiring knowledge. These are instruments quite adequate for the purpose for which they were designed, the exploration of the physical world, and at the best they can only lead us to grasp dimly some knowledge about the infinite and the eternal. Man, if he did but know it, has a higher power which he can use if he chooses. He will never reach God by the path of reason, but through love he can see Him directly. So long as he is occupied with the objects of the sense world, he is not employing the highest power that has been granted to him, that of intuition.

This idea is beautifully phrased by the anonymous author of the *Theologia Germanica*. "The two eyes of the soul of man cannot both perform their work at once: but if the soul shall see with the right eye into eternity, then the left eye must close itself and refrain from working, and be as though it were dead. For if the left eye be fulfilling its office toward outward things—*i.e.*, holding converse with time and creatures—then must the right eye be hindered in its working. Therefore, whosoever will have the one must let the other go; for no man can serve two masters." This is what St. Thomas Aquinas taught in less figurative language about the miraculous state of rapture.

When he has closed the pathways leading into the soul from the outer world, the mystic lifts up his mind to God through prayer and meditation. This, however, is but the first stage in the journey of the soul to God. The next is illumination. The Divine becomes present to the pilgrim, and like the prisoners of Plato's *Republic*, he merges from the shadows and darkness to the sun and allows its rays to shine upon his soul. He has passed from the lower exercise of meditation to the higher activity of contemplation.

Then follows the most terrible ordeal of the mystic pilgrim, the complete purification of the self, sometimes called the mystic death or the dark night of the soul. The seeker has wholly surrendered himself, both intellect and will, to God, and he feels that he is close to the achievement of his quest. Suddenly, the object of his search seems to be withdrawn; at one moment he seems to see clearly, and at the next he seems to be plunged into complete darkness. As the Pseudo-Dionysius had taught, the excess of the Divine Light blinds the soul and produces the paradoxical state of absolute darkness.

Finally, the mystic reaches the end of his pilgrimage and enjoys complete union with God. The self is wholly lost and, in the words of St. Thomas, the soul becomes *deiformis*, completely transformed by God. As Eckhart wrote, "If I am to know God directly, I must become completely He and He, I; so that this He and this I become and are one I."

Most of the mystics believed that the union of the individual soul with God is possible for man in his present life, and often speak of being granted the Divine Vision. As we have already seen, St. Thomas was chary of admitting this except in the two cases authenticated by the Scriptures, those of Moses and St. Paul.

If the Pseudo-Dionysius may be regarded as the Father of Mediæval Mysticism, then St. Bernard of Clairvaux (1090–1153) may be considered its founder, so great was the influence he exercised on those who followed him. His mystical teaching is chiefly found in the latter part of the *De Consideratione* and in his *Homilies on the Songs of Solomon*. St. Bernard sought union with God through love and the humility that springs from it. Through meditation and contemplation the soul passes to the state of rapture in which it is joined so intimately to God that St. Bernard uses the analogies of the drop of wine hidden by the water in which it is mixed, the glowing iron that seems part of the fire, and the air which is rendered transparent by the rays of the sun. At the same time he is careful to emphasize that there remains a real distinction between man and God, even at this supreme moment. The one is the finite; the other the Infinite. It was probably St. Bernard's devotion to the way of contemplation that made him unduly suspicious of the rational approach of Abelard which seemed to him a direct attack upon simple faith.

Dean Inge sums up the influence of St. Bernard as follows. "The great importance of Bernard in the history of mysticism does not lie in the speculative side of his teaching, in which he depends almost entirely upon Augustine. His great achievement was to recall devout and loving contemplation to the image of the crucified

Christ, and to found that worship of our Saviour as the 'Bride-groom of the Soul,' which in the next centuries inspired so much fervid devotion and lyrical sacred poetry."[1]

The greatest mystical theologians of the 12th century were Hugh and Richard of St. Victor, usually known as the Victorines. The school of the Abbey of St. Victor had been founded by William of Champeaux, and it was here that he had retired for a time when worsted in the dialectical contest with Abelard. Hugh, the elder of the two thinkers, was born in 1096 and entered the convent of St. Victor in 1115, where he remained until his death in 1141. He was as opposed to the teaching of Abelard, as was St. Bernard, but although some of his arguments are directly aimed at Abelard, Hugh never once mentions him by name. Hugh made a separation between theology, which is concerned with the Divine, and philosophy, whose business is with this world. He had no particular quarrel with the latter (he was no mean philosopher himself), so long as it confined itself to its proper sphere, but he was not in favour of attempting to reach God through the feeble and hesitating light of reason.

Before man fell from grace he possessed the eye of the flesh to enable him to deal with the visible world, the eye of reason to enable the soul to know itself, and the eye of contemplation through which he could see God and the things about Him. As a consequence of the sin of our first parents, we have lost the eye of contemplation; the eye of reason has become obscured and dim, but the eye of the flesh still belongs to us. Our loss is compensated by the gift of faith by which we believe what we cannot see. Faith, however, is not purely subjective. It stands in need of the objective base of knowledge, even though the latter may be only a general grasp of the being of its object. It is never contradictory to reason, for true faith is always rational or super-rational.

Based upon knowledge, faith rises to an understanding of the nature of its object, and is gradually perfected until it reaches its fruition in heaven. Hugh is especially interested in the increasing depth of the seeker's grasp of the Divine Nature. Starting with thought (*cogitatio*), the seeker passes through meditation to contemplation, which is a direct intuition (*contuitus*) of the Divine.

In a beautiful passage in the first of his *Nineteen Sermons on Ecclesiastes*, Hugh speaks of the seeker in the stage of meditation

---

[1] INGE, W. R., *Christian Mysticism* (Methuen: 1899), p. 140*n*.

I

as being distracted by the contest between ignorance and knowledge. The light of truth shines through a fog of error. The attainment of truth may be compared with making a fire from green wood. It is only with great difficulty that a fire can be started, but once the wood has kindled we see immense volumes of smoke pouring forth, with here and there a leaping flame. As the heat dries the wood and the flames drive away the smoke the "*victrix flamma*, darting through the heap of crackling wood, springs from branch to branch, and with lambent grasp catches upon every twig; nor does it rest until it penetrates everywhere and draws into itself all that it finds which is not flame. At length the whole combustible material is purged of its own nature and passes into the similitude and property of fire; then the din is hushed, and the voracious fire, having subdued all, and brought all into its own likeness, composes itself to a high peace and silence, finding nothing more that is alien or opposed to itself." In a similar manner, the tiny spark within us struggles against the smoke and fog *in cogitatio*, and, gaining in strength, contends in smoke and flame. Then, in the clear flame of contemplation, the smoke is dispelled, until at last the soul reaches out to God and the one-time spark is now become a consuming heat without either flame or smoke.

Richard, the pupil of Hugh of St. Victor, was born in Scotland. He became Prior of St. Victor in 1162 and died in 1173. Richard's teaching was in many respects similar to that of his master, but the chief characteristic of his mystical theology was his elaboration of the stages in the journey of the soul towards union with God. Speaking of both Hugh and Richard, Miss Evelyn Underhill wrote, "Like his master, Hugh, he had the mediæval passion for elaborate allegory, neat arrangement, rigid classification and significant numbers in things. As Dante parcelled out Heaven, Purgatory, and Hell with mathematical precision, . . . so these writers divide and subdivide the stages of contemplation, the states of the soul, the degrees of Divine Love: and perform terrible *tours de force* in the course of compelling all the living spontaneous and ever-variable expressions of man's spiritual vitality to fall into orderly and parallel series, conformable to the mystic numbers of Seven, Four, and Three."[1]

Thus, Richard distinguishes the first three stages according to the functions realized by imagination, reason and intelligence,

[1] UNDERHILL, EVELYN, *Mysticism*, 11th edition (Methuen: 1926), p. 547.

respectively. Imagination and intelligence imply the presence of their object, in the one case a material existence, in the other an intelligible essence. Reason is able to know an object which is not present to the senses or a property which is hidden by other qualities of the object presented—*e.g.*, it starts with knowledge of the effect and arrives at an understanding of the cause. Reason, however, always needs the assistance of the sensible but the intelligence can reach its object directly.

Three further developments are necessary before the mystic attains union with God. These progressive steps in contemplation are the enlargement of the mind (*dilatatio mentis*), by which the mystic sees God under the form of symbols, the elevation of the mind (*sublevatio mentis*), which enables him to see God as a person sees another reflected in a mirror, and finally, the alienation of the mind (*alienatio mentis*), when he sees God as He is. The necessary prerequisite of contemplation is purity of heart. Indeed, the mirror in which the mystic sees God is his own soul. If the latter is besmirched by sin, the subject will obtain only a distorted view of the Divine.

Two of Richard's most important mystical treatises were entitled *Benjamin Major* and *Benjamin Minor*. In his symbolism, Benjamin, the younger son of Rachel, becomes the emblem of the contemplative life. Both works were extensively paraphrased and translated, and strongly influenced the English mystics of the 14th century.

In another treatise, Richard makes use of an allegory which became very popular amongst later mystical theologians. The journey of the soul to God, "the steep stairway of love," as he terms is, it portrayed under the symbolism of earthly courtship and marriage. Thus we have the four progressive stages of the betrothal, the marriage, the wedlock, and the fruitfulness of the soul.

In the latter 13th and the 14th century, mystical theology became the leading characteristic of the German Dominican school which drew its inspiration from St. Thomas Aquinas. This school produced a trio of celebrated mystical thinkers, Meister Eckhart, John Tauler, and Blessed Henry Suso. John Eckhart (1260–1329) entered as a young man into the Order of St. Dominic. At first his talents were rewarded by appointment to high office in his order, but later in life many of his more extravagant statements aroused alarm and suspicion, and he was accused of heresy. Certain propositions collected from his works were condemned as heretical a few months after his death. It was thought that many of his expressions savoured of pantheism, and it is certain that, at the very least, they appeared rash and exaggerated to most men of his age. In defending himself before his accusers, Eckhart insisted upon his loyalty to the Catholic faith and his desire to avoid pantheism, but he admitted that some of his teaching was capable of an interpretation which he did not intend.

Eckhart was a man of considerable scholarship. He knew at first hand the writings of the Fathers, especially St. Augustine and the Pseudo-Dionysius. He was familiar with the works of the 12th-century Scholastics and had studied Arabian and Jewish philosophy. At the same time he was strongly influenced by the teaching of Albert the Great and St. Thomas Aquinas (to whom he always refers as "the Master"), and he was acquainted also with the leading ideas of Duns Scotus.

Eckhart's works fall into two groups: the *Sermons*, which were delivered in German, and the Latin treatises. The latter have been recovered piecemeal and some of them are still not edited, but they show that he was an able philosophical thinker as well as a mystic. The mystical element is most prominent in the German works, which were evidently the only ones available to Dean Inge at the time he produced his book on Christian mysticism, for he wrote, "Eckhart wrote in German; that is to say, he wrote for the public, and not for the learned only. His desire to be intelligible to the general reader led him to adopt an epigrammatic antithetic style, and to omit qualifying phrases. This is one reason why he laid himself open to so many accusations of heresy."[1] Now that we know these treatises to be a written version of his sermons, the looseness in phraseology explains itself.

The key to Eckhart's thought lies in his doctrine of God Whom he compares as the Infinite with the creature who is the finite. In his earlier teaching, Eckhart considered intelligence to be a higher function than that of being (*intelligere est altius quam esse et est alterius conditionis*). Hence, he prefers to speak of God as the Supreme Intelligence rather than as the Supreme Being. In fact, God can be described as Non-Being (*in Deo non est ens nec esse*), and when we speak of being we are referring to creatures.

St. Thomas had identified intelligence and being in the Divine Nature, but Eckhart went a step further, and, using the Neo-Platonic

[1] *op. cit.*, p. 150.

axiom that nothing belonging to the cause is to be found in the effect, he affirmed that God, the Infinite Cause of all being, has nothing of being Himself, but is pure Intelligence. This is the meaning of his statement that non-being is a property of intelligence. "For if the species which is in the soul were a being, we could not know, by means of it, the thing of which it is the species; if it were a being, it would lead to a knowledge of itself and it would substitute a knowledge of the species for a knowledge of the thing."

Some years later, Eckhart developed quite a different doctrine. He brought his theories into line with the generally accepted view that God is Being, but just as he had previously exaggerated the aspect of intelligence, so now he tended to over-state the conception of being. He asserted that God is the one and only existence (*ens tantum unum est et Deus est*), so that nothing exists external to God (*rursus extra Deum, utpote extra esse, nihil est*). Every created being has its own essence which is distinct from the Divine Essence, but existence, which brings these essences into actuality, does not belong to the creature. All creatures derive their being from God.

Eckhart compared the relation between God and creatures to that of form and matter, whole and part, actuality and potentiality. Since the being of created substances is really God's Being, when God loves creatures He is also loving Himself. The Divine Being actualizes all created essences. Therefore, the man who loves creatures for their own sake is really loving what is nothing. Eckhart met with the problem which is common to all thinkers of his type; how can the Divine Unity give rise to the multiplicity of the visible world? We have already seen this difficulty occurring in the thought of Erigena and Nicholas of Cusa. Eckhart's answer was not altogether satisfactory. In the first place, he asserted that the created world, although multiple, has a unity of its own, due to the causal action of God in creation, for every agent views his work as a whole. In modern terms, the world is a unity because, underlying its apparent multiplicity, there is the unfolding of a single plan or design.

Secondly, multiplicity is found also in the Divine Nature. God is One as regards His Substance, but He is also a Trinity of Persons. After the fashion of Gilbert de la Porrée, Eckhart drew an important distinction. Whilst God is a Person Who reveals Himself through the Son, the Godhead is an abstraction. When we have said that the Godhead is One, we have said all that it is possible to say—it is the. desert, the abyss, the immobile silence and the light which reflects upon itself. From another point of view, there is a distinction of Persons in God, but Eckhart often speaks as though they are but moments in an eternal process. An additional distinction is that of the Ideas which exist in the Word. "The ideal world is the complete expression of the thought of God, and is above space and time. He calls it 'non-natured nature', as opposed to '*diu genaturte nature*', the world of phenomena."[1] In this connection, Inge compares his view with that of the *natura naturata* in the *Ethics* of Spinoza. He also shows an important difference between Eckhart's teaching and that of the Neo-Platonists. For Plotinus and Proclus, *nous*, the second principle of the Neo-Platonic trinity, is inferior to the One, and in a similar way the World Soul is subordinate to *nous*. Eckhart refuses to subordinate the Son to the Father, but in doing so the view of the world he adopts is more pantheistic.

As was said above, the mystical teaching of Eckhart is most prominent in his *Sermons*. He held that creation is a downward movement; the One becoming the many in the visible world. Parallel to it is an upward movement; as all beings come from God, they all seek to return to Him. This tendency, unconscious in nature, can become a conscious desire in man whose ultimate end consists in union with the Divine. This could be possible only if there is something of the Divine in man. The eternal light exists as a spark (*scintilla*) in the human soul and it can be fanned until, in its intense heat, it consumes our finitude and the evil desires coming therefrom, so that only the Divine remains.

The conception of the *scintilla* was most significant for the mystical theologians. The idea goes back as far as Tatian and Tertullian. It was implicit in the Augustinian school; the metaphor was frequently employed by St. Bernard, and was also a favourite one with the Victorines. Alexander of Hales employs it and St. Bonaventure speaks of the *apex mentis* or *scintilla*. In the works of the 13th-century theologians it became, "the natural will towards Good, implanted in us all, though weakened by sin. It cannot be extinguished. It was created with the soul, moving the will away from sin and towards virtue, and always seeking the Source from Whom it came. It is a power or potentiality in the soul in which God works directly and unceasingly."[2] Theologians before Eckhart

---

[1] INGE, *op. cit.*, p. 152.   [2] MELLONE, *op. cit.*, p. 157.

had regarded it as a residue of God in man. Eckhart thought of the *scintilla* as God's image in the soul. The Augustinians saw the image of God in the soul in its triple powers of the memory, the understanding and the will. For Eckhart, there is a lower trinity of the sensuous, the spirited and the rational elements (*cf.* Plato). Then follows the higher trinity of the Augustinians. Higher than all these there is the true image of God, the Divine Spark (*scintilla—funkelin*), which is not a residue or power of the soul, but part of its very being. In the moral theology of St. Thomas the *scintilla* became synderesis, and when the Cambridge Platonists in the 17th and Bishop Butler in the 18th century speak of the candle of the Lord within us, this is probably a remnant of the older belief.

At first, Eckhart was inclined to identify the *scintilla* with the Active Intellect, but later he wrote, "There is in the soul something which is above the soul, Divine, simple, a pure nothing; rather nameless than named, rather unknown than known. Of this I am accustomed to speak in my discourses. Sometimes I have called it a power, sometimes an uncreated light, and sometimes a Divine Spark. It is absolute and free from all names and forms, just as God is free and absolute in Himself."[1]

According to Eckhart, the mystic's union with God is effected through knowledge and love when these powers are turned from preoccupation with the external world towards God, the Guest of the soul. Knowledge has its fruition in itself. Its end is knowledge for the sake of knowledge. If it is directed towards any other end, it becomes debased and mercenary. Love, however, is the superior activity, for it concentrates on the one object of love, whilst knowledge has a multitude of objects.

The soul thirsts after God, but God loves the soul because He is the Source of its being. He can enter the inner recesses of the soul only when it has renounced all created objects and even itself. When this has been accomplished, God reveals Himself in His true Essence. The soul is carried into the silent desert where there is no longer effort, doubt, or faith. In knowing God, as He is, we are transformed wholly into Him (*nos transformamur totaliter in Deum*).

Eckhart's pupils were John Tauler (1300–61) and Blessed Henry Suso (1295–1365). Although, in many ways, these two men present contrasting personalities, they are alike in that they drew their inspiration from Eckhart and developed certain aspects of his

[1] INGE, *op. cit.*, p. 157.

teaching. "The distinctive fact about the German mystics of the fourteenth century is the enormous impulse they received from Eckhart, their close acquaintance with his teaching; all use his ideas, modified and warmed through by their own temperament or experience. From him they get their wide horizons, their way of escape from a merely human range of imagery and emotion."[1]

In his earlier life Suso was an ascetic who interpreted Christ's saying, "Where I am, there shall also My servant be," as meaning that only those who endure in themselves the sufferings of Christ can hope to reign with Him in glory. For over sixteen years he inflicted intense tortures upon his body and subjected himself to penances which seem horrible and repulsive to the modern mind. At the end of this period Suso considered that the flesh had been subjugated, and for the remainder of his life he showed himself in his true character as a gentle, lovable and romantic soul.

Shortly before his death, Suso wrote his autobiography, in which he revealed the inner working of his devotional life. Many mystics have declared that they are unable to express in language their most ecstatic and intimate experiences, but this was not the case with Henry Suso, who tells us without reserve and in great detail the visions which he claimed were vouchsafed to him. His great desire was to become the Servitor of the Eternal Wisdom, and in his autobiography he always calls himself by this title. He felt that the accusations made against Eckhart were unjust, and shortly after his master's death he saw Eckhart in a vision. "He signified to the servitor that he was in great glory, and that his soul was completely transformed and made Godlike in God."

A secondary influence upon the development of Suso's mysticism was that of the German women mystics, St. Mechthild of Hackborn, Mechthild of Magdeburg and St. Gertrude. Suso added nothing original to the philosophical teaching of his master, but in his writings he gives us a picture of himself consumed with a most passionate love and longing for God Whom he conceived in the guise of the Eternal Wisdom of the Book of Proverbs. He speaks of Wisdom as "a gentle loving Mistress" who besought him, "My son, give me thy heart."

In contrast to Suso, Tauler was a preacher, a missionary and a reformer. In him the social element was exceedingly prominent.

[1] UNDERHILL, EVELYN, *The Mystics of the Church* (James Clarke: 1925), p. 136.

He was by no means a recluse, for we find him at Strasbourg in 1348 continuing his ministrations at the very height of the Black Death. Tauler was closely associated with that astonishing society the Friends of God. Its members put before themselves the object of transforming and revitalizing the rather decadent life of the German people, and it is noteworthy that the majority of the members of the movement were lay folk. The society had no rigid form of organization; it was held together by the burning zeal of its members who conceived the mystic way as the ideal life for man.

The Friends of God "denounced the numerous and glaring abuses and sins of the time, foretold divine vengeance, demanded realism and sincerity, and practised an often extreme asceticism; regarding themselves as an 'inner Church' of spiritual men, a faithful remnant in an evil generation, directly guided by the Holy Ghost. They taught a mystical form of personal religion, based on the conception of a 'Divine Spark' or Godlike quality latent in every soul. . . . In this doctrine of the Inner Light, the Friends of God anticipated the Quaker position; but they never broke with institutional religion, and seem to have felt peculiar reverence for the sacraments."[1]

The monument bequeathed to us by the Friends of God is the beautiful *Theologia Germanica*. This little book, so spiritual in its outlook, is by an unknown author or authors and has always been regarded as one of the most exquisite gems of devotional literature. Its influence was far-reaching and affected even Henry More and the Cambridge Platonists of post-Reformation days. Tauler had severely criticized some of the manifestations of false mysticism in his day, and the authors of the *Theologia Germanica* are no less drastic in their condemnation. The tree is known by its fruit, and no one can hope to be united to Christ unless he lives a life of love, purity, and good works.

Contemporary with Suso and Tauler was John Ruysbroeck (1293–1381), the great mystic of the Low Countries. For the first half of his life Ruysbroeck was a priest of the Cathedral of St. Gudule at Brussels. When he was middle-aged, the desire for seclusion drove him with some chosen companions into the forest of Soignes, where he founded a small community under Augustinian rule of which he was prior until his death.

Ruysbroeck was much less of a philosopher than Eckhart, and in

---

[1] UNDERHILL, EVELYN, *op. cit.*, pp. 137

his emotional fervour was more akin to Suso. He was also strictly orthodox. He carefully guarded himself against any taint of pantheism and received from the Church the title of Doctor Ecstaticus. Miss Underhill describes him as "both saint and seer; truly a God-intoxicated man." Ruysbroeck revived the practice of the Victorines of mapping out in threes or sevens the stages on the road to union with the Infinite. "This arbitrary schematism is the weakest part of Ruysbroeck's writings, which contain many deep thoughts. His chief work, *Ordo spiritualium nuptiarum*, is one of the most complete charts of the mystic's progress which exist."[1]

The tendency to minute classification was also very pronounced in Jean Gerson (1363–1429), who became Chancellor of the University of Paris in 1395. On the philosophical side Gerson was sympathetic to the doctrines of Ockham, and in politics he supported the Conciliar theory against the Papacy. Part of his life was spent in Brussels, where he came into contact with some followers of Ruysbroeck. Gerson's mystical writings make laborious reading. He tried to reduce mysticism to an exact science by distinguishing between symbolical, natural, and mystical theology. In his account of the latter, the "mystic numbers" again come into prominence. There are three cognitive faculties to which correspond the same number of affective faculties and three activities of contemplation, meditation, and cogitation. There are also seven means of mystical theology.

Before closing this brief sketch of mystical theology, there are two interesting developments which should be mentioned. The first is the prominent part played by women mystics. Thus, in Germany, we have the early period dominated by St. Hildegarde (1098–1179) and St. Elizabeth of Schoenau (1138–65). These two remarkable women were not only mystics and visionaries but active political reformers. The former was a wonderful person. "Of abnormal psychic make-up, weak bodily health, but immense intellectual power, Hildegarde's personality and range of activities would be startling at any period. She founded two convents, wrote a long physical treatise in nine books, including a complete guide to the nature and properties of herbs, was skilled in medicine, deeply interested in politics, sternly denounced ecclesiastical laxity and corruption, and corresponded with and often rebuked the greatest men of her day. She was also a musician and poet, and over

[1] INGE, *op. cit.*, p. 169.

sixty hymns are attributed to her. In later life she travelled hundreds of miles in the course of her duties—a considerable matter for an elderly nun of the twelfth century. Yet she remained first and foremost a contemplative, whose actions were always dictated by inward commands, and whose sources of power lay beyond the world."[1]

Italy provided St. Catherine of Siena (1347–80) and St. Catherine of Genoa (1447–1510). Both of these women were prominent in the life of action as well. The former was one of the most remarkable characters in history. When still an adolescent, she resolved to dedicate her life to God, and she devoted herself to prayer and self-mortification. Very soon she began to experience mystical visions which culminated in her Mystical Marriage with Christ. The Divine Voice urged her to pass on to other people the grace which she had received. Coming out of her seclusion, Catherine began to spend her days in comforting and nursing the sick and poor of Siena. She acquired enormous influence, and through her agency many souls were turned towards a religious life.

In spite of giving up her time to works of mercy, Catherine still found opportunities for contemplation, and in 1370 she experienced a trance which lasted for four hours. When she returned to normal consciousness, she declared that although her soul had crossed to the life beyond, it was returned to this world to minister to others. "Thou shalt bear the honour of My name and witness to spiritual things before small and great, layfolk, clergy and religious; and I shall give thee words and wisdom none shall be able to withstand."

The remaining ten years of Catherine's life present a truly amazing spectacle. This woman, who had sprung from a family of artisans and who had but little education, became one of the greatest spiritual forces in Europe. She realized the evils that beset the Church and, inspired by Divine Power, she set about the task of reform. No person was too great or powerful for her to approach. She scourged the dignitaries of the Church for their unworthy lives, travelled over a great part of Italy to persuade rebellious cities to make their peace with the Papacy, and became the counsellor of the most important politicians of the day. The greatest scandal was the residence of the Papal court at Avignon, and it was due largely to her influence that Gregory XI was persuaded to return to Rome.

[1] UNDERHILL, op. cit., p. 75.

In a letter to the Pope, she urged, "Answer the summons of God, Who is calling you to come, hold, and possess the place of the glorious shepherd St. Peter, whose vicar you are."

St. Catherine of Genoa was a teacher and philanthropist who founded in 1477 the first hospital in Genoa and managed it for more than twenty years. "Her accounts were never a farthing wrong, nor was she ever known to fail in her duties through absorption in spiritual joys. When the plague came to Genoa, she was the centre of a devoted band who went through the city nursing the victims, and in many cases sacrificed their own lives. . . . Some of her sayings of this period are among the strangest which the Christian mystics have left to us, and seem almost to imply the claim to an actual trans-mutation of her personality; that which is known in mystical theology as the 'transforming union' of the soul with God. 'My me is God, nor do I know my selfhood, save in Him.' 'My being is God, not by simple participation but by a true transformation of my being.' 'God is my being, my self, my strength, my blessedness.'"[1]

The other remarkable feature is the contribution to mysticism made by English people. On this topic, Dean Inge remarks, "I have come across the statement repeated in many books, that England has been a barren field for mystics. It is assumed that the English character is alien to mysticism—that we have no sympathy, as a nation, for this kind of religion. Some writers hint that it is because we are too practical, and have too much common sense. The facts do not bear out this view. There is no race, I think, in which there is a richer vein of idealism, and a deeper sense of the mystery of life, than our own."[2]

In addition to the large number of English mystics in the Middle Ages, in assessing the contribution made by Englishmen we have to take into account the 17th-century mystic poets, Vaughan, Herbert and Traherne, the Cambridge Platonists of the same period, Fr. Augustine Baker and his pupil Dame Gertrude More, George Fox the Quaker, John Woolman, William Law the Non-Juror, and many of the English poets, especially Blake, Wordsworth and Browning. Altogether an impressive list, and one which bears out Dean Inge's contention.

[1] UNDERHILL, op. cit., pp. 164-5.
[2] INGE, op. cit., p. 197. Dean Inge is thinking of such statements as: "Our island would be but a spare contributor to a general exhibition of mystics. The British cloister has not one great mystical saint to show."—R. A. VAUGHAN, Hours with the Mystics (Strahan: 1879), vol. ii, p. 301.

In mediæval England, as on the Continent, the 14th century was the golden age of mysticism, just as the 13th saw the culmination of Scholastic philosophy. There are numerous reasons to account for the flowering of mystical theology at this particular time. Institutional religion and official philosophy were being overcome by a deadness which for years to come was to increase rather than diminish. An acute thinker like Gerson perceived the symptoms of the age, and as Professor Gilson has shown, used all his learning and eloquence to point out to the philosopher and theologian their respective fields and to warn the logician of the dangers of intruding into the domain of metaphysics or religion and *vice versa*. Probably this accounts for Gerson's attempt at a rigid demarcation of the divisions of theology and the cataloguing of each step in the mystic way.

The growing laxity in the lives of the clergy, especially in high places, accounted for the failure of this age to produce the leaders who were needed. Moreover, the latter 14th century had its fill of wars and social discontent. England was almost continuously at war with either Scotland or France, and this involved campaigning of a type which wrought great devastation in the lands of the weaker. The middle of the century saw the population of Western Europe more than decimated by the ravages of the Black Death and similar plagues, and when this terror had passed, it was succeeded by a period of intense and widespread discontent and sometimes armed rebellion, as exemplified by the Peasants' Revolt of 1381. The whole social order was changing and changing rapidly. Some saw the remedy in revolution, both social and spiritual. Hence the spread of Lollardry in England and, later, the Hussite movement in Bohemia. Such movements were fanned by the "Babylonish" captivity at Avignon and the beginning of the Great Schism in 1378.

Small wonder, then, that devout Christians, both simple and scholarly, turned away from this world, in which they saw nothing but suffering, apathy, decadence and dissension, to find secure peace and quiet in the realm of the spirit. Christianity has always been a religion of other-worldliness, and Christians of this period, in what we now know was the beginning of the end for the Middle Ages, imitated those earlier Christians at the break-up of the Roman Empire in the West. Hence the appearance of the great German mystics, Eckhart, Suso and Tauler, the teaching of

Ruysbroeck in Flanders, and, on the practical side, the coming together of the Friends of God.

A parallel movement took place in England. This country in the 14th and 15th centuries was peculiarly rich in mystics. Some were simple souls leading a life of prayer and meditation in their anchorages apart from the activities of everyday life. Others were scholars, familiar with the works of Augustine, Dionysius, St. Bernard, the Victorines, St. Bonaventure and the contemporary thinkers on the Continent. They freely chose the mystic way and committed their experiences to writing, not only to show to others the path they had followed, but also to prove that, through the mystic means of knowledge, they had obtained the key to answering those ultimate problems which had baffled generations of philosophers. In a history with this title, it is with these speculative mystics alone that we are concerned.

One of the earliest English mystics was Richard Rolle (1290–1349). His birthplace is believed to have been Thornton-le-dale, near Pickering in Yorkshire. Richard's parents, though of good family, were not rich, but with the assistance of the Archdeacon of Durham, they were able to send their son to Oxford, where he came under Franciscan influence. Richard was no mean scholar. He wrote in both English and Latin, and his works show that he was familiar with the writings of St. Augustine, the Victorines and St. Bonaventure. There is a possibility that, after studying at Oxford, Rolle took his doctorate in theology at Paris. According to some writers, he was never ordained, but since he was allowed to preach in churches and to act in the capacity of spiritual guide to nuns and anchoresses, it seems probable that he was a priest.

Richard returned to Yorkshire fired with the Franciscan ideal of renunciation and determined to live the life of a hermit. He persuaded his sister to meet him in a wood near his home and to bring with her two of her old tunics, one white and the other grey. "Rolle begged of his sister, to whom he was united by close affection, her white and grey frocks. When therefore he had taken them, he forthwith amputated the sleeves of the grey one, and cut off the buttons from the white one, and sewed together as best he could the sleeves of the white tunic, so that they might be to some extent adapted to his purpose. Then he put off his own garments and put on the white frock next his skin; over which he put the grey frock with the amputated sleeves, thrusting his arms through the holes which this amputation had made; then he drew over all this a rain-cloak (with hood); in order that, to some extent, after his own fashion, he might shape himself roughly into the likeness of an hermit, so far as was possible at that moment. When his sister saw this she was filled with amazement, and cried: 'My brother is gone mad, my brother is gone mad!' At which words he drove her from him with threatening gestures, and fled forthwith without delay, lest his friends and acquaintance should lay hands on him. Thence Rolle went into a neighbouring church [Topcliffe], and was found absorbed in prayer in Lady de Dalton's pew."[1]

His first hermitage was near the home of the Daltons, and he spent some time here in prayer, fasting and meditation in preparation for the ecstatic experiences he was to enjoy later. After nearly three years of self-discipline, he tells us that the "heavenly door" was opened to him. According to his own account, Richard experienced the ecstatic union on several occasions, but when he attempts to describe the unitive life words fail him and all that he can do to express his experiences is centred round the three words *canor*, *calor*, and *dulcor*—song, warmth, and sweetness.

Although many of Richard's longer works were written in Latin, he was the first to use the vernacular to any extent, and in consequence he has been described as the Father of English Prose. He was also a poet. "His verse is, by modern standards, crude and irregular. He was not writing the laboured poetry of the poetaster for fame as a poet. His verse is the rushing forth of the melody that is within him, a melody of inspiration, however feebly the expression of it may read. That inward melody gives music to his prose; it is partly expressed in the alliteration, and even the repetitions, which strike one on first reading as redundancies, are afterwards seen as part of a larger rhythm."[2]

Until recently, the metrical *Pricke of Conscience* was attributed to him, but it is now regarded as a production of one of his followers. *The Fire of Love* and *The Mending of Life* were translated into English by the Carmelite Richard Misyn about 1460. In the prologue to *The Fire of Love*, he tells us the purpose of the book. "This book I offer not to philosophers or wise men of this world,

---

[1] COULTON., G. G., *Mediaeval Panorama* (C.U.P.: 1938), pp. 524–5.
[2] HESELTINE, C. G., *Selected Works of Richard Rolle* (Longmans, Green: 1930), p. xxviii.

nor to great divines lapped in infinite questions, but unto ignorant and untaught men, more busy to learn how to love God than to know many things."[1]

Rolle's later life was spent at Hampole near Doncaster, and in his anchorage he communed with the love that filled his soul, occasionally wandering further afield, preaching and giving advice to the people of the neighbourhood. In his writings we find a strong vein of common sense. He was opposed to excessive mortification, since he believed that it merely weakened the body and laid the individual open to temptation. He advises, "It behoves him to be truly strong that will manfully practise love of God. When the flesh is made very feeble with great discomfort, a man oftentimes cannot pray, and so he is the more unable to lift himself to high things with fervent desire. I would rather therefore that a man failed for greatness of love than for too much fasting."[2]

In his teaching about contemplation Rolle falls into line with the majority of the mystics. "Contemplative life or contemplation has three parts: reading, prayer, and meditation. In reading, God speaks to us; in prayer, we speak to God; in meditation, angels come down to teach us, that we err not. In prayer they go up and offer our petitions to God, rejoicing in our progress; they are messengers between God and us. Prayer is, indeed, a devout disposition of the mind directed to God, with which He is pleased when it comes to Him."[3]

Although Rolle freely chose the contemplative life, in his counsel to Margaret the Anchoress he admits that the active life also has its merits, but "Two lives there are that Christian men live. One is called active life, for it is more in bodily work. The other, contemplative life, for it is more in spiritual sweetness. Active life is much outward, and in more travail and peril because of the temptations that are in the world. Contemplative life is much inward, and therefore it is more enduring, and securer, more restful, more delectable, lovelier and more meritorious."[4]

Richard's works became widely known, and he was followed by a series of mystical writers of whom space forbids the selection of more than three for mention. The first is the *Cloud of Unknowing*, written in the East Midland dialect, the language of Chaucer, by

[1] ROBINSON, GERTRUDE, *In a Mediaeval Library* (Sands & Co.: 1918), p. 87.
[2] *The Mending of Life*, c. iv.
[3] *ibid.*, c. xii.
[4] *The Form of Living*, c. xii.

an unknown author. Many attempts have been made to discover his identity. Some writers have ascribed the work to Walter Hilton, but internal evidence shows that this is improbable. The writer may have hailed from East Anglia, and he describes himself as a university scholar, probably of Cambridge. Despite its anonymity, *The Cloud of Unknowing* remains as one of the choicest examples of mystical literature. The same author has also given us an English translation of the *Mystical Theology* of Dionysius, and it is upon the Areopagite that he bases his teaching. He also shows a knowledge of Augustine, Gregory, Bernard and the Victorines. Although the book is distinguished by a seeming simplicity and a beauty of style, it is one of the most profound of the mystical treatises. Its title shows that the teaching of Dionysius is the predominant element, and the book itself is addressed to a young man of twenty-four who has just adopted the religious life. Miss Underhill says, "If Rolle and Hilton show us the English layman of the fourteenth century as his spiritual teachers saw him, we get from this nameless mystic a vigorous and amusing picture of the fourteenth century cloister, with its ardent, sanctimonious, hypo-critical, fidgety, and variously tiresome inhabitants."[1] Thus he describes the behaviour of some of his fellow religious. "For some men are so cumbered with nice curious gestures in their bodily bearing, that when they shall aught hear, they writhe their heads on one side quaintly, and up with the chin; they gape with their mouths, as though they would hear with their mouths and not with their ears. Some, when they should speak, point with their fingers, either on their fingers, or on their own breasts, or on theirs that they speak to. Some can neither sit still, stand still, nor lie still, unless they be either wagging with their feet, or else somewhat doing with their hands. Some row with their arms in the time of their speaking, as though they needed to swim over a great water. Some be evermore smiling and laughing at every other word that they speak, as they were giddy girls or silly jesting jugglers lacking behaviour. Better far were a modest countenance, with sober and demure bearing of body and honest mirth in manner."[2]

Walter Hilton, first a Carthusian and later an Augustinian canon, died in 1396. He was an inmate of the priory of Thurgarton in Nottinghamshire. "The writings of Walter Hilton . . . were read in manuscript by large numbers of people, and his teaching

[1] *The Mystics of the Church*, p. 120. [2] *The Cloud of Unknowing*, c. 53.

was spread through word of mouth by his readers. His chief book, *The Scale of Perfection*, was a favourite book with the King's mother; and it seems to have been eagerly read by rich and poor, learned and unlearned. It opened men's minds to a truer standard of values than the political and military leaders could know. Such opening of the mind is, in itself, a revolution."[1]

The Scale of Perfection was addressed to an anchoress and was intended as a complete guide to the contemplative life. Hilton also wrote a second book, the *Treatise on Mixed Life*, which was addressed to the ordinary man who wished as far as he could to follow the path of the mystic. In the latter, Hilton distinguished between three modes of life, the active, the contemplative and the mixed. The latter is a combination of the first two. He describes the mixed life as follows: "The third life, that is mingled life, it belongeth to men of Holy Church as to prelates and to other curates, the which have care and sovereignty of other men, for to teach and rule both their bodies and their souls. . . . Also it belongeth to some temporal men the which have sovereignty with much having of worldly goods and have also as it were lordship over men to govern and sustain them as a father over his children, a master over his servants, a lord over his tenants, which men have also received of our Lord a gift of grace and devotion and, in particular, savour of ghostly occupation: unto these men belongeth a mingled life that is both active and contemplative."[2]

Hilton was both a contemplative and a practical man. He had nothing but scorn for those who are so wrapt in meditation that they neglect the simple duties and charities of ordinary life, "tending God's head and neglecting His feet," as he terms it. In his *Song of Angels* he tells us, "Whoso then will hear angel's song and not be deceived by feigning of himself nor by imagination, nor by the illusion of the enemy, him behoveth for to have perfect Charity, and that is when all vain love and dread, vain joy and sorrow, is cast out of the heart, so that it love nothing but God, nor joyeth nor sorroweth nothing but in God and for God. Whoso might by the grace of God go this way, he should not err."[3]

The last and, in many ways, the greatest of the English mystics we are considering was Dame Juliana, an anchoress whose

[1] HOPKINSON, A. W., *Mysticism: Old and New* (Nisbet: 1946), p. 61.
[2] ROBINSON, *op. cit.*, pp. 185–6.
[3] Quoted by UNDERHILL, EVELYN, *The Mystic Way* (Dent: 1913), p. 207.

cell was attached to the Church of St. Julian at Norwich. We know
nothing more about her than what she has to say concerning herself
in her book, *The Revelation of Divine Love*. From this, we gather
that she was born in 1343 and that her early life was not altogether
happy. She often wished for "a grievous illness almost unto death,"
so that she could lay aside her attachment to the world and gain a
surer grasp of spiritual realities. Her wish was granted at the
age of thirty, when she became so seriously ill that her friends
thought she was dying. They held a crucifix before her eyes, and it
seemed to her that the figure on the Cross became alive. This was
the first of many visions that came to her, sometimes when asleep
but more often in her waking hours. We do not know the date of
her death, but it is said that she lived to a ripe old age and was still
alive in 1413.

Two different manuscripts of *The Revelation of Divine Love* are
extant, a shorter, written soon after she experienced her visions,
and a longer, when she had fifteen or twenty years to ponder over
their meaning. She describes herself as "a simple creature,
unlettered," but this is not to be understood in the sense that she
was nearly illiterate, but rather in the meaning of not having
received a regular training in theology or philosophy. In fact, she
possessed a wonderful command over language and showed great
artistry in expression. Tradition states that she was an inmate of
the nunnery of Carrow, which had long been known as a place
of education for the daughters of well-to-do people living in the
diocese of Norwich. In any case, her rule enjoined a certain
amount of reading and study, and she not only knew the works of
Hilton and other contemporary mystics, but was familiar with the
Christianized Platonism of Augustine. Thus we find in her
writings the reference to the spark or *scintilla*. "I saw and understood full surely that in every soul that shall be saved there is a
godly will that never assented to sin, nor ever shall; which will is
so good that it may never work evil, but evermore continually it
willeth good and worketh good in the sight of God."

Like all the English mystics of this period, Juliana's views were
entirely free of any trace of pantheism. In the most intimate
union with the Divine, the distinction between the finite and the
Infinite is preserved and her love of God is expressed through a
personal devotion to Christ as true God and true man. Few
mystics have described with such philosophic insight the vision

of God as does Dame Juliana in the words, "After this I saw God in a Point, that is to say in mine understanding—by which sight I saw that He is in all things. . . . For I saw truly that God doeth all-thing, be it never so little. And I saw truly that nothing is done by hap nor by adventure, but all things by the foreseeing wisdom of God: if it be hap or adventure in the sight of man, our blindness and our unforesight is the cause. . . . Wherefore me behoveth needs to grant that all-thing is done, it is well-done; for our Lord God doeth all. For in this time the working of creatures was not shewed, but the working of our Lord God in the creature: for He is in the Mid-point of all thing, and all he doeth."

In concluding this brief outline of the development of mediæval philosophy, two things remain to be said. The first is that the reader should have discovered that in one sense the term mediæval philosophy is a misnomer. There was no mediæval philosophy; there were mediæval philosophies. In other words, the term mediæval philosophy is merely a convenient way of classifying all those diverse systems of thought which flourished during the period we know as the Middle Ages. Amongst these different thinkers, certain stand out as though related by some family resemblance. A line of philosophers from St. Anselm to William of Ockham, although differing greatly in the particular views they held, all seem to fit in a kind of general pattern. They present similarities in their teaching; their view of the relations between philosophy and theology is approximately the same; they more or less adopt the same teaching methods, and they all make considerable use of the common classical heritage, especially Aristotle. Thus in spite of the many important differences between, say, St. Thomas and Duns Scotus, we can recognize the pattern, but the same could not be said about David of Dinant or Averroes. It is customary to apply the name Scholastic to this body of thinkers, and certain writers, such as De Wulf, have attempted to give an even more precise meaning to the term.[1]

The second point consists in the reasons for the rapid decline and subsequent oblivion that overtook Scholastic philosophy until its revival in the 19th century. This is a problem that cannot be adequately answered in a book of this kind; it is a research in

[1] In the later editions of the *History of Medieval Philosophy*, De Wulf has modified his view. See vol. i, 6th edition (1934), Preface and Introduction.

itself. All we can say is that for practical purposes, after the close of the 15th century, Scholastic philosophy occupied a very unimportant place in the progress of thought. One exception to this statement occurred in Spain, where there was a short-lived but brilliant revival led by Suarez (1548–1617). One might also mention Cajetan (1468–1534) and Gabriel Vasquez (d. 1604) in Italy and John Major (1478–1540) in Scotland.

The Scholastics of the 16th and 17th centuries had mainly themselves to blame for the ruin that came upon them. They deliberately shut their eyes to the new advances that were being made in mathematics and the natural sciences and to the humanistic influences of the Renaissance. It is said that some of his contemporaries refused to look through the telescope of Galileo lest they should be convinced against their will. All power of origination seems to have passed from the Scholastics of these later days. A St. Thomas or a Grosseteste would have taken a leading part in the revival of letters and would have hailed each new scientific discovery with gladness. Not so these men. They were infected by the worst influences of the school of Ockham and concentrated their interest upon the formalities of logic, introducing over-elaborate classifications until they mistook the shadow for the reality.

On their side, the scientists retorted by asserting that Scholastic philosophy was bound up with an outworn view of the universe and wedded to such false notions as a belief in the theory of natural places, the difference between the matter of the heavenly bodies and terrestrial matter and the idea that circular motion is the most perfect. We know now that the main body of Scholastic thought was independent of the scientific views of the age. St. Thomas was aware of this when, in the course of discussing the theory that the planets are moved by intelligent motors, he wrote, "It is agreed that by adopting such hypotheses the appearances are saved, but one ought not to say that these theories represent the true explanations, for it may come to pass that the appearances about the stars may be saved by some other explanation not yet known to men."

In addition, owing to the doctrinal differences of the Reformation, Scholasticism, at least to those who lived in the countries which had adopted Protestantism, appeared to be bound up with the doctrinal system of the Roman Church. But the essential cause of the decline was expressed by De Wulf when he wrote, "Scholasticism succumbed for want of men, not for want of ideas."[1]

SUGGESTIONS FOR FURTHER READING

For the understanding of mysticism, the student should read W. R. Inge's *Christian Mysticism* (Bampton Lectures, 1899: Methuen). This book was responsible for the revival of interest in the subject in modern times. The same author's *Studies of English Mystics* (St. Margaret's Lectures, 1905: John Murray) is a sympathetic historical account.

The greatest modern authority on mysticism was Evelyn Underhill. In *The Mystics of the Church* (James Clarke: 1925) she gives a simple historical account of mysticism. Her book *Mysticism* (Methuen: 1926) is one of the most complete studies that has been made. In *The Mystic Way* (Dent: 1913) she shows that Christian mysticism is inherent in the Christian religion and the liturgy of the Church and that the Neo-Platonic element is not an essential of it.

Many translations and editions of the mystics have been published.

The following is a short selection:

McCANN, J., *The Cloud of Unknowing* (Burns, Oates and Washbourne: 1924).

GARDNER, B., *The Cell of Self-Knowledge* (London: 1910); *St. Catherine of Siena* (London: 1907).

UNDERHILL, E., *Walter Hilton, The Scale of Perfection* (London: 1923); *Ruysbroeck* (London: 1915).

WARRACK, G., *Julian of Norwich, Revelations of Divine Love* (Methuen: 1901).

COMPER, F., *Richard Rolle, The Fire of Love* and *The Mending of Life* (Methuen: 1914).

HESELTINE, C. G., *Selected Works of Richard Rolle* (Longmans, Green: 1930).

[1] *op. cit.*, 3rd edition, trans. P. Coffey (Longmans, Green: 1909), p. 505. For a fuller discussion of the causes of the decline of Scholasticism, see De Wulf's *Scholasticism Old and New*, trans. P. Coffey (Longmans, Green: 1910), chapter iii.

CHIEF PHILOSOPHICAL WORKS OF ST. THOMAS AQUINAS

(In some cases the chronology is still unsettled)

Commentary on the Sentences, 1254–56.

De Principiis Naturæ, 1255.

De Ente et Essentia, 1256.

Contra Gentiles, 1258–60.

Commentary on the Divine Names, 1261.

Questiones Disputatæ :

      De Veritate, 1256–59.

      De Potentia, 1259–63.

      De Malo, 1263–68.

      De Anima, 1269–70.

Quæstiones Quodlibetanæ, 1263–73.

The Rule of Princes, 1265–66.

Commentaries on Aristotle, 1265–73.

De Unitate Intellectus, 1270.

De Substantiis Separatis, 1272.

Summa Theologica, 1267–73.

INDEX

A

Abelard, Peter, 55–69, 81, 87, 186, 257
Active and passive qualities, 143–4
Adam du Petit Pont, 82
Aesthetics, theory of Aquinas, 198–200
Albert of Saxe, 243–4
Albert the Great, 46–7, 117, 129–33
Alcuin, 33n, 99, 102
Alexander of Hales, 96, 124–6, 203, 262
Alfarabi, 109
Alkindi, 109
Amalric of Bene, 45–6
Analogy, 22, 29, 168–72, 227
Anselm of Canterbury, 70–9, 164
Anselm of Laon, 56, 88
Anti-realism, 50, 52, 63–4
Aquinas, St. Thomas, 12, 26, 33, 47, 49, 69, 79, 93, 94, 96, 114, 116–7, 134–200, 223–5, 227, 249, 254, 255, 263
Arabian philosophy, 105–15
Aristotle, 13, 31, 49, 86, 105, 106, 107–8, 115–16, 120–23, 136, 143, 144n, 146, 166, 173, 185, 186, 187, 190, 193, 196, 204
Arnold of Brescia, 60
Augustine, St., 12, 13–20, 204, 206
Avempace, 111
Avencebrol, 47
Averroes, 111–15, 147
Averroists, Latin, 117–19, 122–3
Avicenna, 110–11, 124

B

Bacon, Roger, 122, 127, 208–16
Beatific Vision, 172–9
Berengar of Tours, 53

Berkeley, Bp., 38
Bernard of Chartres, 54
Bernard, St., of Clairvaux, 28, 54, 59–60, 65, 256–7, 262
Boethius, 12, 31–4, 35, 105
Bonaventure, St., 202–8, 263
Buridan, John, 242–3
Butler, Bp., 263

C

Cajetan, 277
Cassiodorus, 31, 33
Catherine of Genoa, St., 268
Catherine of Siena, St., 267–8
Cause and effect, 234, 240
Chartres, school of, 53, 54, 81–2, 88, 127
Cicero, 13
Cloud of Unknowing, 272–3
Conceptualism, 50, 231, 235–7
Conscience, 188–9
Constance, Council of, 245
Cousin, Victor, 11, 60

D

Damian, Peter, 53–4, 163
Dante, 28, 111, 112, 121–2, 178–9, 196–7n
D'Arcy, M.C., 169–70, 183
David of Dinant, 46–7
De Burgh, W. G., 181–2
De Wulf, M., 36, 44, 46, 103, 131, 276, 278
Decline of Scholasticism, 277–8
Descartes, 15, 79, 160, 253
Divine Illumination—in St. Augustine, 16–18; St. Bonaventure, 203–7; Roger Bacon, 211
Dominicans, at the universities, 94–7, 117
Donatus, 102
Duns Scotus, 183, 217–28
Durandus of Saint-Pourçain, 229–30

E

Eckhart, 256, 259–63, 264
Eric of Auxerre, 52
Erigena, 35–47, 246, 247, 248

Essence and existence, 126, 164, 223-4
Ethics—Abelard, 65-9; Aquinas, 181-9; William of Ockham, 239
Eton College, 92
Eucharistic controversy, 37
Existence of God—in St. Augustine, 14-15; St. Anselm, 74-6, 79; St. Thomas Aquinas, 165-7; Duns Scotus, 226-8; Ockham, 238

F

Form—*see* Matter
Formal distinction, 223-5
Franciscans, at the universities, 94-7, 117
Fredegis, 50
Friends of God, 265
Fulbert of Chartres, 53

G

Gaunilon, 76-9
Gerbert, 53
Gerson, Jean, 266, 269
Gilbert de la Porrée, 54-5
Giles of Rome, 116
Gilson, E., 119, 120, 127, 131, 203, 204-5, 241, 269
Gottschalk, 37
Grosseteste, Robert, 126-9, 208, 211, 215

H

Haecceitas, 222-3
Hauréau, 11
Hegel, 79
Héloïse, 57, 58, 60
Hildegarde, St., 266-7
Hilton, Walter, 273-4
Holkot, Robert, 239
Hugh of St. Victor, 257-8

I

Identity theory, 61
Indifference theory, 62
Individual existence, 146-53, 222-3, 225, 230, 231, 233-6
Inge, W. R., 256-7, 268
Intellect, Active and Possible, 107-10, 112-14, 117-23, 125, 156-63, 204-5, 211, 225-6

Intellect, controversy on, 107-10, 112-14, 117-23
Intelligible species, 158-9, 162-3
Isidore of Seville, 33, 35*n*
Itinerarium Mentis, 205-7

                                    J

John of Salisbury, 54, 64, 81-86, 115
Juliana of Norwich, 274-6
Justinian, 187

                                    K

Kant, Immanuel, 38, 66, 78, 108, 156, 158, 161, 164, 200, 251
Kepler, 252
Kilwardby, Robert, 117, 122

                                    L

Lanfranc, 53, 70
Law; view of Aquinas, 187-9, 198
Leibnitz, 79

                                    M

Maimonides, 115
Major, John, 277
Mandonnet, P., 117, 118
Manegold of Lautenbach, 85, 192*n*
Marsiglio of Padua, 192*n*
Matter and Form, 19-20, 125, 132, 159, 219-21
Mill, J. S., 213
Mysticism, mediaeval, 12, 29-30, 174-6, 254-76

                                    N

Nardi, Bruno, 119
Neo-Platonists, 13, 25, 107, 252
Nicholas of Autrecourt, 239-41
Nicholas of Cusa, 12, 45, 47, 245-53
Nicholas of Oresme, 244
Nominalism, 50

                                    O

Odo of Tournai, 51

Ontological argument—in St. Anselm, 74–6; Objections of Gaunilon, 76–8; Anselm's reply, 79–80; Rejection by Aquinas, 164; by Duns Scotus, 226–7

P

Peter Aureolus, 230–1
Peter Lombard, 93*n*
Plato, 13, 31, 49, 136, 204, 255, 263
Platonists, Cambridge, 263, 268
Political theory—Aquinas, 190–98; John of Salisbury, 83–6; Dante, 196–7*n*
Porphyry, 33–4
Predestination, controversy on, 37
Pseudo-Dionysius, 12, 20–30, 36–7, 43, 57, 136–7, 143, 167–8, 173, 199, 246, 247, 248, 256, 273

R

Rationes seminales, 20, 132, 208, 220
Ratramnus, 37
Realism—extreme, 49; moderate, 49–50, 86
Remi of Auxerre, 51
Renan, E., 113, 117, 211
Richard of St. Victor, 258–9
Robert de Sorbon, 91, 96
Rolle, Richard, 270–2
Roscelin, 52–3
Ruysbroeck, 265–6

S

Schools—grammar, 98–104; chantry, 99; monastic, 99; palace, 99; public, 101; song, 100
Science and mathematics, mediaeval, 127–9, 129–30, 210, 212–15, 241–4, 249–53
Scintilla, 262–3, 265, 275
Seven Liberal Arts, 32–3, 102
Sic et Non, 58–9, 124
Siger de Brabant, 117–22
Simon de Montfort, 197
Spinoza, 45
Suarez, 277
Suso, Henry, 263–4
Synderesis, 188–9

T

Tauler, John, 263, 264–5
Terminism, 237–9
Theoderic of Chartres, 54
Thèry, G., 46–7

U

Underhill, Evelyn, 258, 273
Unity of forms, 139–40
Universals controversy—meaning of universals, 48–50; origin of contro-
    versy, 33–4; history of, 50–65; Albert's solution, 132–3
University, meaning of, 87–8; degrees, 88–9, 92–3; teaching at, 93–4
Universities—Bologna, 87; Cambridge, 89, 90, 95, 98; Oxford, 89, 90, 91,
    95, 97–8; Paris, 87, 89, 90–1, 3, 95, 96, 97–8, 117; St. Andrews, 90;
    Salerno, 87

W

Wicksteed, P., 44, 150–1
William of Auvergne, 209
William of Champeaux, 55–6, 61, 62, 88, 257
William of Conches, 54
William of Moerbeke, 116, 137, 215
William of Ockham, 231–9, 241–2, 266
Winchester College, 91–2
Woodham, Adam, 239
Wykeham, 91–2